Robert Boston

Close Encounters
with the
RELIGIOUS RIGHT

**Journeys
into the
Twilight
Zone
of Religion
and
Politics**

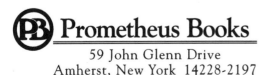

Prometheus Books

59 John Glenn Drive
Amherst, New York 14228-2197

Published 2000 by Prometheus Books

Inquiries should be addressed to
Prometheus Books, 59 John Glenn Drive, Amherst, New York 14228–2197.
VOICE: 716–691–0133, ext. 207.
FAX: 716–564–2711.
WWW.PROMETHEUSBOOKS.COM

04 03 02 01 00   5 4 3 2

Library of Congress Cataloging-in-Publication Data

Boston, Rob, 1962
    Close encounters with the religious right : journeys into the twilight zone of religion and politics / Robert Boston.
        p.   cm.
    ISBN 1–57392–797–X (paper : alk. paper)
    1. Conservatism—Religious aspects—Christianity—History—20th century.
2. Christianity and politics—History—20th century. I. Title.

BR526.B575 2000
320.5'5'0973—dc21   99–058537
                                                                          CIP

Printed in the United States of America on acid-free paper

In loving memory of my father,

Robert E. Boston

1926–1998

CONTENTS

ACKNOWLEDGMENTS

This book was made possible by the kind indulgence of two key staff members at Americans United for Separation of Church and State, Joseph L. Conn, director of communications, and the Rev. Barry W. Lynn, executive director, who gave me time off to write it.

Few people in America know more about the Religious Right than Joe Conn and Barry Lynn. Thankfully, they are on our side. Joe is Americans United's longest-serving employee still on staff (I'm number two), and Barry, who has been with AU since 1992, has had a lifelong commitment to religious freedom and civil liberties. It has been a pleasure to work for both of them, and I have learned more than I can express under their joint tutelage.

The entire Americans United staff deserves my thanks. It has been a pleasure to work with individuals of varied talents over the past thirteen years. The organization has changed and grown over those years, as we have assumed new responsibilities and projects to defend the separation of church and state. Not surprisingly, much of our work these days centers on the Religious Right, an aggressive movement that has launched countless mean-spirited and ill-informed attacks against the constitutional principle of church-state separation.

Americans United's budget is nowhere near that of the major Religious Right organizations, yet we have managed to be an effective, increasingly active force for countering Religious Right calumny and organizing opposition to groups like the Christian Coalition. That is only possible because of the dedication and hard work of the AU staff, all of whom are committed to this cause. I appreciate the efforts of each and every one.

While I am grateful for the efforts of everyone on the AU staff, I must single out two others for special thanks. Research Coordinator Steve Benen, friend, colleague, and wizard of the World Wide Web, provided me with valuable research services that helped make this book possible. Susan Hansen, assistant to the AU Communications Department, made sure all of my documents looked like they ought to, got things out in the mail on time, and performed countless other tasks that made this project go a lot more smoothly.

Americans United's oversight boards, our Board of Trustees and National Advisory Council, also play an important role in our efforts. Through their time, effort, and commitment, this diverse body of individuals helps Americans United achieve its mission of defending religious liberty by advocating for the separation of church and state. I salute them.

But my deepest thanks go to Americans United's members. They are what it's all about. Membership in Americans United has grown in recent years, a trend I am happy to see. We are always looking for new support, however, as the struggle against the Religious Right and the effort to keep America's Bill of Rights intact will never truly be over. In my travels around the country, I have met hundreds of Americans United members, including people who have been with the organization since our founding in 1947. I have corresponded through the U.S. mail and e-mail or talked on the phone to countless others. The dedication of all of Americans United's members to this cause is always an inspiration, and I thank them all, from new members to longtime supporters.

On the home front, I extend gracious thanks to my wife, Carol, who cheerfully puts up with my rants whenever I come home from a Religious Right gathering. I also thank Carol for acting as a sounding board for some of the ideas in this book. I couldn't keep at this without her support.

My children, Claire, age five, and Paul, twenty-two months (at this writing), are crucial to helping me keep a sense of perspective and to remembering what this "family values" debate is really all about. Claire and Paul serve as constant reminders to me of why we must respond forcefully to the Religious Right—for the sake of the next generation. So much of what the Religious Right tries to pass off as "family values"—censorship, attacks on public education, gay bashing, criticism of our public libraries, forced religious worship, and so on—is in my view the antithesis of real family values. If only for the sake of our children, the Religious Right must be stopped.

Thanks as always to my mother, Alice R. Boston, and to my late father, Robert E. Boston. My father was never one to suffer fools gladly, and he would never have fallen for the type of scam Religious Right groups constantly put over on their supporters. I'd like to think that some of his innate common sense and his finely tuned "baloney detector" rubbed off on me.

One final word: I compiled this book from many different sources, and accepted help from lots of people. For that I am deeply grateful. But there's no passing the buck: I am responsible for the contents and cheerfully accept the credit—and blame—for all within.

Robert Boston
September 1999

Introduction

THAT'S THE SIGNPOST UP AHEAD

When I was in college studying journalism, I used to think it would be interesting to work for an activist organization and spend my days exposing the forces that seek to tear down American freedoms.

The Religious Right was all the rage in the early 1980s when I was a student. I didn't think much of it. Like a lot of people, I believed the entire movement was a passing fad that would soon blow over. But that didn't happen, and in a sense I came of age just as the Religious Right did.

After graduating, I did what most of my peers in journalism did—looked for a job on a newspaper. I accepted a position as a general-assignment reporter with a small daily in central Pennsylvania. I covered school boards, borough councils, township boards of supervisors, and all manner of local news. (I once found myself in the middle of the night photographing a bear that some people in a rural area had chased up a tree. This was real small-town news.) When I grew tired of that, I set out for Washington, D.C.

After two years of routine editing and writing for a trade association, I landed at Americans United for Separation of Church and State. Suddenly that weird dream I had once had in college had come true. Tracking the Religious Right and defending the separation of church and state was my full-time job. Now the question facing me was how best to fulfill this mission.

As a kid, I remember being fascinated by nature documentaries on public television. I was always amazed at the things caught on camera—especially when the animals in question were big and dangerous, like grizzly bears and lions. The photographers, I learned, really did risk life and limb in some cases to bring back footage that was "up close and personal."

Eventually, I decided that fieldwork was the best way to study the Religious Right as well. You could read Religious Right magazines, watch its videos, and listen to Religious Right leaders' speeches on tape—but to get a feel for the real thing it would be necessary to travel deep into Religious Right territory. Just as a good scientist tracking a wild animal goes into the habitat, I would have to do the same.

At Americans United, we believe that the only way to really find out what the Religious Right is up to is to attend its meetings. I've been to several of the Christian Coalition's "Road to Victory" conferences. I spent two days with the Promise Keepers in a football stadium. I rubbed shoulders with devotees of TV preacher D. James Kennedy in Florida. For a while I even attended local Christian Coalition chapter meetings in the Maryland county where I reside. (I am by no means the only one who does this for AU. Other staffers and supporters attend these events as well. There is always a hefty dose of "observers" at every Religious Right gathering, just as I always assume there are Religious Right supporters at AU's annual conferences.)

There is nothing unethical or underhanded about attending these events. The Christian Coalition, Kennedy's Coral Ridge Ministries, and other Religious Right organizations actively promote their events and seek attendance among the general public. I am a member of the general public. I'm only doing what they want me to do.

Also, it would be naive of the leaders of these organizations to think that everyone in the audience is an enthusiastic supporter of the Religious Right. We're all adults, and it's not news that both sides keep tabs on one another. Opponents of Americans United attend our annual conferences. We do not try to screen them out or harass them once they show up. They are welcome to be there. We have nothing to hide.

In addition to attending Religious Right gatherings, I've had the opportunity to interview some Religious Right leaders or debate them in the media. In other words, I've seen these people like those wildlife photographers see the animals—"up close and personal."

Americans United monitors Religious Right groups in other ways. We read the books, magazines, and newsletters they produce. We watch their videotapes and listen to their audiotapes. We collect their fund-raising letters and compile articles written about these groups and the people who run them. In other words, we're watchdogs of the Religious Right.

People often ask me how I can stand being immersed in the Religious Right's world—even for just a while. I tell them that I try to look on the bright side. I like to travel, and tracking the Religious Right has taken me to some parts of the country I probably would not have seen otherwise. Also, I remind myself that no matter how hateful or mean-spirited a particular Religious Right group is being, its words will be used for good effect when Americans United tells the country what these groups are really trying to do. The short answer: It's for a good cause.

Of course not all of my travel is to visit Religious Right groups. I often speak to Americans United chapters, allied organizations, or other folks who are interested in our issues. I've given speeches, sat on panel discussions, engaged in debates, and done local and national television and radio appearances. I appreciate having these opportunities, enjoy public speaking, and like meeting people all over the country. I consider myself fortunate.

The difference between speaking to an AU chapter or an allied group and attending a gathering of, say, the Christian Coalition is jarring. I'm always amazed at how gullible some followers of the Religious Right are and how willing they are to accept things uncritically. They really do vest their leaders with a lot of author-ity—an unhealthy degree of it, I think.

AU's critics sometimes assert that we are too obsessed with the Religious Right. I reject this assertion. Americans United was founded to defend the separation of church and state and educate the American public about the importance of that principle to our way of life. Religious Right groups, almost without exception, attack the separation of church and state, often employing vocif-erous and nasty language. To fail to respond would make us remiss in our duties.

Serving as a watchdog also means we have to keep an eye on some issues that are not, strictly speaking, related to the separation of church and state. In this book I recount the incident of Jerry Fal-well "outing" Tinky Winky, the purple Teletubby®. Some right-wingers criticized Americans United after we gave this information to the press, saying we were only trying to embarrass Falwell; they charged that Falwell's statements about a children's television show had nothing to do with separation of church and state.

Perhaps so, but consider these two points: First, we didn't em-barrass Falwell; he embarrassed himself (but more on this later). More importantly, our actions were completely appropriate, and here's why: When we point out that Falwell has odd views on a topic like the sexual preferences of fictional characters from children's TV, it will, we hope, cause people to stop and think for a moment when they hear Falwell expounding on other topics. In other words, when Americans hear Falwell attacking the separation of church and state I want them to pause for a minute and think, "Hold on. Isn't this the same guy who once said one of the Teletubbies is gay?"

Is Americans United trying to discredit the Religious Right? No. We don't have to do that. The Religious Right has already discredited itself. We are merely bringing that information to light. I will not apologize for doing so.

Recently some books have come out arguing that the Religious Right isn't really so bad. Worse yet, some commentators have asserted that this movement has lost or is losing its steam. I dispute those assertions. In fact, I think they are dangerous because they can lull people into a false sense of complacency.

Some writers are mere visitors to the world of the Religious Right. They drop in, talk to some people who appear to be decent, nice, and reasonable, and then go home. Subsequently, they draw inaccurate conclusions about the movement.

No one can spend a day, a week, or even a few weeks hanging out with Religious Right groups and presume to be an expert. It takes a lot more than that. I am not a visitor to the world of the Religious Right; I'm more like a permanent resident alien. I will never truly fit in because I disagree with so much of the Religious Right's politics and theology, but I've been to their neighborhood enough times to know what the terrain is really like; I know my way around.

Plus, I've done the research others have not—read the books, looked at the fund-raising mail, talked to people face to face. With all due respect to those who have merely dropped in on the Religious Right for a quick visit, I must point out that it takes years of study to really understand this religio-political movement. I have been doing this work for twelve years, and I acknowledge that I still have much to learn.

Does this mean that I believe that every person involved in Religious Right groups is mean-spirited and hateful? Not at all. One thing I have learned from my travels is that good people are quite capable of following bad leaders. I have met good people at Religious Right gatherings, the kind of folks you'd like to have for neighbors—caring parents, loving spouses, and so on. (Of course, I've also met plenty of people who really are mean-spirited and full of hate.)

When I condemn or criticize the Religious Right, I am directing my words to the movement as a whole. I believe that if the Religious Right's agenda were implemented, millions of Americans would have their constitutional rights violated or be oppressed in various ways. The outcome would be uniformly negative. Yet some good people are laboring to bring about the Religious Right's agenda. Just as good people are capable of following bad leaders, they are also capable of advocating for bad causes. Perhaps they have been misled; perhaps they truly do not understand the consequences of their actions. But this is irrelevant. The fact that they are good people does not excuse their complicity. And the fact that they are nice does not mean they should not be opposed. Some of the people in the Religious Right are nice. But their agenda is dangerous and wrong for America, and it must be stopped.

Let me say a few words about the title of this book: Although it's probably not a good idea to mix science-fiction metaphors, I wanted to work the phrase "Twilight Zone" into the title because to me, that adequately expresses some of the feelings I have had while attending Religious Right meetings. *The Twilight Zone* TV series was in frequent syndication when I was growing up, and I believe I have seen every episode at least once. Readers might recall that episodes open with narration by the series' creator, writer Rod Serling: "You're traveling through another dimension—a dimension not only of sight and sound, but of mind. A journey into a wondrous land whose boundaries are that of imagination. That's the signpost up ahead—next stop, the Twilight Zone!"

Going to a Religious Right gathering is a lot like traveling though another dimension, all right, but I wouldn't necessarily call it wondrous. In any case, that sense of unreality is what I hoped to capture in the title of this book.

In most *Twilight Zone* episodes there is a point when the protagonist first begins to notice that something isn't right. It's as if the normal laws that govern the universe have been suspended—which, of course, in the Zone, they have. Serling was a master at capturing that creepy sense of how it feels to first discover that something is horribly amiss. And from there, those feelings of being out of place just build until, in a *Twilight Zone* episode, they can become outright terror.

I won't say I've felt terror at Religious Right meetings—repulsion, disgust, anger, yes—but not terror. But I definitely got that creepy feeling of something not being right. But it wasn't gradual. When you enter a Religious Right gathering, you know right away you're in the Twilight Zone.

One *Twilight Zone* episode I remember well concerned a group of individuals in odd outfits who found themselves trapped in some type of large room with no doors or windows. They didn't know how they had ended up there or how they could get out. In the end, it turned out they were a collection of a child's dolls, trapped in a toy box—and they wouldn't be getting out.

Thankfully, you can always get "out of the box" at a Religious Right gathering. Eventually the meetings end. There are breaks for meals. You can always walk out on a dull speaker and take a breath of fresh air. You're not trapped in the Zone forever.

But when you're in the room, surrounded by the faithful, a sense of unreality can come upon you. You hear things said that you know very well are not true, yet thousands of heads nod in approval. People ask prying questions about your religious beliefs—questions that I was taught were not asked in polite society. Certain things are just assumed about you—that you hate Democrats, can't stand the public schools, think Robert Bork is a great legal mind, or whatever—and these assumptions become the opening gambit for conversations.

As I said, the rules of polite society are suspended. In normal society, you would probably rarely ask an almost total stranger a personal question like, "What church do you go to?" But I cannot tell you how many times I've had strangers ask me this at Religious Right conferences. It took me a while to figure it out, but eventually I realized that many of the people who attend these gatherings have a type of religious pecking order in their heads. At Christian Coalition gatherings, it's not uncommon to run across a lot of Pentecostals. They were less common at D. James Kennedy's gatherings. (How do I know? At Coalition meetings, it's common to see half of the crowd with their hands in the air during the emotional parts. Practically no one did that at Kennedy's event.) Basically, these folks believe that your choice of church tells more about you than you yourself can say.

Despite the religious third-degree, it's always worthwhile to be friendly and open (although as circumspect as possible in my case) at these gatherings. One learns interesting things. The first day of D. James Kennedy's "Reclaiming America for Christ" conference, the man next me struck up a conversation as we waited for things to get under way. Almost immediately he launched into a diatribe explaining why democracy is the worst form of government.

And, as I've said, I'm also frequently amazed—and discouraged—at the low levels of skepticism at these meetings and how readily people uncritically accept what Religious Right leaders say. People basically swallow everything they are told from the podium. At one point during Kennedy's gathering, we were each given a "life card" listing four companies we were supposed to boycott for giving money to Planned Parenthood, which the card described as "the world's largest abortionist." One of the companies was Target department stores. An elderly gentleman sitting next to me turned around to say, "I'm sorry to see Target on this list. I shop there, but I guess I'll have to quit."

I decided to have a little fun with him. "You know," I said,

"Planned Parenthood doesn't just provide abortions. Maybe the money is being used for other types of medical services, like prevention of venereal diseases."

But the old guy would have none of it. "They're up to something," he said, "or they wouldn't be on this card."

I stopped trying to plant a seed of doubt. His mind was made up. There's an old fundamentalist bumper sticker that says, "The Bible says it, I believe it, end of discussion." (I saw a kid who looked to be about eleven wearing a T-shirt with the same slogan during my visit to James Dobson's Focus on the Family.) To suit today's Religious Right, those first few words should be changed to read, "Pat Robertson said it . . ." or "Bill Bennett said it. . . ."

It is also amazing to me to sit and listen to words and phrases take on new definitions at Religious Right gatherings. "Pro-family" and its variants are my favorites. Devotees of the Religious Right seem to believe that upholding a narrow right-wing political agenda is always "pro-family," no matter how many people it may hurt.

To be honest, I eavesdrop at these meetings. You hear interesting things that tell you a lot about the mindsets of the attendees. At Kennedy's gathering, I heard an elderly woman behind me recount, with great disgust, that her son had attended his daughter's lesbian wedding ceremony. "I understand the way she is," said the woman, "but why does she have to flaunt it?"

To me, accepting your children and giving them all of the love you can is the true "pro-family" stance. Disowning them, alienating them, and treating them like undesirables because of factors they cannot control isn't pro-family. In fact, it's downright unkind. It saddened me to think that this woman was missing out on enjoying a positive relationship with her granddaughter because of prejudices fed by Kennedy and his ilk.

Kennedy's party line is that homosexuality is a "lifestyle choice" and that people can choose to leave it if they just accept Jesus. Because people like the woman I quoted above refuse to even entertain the possibility that homosexuality may be a predetermined factor, like being left-handed or having brown eyes, they are caught in a trap of their own absolutist thinking. They cause pain for families and divide them unnecessarily. This is pro-family?

In fact, few if any of the Religious Right's views are really "pro-family." Believing that your religion should be forced onto others through the public school system or through government action is not pro-family. Denying young people access to information about birth control or evolution is not pro-family. Teaching Bible stories as literal history is not pro-family. Demonizing people of liberal or moderate political opinions is not pro-family. Turning churches into cogs in a power-hungry television ministry's political machine is certainly not pro-family.

Now I come full circle. How can I stand it? The answer is often I can't. But since I started working at Americans United my life has changed in many ways. Chiefly, I got married, and I now have children of my own. I remember them when I'm in these meetings or debating a Religious Right honcho on talk radio. I don't want my children to grow up feeling like lesser Americans, like second-class citizens, because they are the "wrong" religion. I don't want them judged by the standards of right and wrong laid down by Pat Robertson, Jerry Falwell, James Dobson, or D. James Kennedy.

Conversely, I remember what I want for them: I want a public school system that welcomes and encourages all young minds, irrespective of what they believe or don't believe about God. I want a curriculum free from sectarian dogma. I want public libraries unrestrained by fears of religious censorship. I want open inquiry and the right to discuss, debate, and disagree about religion.

I want what Thomas Jefferson promised us a long time ago: A First Amendment that guarantees "a wall of separation between church and state."

Before we get into the meat of things, I should say a few words about terminology. I am well aware that not everyone is happy with the term "Religious Right." Some groups and individuals who oppose this movement argue that the terms "religion" and "religious" have a positive connotation to most Americans, as does the term "right." They also argue that calling the movement the "Religious Right" concedes too much because the movement is primarily political, not religious.

These are all good points. Unfortunately, I think we are stuck with the term "Religious Right." I find the most commonly used substitute, "religio-political extremists," to be a bit of a mouthful. Like it or not, "Religious Right" is the term in common parlance in the media and the larger culture. I acknowledge its limitations, but it's the term I use in this book.

Also, while this book is critical of the Religious Right, it is not my intention for it to be critical of the general conservative movement. There are such people as fiscal conservatives and Republican moderates who disagree with the Religious Right on social issues. Some polls show the majority of registered Republicans falling into this camp. Although I sometimes use terms like "conservative Christians," "ultraconservatives," and "right-wing" in this book, I have tried to limit the use of them to descriptions of the Religious Right. Of course a person can be "right-wing" on taxes and economic issues but disagree with the Religious Right on social issues. I have no beef with these folks and do not intend to criticize them here or lump them in with the Religious Right.

I also believe it is obvious that I intend for nothing in this book to be critical of Christianity or religion, but in case there is any doubt about that let me reiterate the point here: The United States is an overwhelmingly religious nation. Christianity, in all of its forms, is the predominant religion of the country. Christianity has inspired many people to do great things, such as combat racism and poverty and work for social justice. But Christianity, like any other doctrine, can also be twisted and perverted and used like a club against others. I believe this is what the Religious Right has done.

They have corrupted the system of religion known as Christianity, not the other way around.

Now it's time for our travels to begin. Fasten your seatbelt. The signpost is looming up ahead. Our next stop is the Religious Right's Twilight Zone world of religion and politics.

Chapter 1

RECLAIMING AMERICA FOR RIGHT-WING, HOMOPHOBIC ZEALOTS

D. James Kennedy's Big Adventure

T ry as I might, I will never understand why some people consider television preacher D. James Kennedy a charismatic or interesting individual. To me, he is grim and dour, with all the charm of a minor bureaucrat.

I wanted to be fair to the man. Perhaps I just hadn't paid close enough attention. After all, my encounters with Kennedy were mostly limited to an occasional Sunday morning visit while channel surfing. Maybe I needed to see him up close and personal. It was time to go and make a visit.

Under normal circumstances, I would have no objection to traveling to south Florida at the end of February. Washington winters tend to be bearable, but I figure any time you can exchange temperatures in the 30s for ones in the 70s you're making the right move.

Still, as my plane descended into Fort Lauderdale's international airport, my emotions were decidedly mixed. Florida winters are nice, but visiting Kennedy probably would not be.

I had come to spend two days at Kennedy's "Reclaiming

America for Christ" conference, an annual event that the Fort Lauderdale–based televangelist has been sponsoring since 1993.

I wasn't sure what to expect. Kennedy is not nearly as well known as other Religious Right figures, such as Pat Robertson or Jerry Falwell. Yet he has been quietly building his own Religious Right empire in south Florida and clearly has national ambitions. I knew enough about him to realize that Kennedy is an old-fashioned, unreconstructed, hard-line fundamentalist with no pretenses of being a moderate and a "take-no-prisoners" attitude. I figured it was time to check him out.

As I said, Kennedy is charismatically challenged. In fact, he's downright stern. His tight grin, silver-flecked hair, and pancake makeup do not add up to a magnetic package. Despite his sullen demeanor, Kennedy, like a lot of TV preachers, has a significant following. (Some people, I guess, just like to be reminded how wicked they are.) No matter where you are in the country on Sunday morning, you can usually tune him in if you just do enough channel surfing. Kennedy stands there in a robe, stiffly gesticulating, railing against evolution, legal abortion, gay people, or some other Religious Right target of the day.

What does Kennedy want? My belief is that Kennedy wants to be as famous as people like Robertson and James Dobson. To that end, he is working to amass a Religious Right empire that could one day rival Focus on the Family or the Christian Broadcasting Network. He doesn't have it yet, and Kennedy, who is close to seventy, may not achieve it in his lifetime. Still, he's giving it a good try.

Born on November 3, 1930, in Augusta, Georgia, Kennedy is a onetime Arthur Murray Studios dance instructor who became a "born-again" Christian at age twenty-four. As Kennedy himself tells it in his book *The Gates of Hell Shall Not Prevail*, he was awakened by a radio alarm clock one morning after a night of heavy partying. The radio was blaring a sermon, and Kennedy was drawn in by the preacher's words. Within a week, Kennedy had converted and eventually decided to enter the ministry himself. He graduated with honors from Columbia Theological Seminary in 1959 and assumed the pastorate that same year of Fort Lauderdale's Coral Ridge Presbyterian Church, a congregation affiliated with the ultraconservative Presbyterian Church in America. (Kennedy has earned a number of other degrees as well, including a Ph.D. from New York University.)

Coral Ridge has grown rapidly under Kennedy's oversight, and the church now claims just under ten thousand members. He began broadcasting on television in 1974 and today reaches millions all over the country with a regular Sunday morning program, *The Coral Ridge Hour*, which is carried by more than five hundred TV stations. In addition, Kennedy has a radio program, *Truths That Transform*, heard daily on more than five hundred stations. A second daily Kennedy program, the ninety-second *Kennedy Commentary*, is heard on more than three hundred radio stations. He is the author of several books.

According to the Evangelical Council for Financial Accountability, an oversight group for evangelical ministries, Kennedy's TV ministry, Coral Ridge Ministries Media, Inc., had a total income of $24,555,110 as of December 31, 1996, the last year for which figures are available. In addition, Kennedy's Coral Ridge Presbyterian Church, which is incorporated separately, had an income of $16,586,074 for the same period.

Recently his broadcast ministry branched out into politics. In 1996 Kennedy founded the Center for Reclaiming America in Fort Lauderdale. Directed by Janet Folger, a thirty-something former antiabortion lobbyist from Ohio, the center says its mission is to provide "nonpartisan, interdenominational information, training, and support to enable Christians to have a positive role in developing a biblical virtues–based culture in their communities and in our nation."

What does this mean? Lots of Religious Right groups hide behind lofty-sounding rhetoric. In reality, the center is just another

Religious Right outfit obsessed with opposing legal abortion and gay rights and with bashing public education. For the time being, the center has chosen, under Folger's leadership, to focus chiefly on fighting the "homosexual agenda." This is a crowded field in Religious Right circles these days, but Folger found a new twist: She has played a lead role in bringing "ex-gays" into the public eye. These are people who say they used to be gay but aren't any more because they found Jesus. According to Folger, the existence of these people is proof that sexual orientation is chosen, not determined by biology, in contrast to the scientific research that leans toward a biological basis for homosexuality.

Although located in Florida, Kennedy has a Washington presence through the Center for Christian Statesmanship, which is also a project of his television ministry. Located on Capitol Hill, the center, which opened in 1995, sponsors Bible studies and other evangelical activities for members of Congress and their staffs. Its weekly fax newsletter, *Compass*, is designed to "help today's leaders apply the principles of God's Word to their official duties." The center also runs newspaper ads "that present the Gospel and challenge today's leaders to become modern-day Christian statesmen." Its director is Dr. Frank Wright.

In addition, Coral Ridge runs a school for grades K through 12 in Fort Lauderdale called Westminster Academy, which serves about one thousand students. Coral Ridge also sponsors the Knox Theological Seminary and owns a radio station, WAFG-FM. That, in a nutshell, is the Kennedy empire.

Kennedy's ministry has always promoted right-wing politics. It isn't uncommon to tune into *The Coral Ridge Hour* and hear him railing against legal abortion, antidiscrimination protection for gays, or the teaching of evolution in public schools. (He *really* hates evolution. He doesn't understand it, in my view, but that's another story.) The ministry frequently sends out lurid fund-raising appeals. One recent letter begged for funds to stop public broadcasting stations from airing a "homosexual-propaganda program" called *It's Elementary*. (Many stations aired it anyway.) In 1996, Kennedy told the evangelical magazine *World* that it has become "increasingly difficult for a genuine Christian to support" the Democratic Party.[1] (So much for that claim in the mission statement of nonpartisanship!)

What does Kennedy think about the separation of church and state? He doesn't like it. Kennedy's 1994 book, *Character & Destiny: A Nation In Search of Its Soul* (written with Jim Nelson Black), is riddled with attacks on the constitutional principle. Among other things, Kennedy calls church-state separation "diabolical," a "false doctrine," and "a lie" propagated by Thomas Jefferson. Kennedy also lapses into Red-baiting, writing, "This phrase does not appear in the United States Constitution at all, but in Article 52 of the Constitution of the Soviet Union—now the Soviet *disunion*. Defunct, because they tried to get rid of God."[2]

I had to sigh when I read that line. When will these right-wingers get some new ideas? This tiresome, unoriginal example of Red-baiting is thoroughly debunked in my first book, *Why the Religious Right Is Wrong About the Separation of Church and State*. The short answer is that Jefferson, who was not a communist, used the phrase in 1802, quite a few years before Marx and Lenin appeared on the scene.

A 1996 Kennedy tome, *The Gates of Hell Shall Not Prevail: The Attack on Christianity and What You Need to Know to Combat It* (coauthored with Jerry Newcombe), calls the wall of separation a "great deception [that] has been used to destroy much of the religious freedom and liberty this country has enjoyed since its inception."[3]

In his 1994 book, *Character & Destiny*, Kennedy asserts that although the United States was once a "Christian nation," that is no longer the case because today "the hostile barrage from atheists, agnostics, and other secular humanists has begun to take a serious toll on that heritage. In recent years, they have built up their forces and even increased their assault upon all our Christian institutions, and they have been enormously successful in taking over the 'public square.' Public education, the media, the government, the courts, and even the church in many places, now belong to them."[4]

Elsewhere in the book, Kennedy writes, "Our job is to reclaim America for Christ, *whatever the cost.*" Kennedy's triumphalist rhetoric has led to speculation that he may be sympathetic to "Christian Reconstructionism," an extreme Religious Right movement that seeks to establish a theocracy in America based on the Old Testament's harsh legal code.

Kennedy has denied being a Reconstructionist, but in May of 1996 he addressed a banquet held by American Vision, a Reconstructionist group based in Georgia and led by Gary DeMar. The group's newsletter, *A.V. Report*, noted that, "American Vision has enjoyed a wonderful friendship and working relationship with Dr. Kennedy and others at Coral Ridge for many years."

Are Kennedy's views extreme? Judge for yourself. Here is a sampling of Kennedy's opinions, taken from his 1994 book, *Character & Destiny*:

The Culture War

Christians did not start the culture war but . . . we are going to end it. That is a fact, and the Bible assures us of victory. (p. 76)

Deceitful Educators

Not all the educators in our public schools and universities are deliberately deceitful, not all of them want to destroy this nation, but many do. The major teachers' unions certainly do. (p. 75)

The United States as a Christian Nation

But the fact is, the United States of America *was* conceived and brought forth by Christians, and history tells us that story in no uncertain terms. . . . Anyone who reads about the values upon which this nation was founded understands perfectly well that this was, from the start, a Christian nation. (p. 71)

Communist Professors

Just a few years ago, there were as many as ten thousand Communist professors in American universities. The average person never saw any of them, and many would doubt the truth of that statistic. But I can assure you it is true. (p. 63)

Secular Sinners

Modern secularists and agnostics do not want to admit that the Christian religion is true, because that would mean that they are sinners; and they have no intention of giving up their right to sin. (p. 46)

Public School Immorality

Teachers in many of our public schools have acceded to the policies of the liberal teachers' unions to make sure that students from kindergarten through high school will be stripped of any sense of moral or ethical absolutes. Right and wrong are non-issues in our public schools. (p. 26)

Evolution: Into the Slime

Every new advance and every step taken by science confirm not evolution but the Genesis account of creation. Yet evolution still continues to be taught as fact. . . . Thus, the honorable place that had been given to human beings by God is surreptitiously aborted, and they are dragged down into the slime. (p. 178)

Dismantling the Wall of Separation

If we are committed and involved in taking back the nation for Christian moral values, and if we are willing to risk the scorn of the secular media and the bureaucracy that stand against us, there is no doubt we can witness the dismantling of not just the Berlin Wall but the even more diabolical 'wall of separation' that has led to increasing secularization, godlessness, immorality, and corruption in our country. (pp. 126–27)

Engaging the Enemy

God forbid that we who were born into the blessings of a Christian America should let our patrimony slip like sand through our fingers and leave to our children the bleached bones of a godless secular society. But whatever the outcome, one thing is certain: God has called us to engage the enemy in this culture war. That is our challenge today. (p. 91)

This Is Our Land

This is our land. This is our world. This is our heritage, and with God's help, we shall reclaim this nation for Jesus Christ. And no power on earth can stop us. (p. 85)

Reclaiming America for Christ

How much more forcefully can I say it? The time has come, and it is long overdue, when Christians and conservatives and all men and women who believe in the birthright of freedom must rise up and reclaim America for Jesus Christ. (p. 80)

Note how often Kennedy simply asserts something as fact and expects his readers to accept it without question—no matter how fantastic the claim may be. I was especially struck by his assertion that ten thousand communist professors were running amok on America's college campuses "just a few years ago." (Again I say: Will these right-wingers never give up on their tiresome Red-baiting?) His claim that every new scientific finding supports creationism is similarly nonsense, absolute bunk. Just the opposite is true.

Like many Religious Right leaders, Kennedy never bothers to offer any proof for his most outrageous claims. The claim about communist professors is startling, yet we are expected to accept it on face value. Why? Because D. James Kennedy said so. This is the old "appeal to authority" argument: "It's true because I said so, and I'm an authority, so I ought to know." There are two things wrong with the argument in this case: One, authorities can be wrong, and two, Kennedy isn't an authority on communism or American universities. In fact, he's just a TV preacher who found someone to help him write books containing outrageous, unsubstantiated claims.

Could we get a footnote? No, Kennedy can't be bothered to document something this inflammatory. We're supposed to believe it because "I can assure you it is true." Maybe that works for his followers, who are trained not to question Kennedy, but anyone with a more questioning outlook should remember the first rule of the skeptic, "Extraordinary claims require extraordinary evidence." (Although in this case, I would allow that just plain old evidence would be fine, too.)

Actually, even if there were a footnote, I doubt it would do much good. Kennedy may be many things, but legitimate historian or plausible social critic are not among them. In the case of Kennedy's books, his claims are only as good as his sources—and they're lousy. Kennedy relies primarily on other far-right fundamentalist writers, not legitimate historians. These writers publish books not to uncover the truth but to buttress their preconceived biases. Like creationists, they selectively interpret data and exclude anything that undermines their position. Sometimes, they rely on historical anecdotes or quotations supposedly uttered by famous figures that are completely fictitious.

I am especially amused by Kennedy's retelling of U.S. history and how our country was founded to be a "Christian" nation. (Funny how the framers forgot to put that in the Constitution.) I have seen this Religious Right revisionist history reprinted time after time in books by other Religious Right leaders. It consists of errors of interpretation, selective interpretation of the facts, falsified quotes, and cut-and-paste revisionism.

Kennedy probably believes it's true. He did not personally make the stuff up. Someone else did, and Kennedy probably just lifted it from other sources. He may have footnotes to cite sometimes. The problem is his sources are wrong to begin with.

Let me give you an example of Kennedy's shoddy research. This one does not deal with U.S. history, but it's a good illustration of how Kennedy gets it wrong and misleads his readers: In Kennedy's 1996 book, *The Gates of Hell Shall Not Prevail*, he includes a little information about Julian II, sometimes called Julian the Apostate, the last pagan emperor of Rome. Julian, who ruled from 351–353 C.E., tried unsuccessfully to reverse the Christianization of the empire put into place by his uncle Constantine the Great. He was killed in battle with the Persians after being speared. According to Kennedy, when hit by the spear, Julian pulled it out, threw a handful his own blood into the sky and shouted, "Thou hast conquered, Galilean!" The point is that even this heretical emperor had to acknowledge the superiority of Jesus in the end.[5]

It's an interesting story, but unfortunately for Kennedy, it's completely fictitious. The ancient world is an interest of mine, and I've read several books on ancient Rome, including two scholarly biographies of Julian. No real historian believes this story. It was invented years after Julian's death by Christian writers who, for obvious reasons, wanted to show that in the end even Julian had to come around.

In fact, Julian's last words were not recorded. Some say he gave a lengthy speech as he lay dying. The speech is recorded in Edward Gibbon's *Decline and Fall of the Roman Empire*, but alas, this too is probably an invention. It's unlikely that a man dying of a serious spear wound had the wits or strength to croak out lengthy, eloquent remarks off the top of his head. The best evidence is that Julian asked for a drink of water and then collapsed. Kennedy cites a book that tells the "Thou hast conquered, Galilean!" story, but that source is wrong—like so much of the "history" Kennedy tries to pass off.

(Another Kennedy book, *Character and Destiny*, contains a fictitious quote by James Madison lauding the Ten Commandments. For a complete debunking of this alleged quotation, see my section on David Barton in chapter 8.)

I think fair-minded readers can understand why I was a tad reluctant to spend two days with the followers of this man. But nevertheless there I was, surrounded by about eighteen hundred people who showed up at the event in Fort Lauderdale on February 26 and 27, 1999, at the Broward County Convention Center. The crowd, overwhelmingly white and mostly over sixty, was heavy with Floridians. Like many other Religious Right gatherings I've attended, the format was simple: a giant stage and a revolving cast of speakers. We heard a parade of them on the first day.

Kennedy himself led off. At the time, the Religious Right world was abuzz because one man, Paul Weyrich, a longtime right-wing strategist who helped found the Moral Majority all those years ago, had dared to express the apostate view that maybe salvation doesn't come from right-wing politics.

Truth be told, Weyrich's message wasn't even that radical. Just weeks before the conference, he had issued a memo to supporters (also posted on the Internet) asserting that in the wake of the failed attempt to remove President Bill Clinton from office, Americans have shown themselves to no longer be a moral people. The culture is so debased, Weyrich asserted, that right-wing Christians would do better to withdraw a bit from the secular world and create their own institutions—send their children to private Christian schools, watch Christian videos instead of television, get filters for the Internet, patronize Christian book stores, and so on. Weyrich was not calling for a total withdrawal from politics, just a tactical retreat. He got blasted all the same.

At the same time, right-wing columnist Cal Thomas had penned a book called *Blinded by the Might*, which asserted that Religious Right activists had erred by placing too much emphasis on politics when they should have been saving souls. Thomas's book, coauthored with Christian minister Ed Dobson (no relation to James Dobson of Focus on the Family), was released just before the Kennedy event. Thomas had been scheduled to be a lead-off speaker on Friday morning. Instead he found himself disinvited. It would appear that Kennedy wanted no part of Thomas's new message.

Thomas had learned a hard lesson about what it's like to be an apostate. It's not like Thomas had suddenly become a liberal. Far from it. *Blinded by the Might* is loaded with standard-issue Religious Right slogans, such as crude attacks on public education. And, having seen mile-high stacks of a previous Thomas book, *The Things that Matter Most*, in the discount section of a local book store festooned with red stickers reading "$4.00," I had to wonder if Thomas's sudden decision to criticize the Religious Right didn't have more to do with sparking book sales than principle. Whatever the story, Thomas had dared to say some things that Kennedy did not like—and that got him booted off the program.

Thomas later told the *Washington Post* that he called Kennedy after the disinvitation and tried to talk his way back on to the invite list. He even promised not to talk about his new book. Kennedy would have none of it. Thomas bitterly reflected to the *Post* that he was having one of his first bouts with censorship, and it was coming from the Right, not the Left.[6]

At the "Reclaiming America for Christ" conference, attendees weren't told the whole story behind Thomas's no-show. As we shuffled en masse into the conference hall Friday morning, we were handed a "Revised Schedule" announcing good news: House Majority Leader Dick Armey (R-Texas) had joined the program. But there was bad news, too: "Unfortunately, Cal Thomas will not be with us today—we share your disappointment."

I am always amused when Religious Right operatives, who constantly bemoan America's embrace of moral relativism, lie through their teeth. "We share your disappointment." What disappointment? Kennedy had personally removed Thomas from the lineup of speakers. *He* certainly wasn't disappointed. The way the flier read, one could assume that Thomas had come down with the flu or just decided at the last minute to fly to Wichita to address the Women's

Christian Temperance Union instead of Kennedy's "Reclaiming America for Christ."

To Kennedy, talk like Thomas's is heresy. He blasted Weyrich and Thomas for daring to suggest it, though not by name. During brief opening remarks, Kennedy made it clear that he doesn't buy into the talk emanating from some circles in Washington these days that the Religious Right has lost the so-called culture wars. To Kennedy, it was a time to declare "spiritual war," not run up the white flag of surrender.

"Not only are the culture wars not over, and not only have we not lost, but the fact is we are winning," Kennedy told the crowd. His evidence for this was that supposedly the number of daily conversions to Christianity around the world was skyrocketing, reaching one hundred thousand per day in 1995. Unfortunately, no source was given for such an astounding figure.

Kennedy made clear his disagreement with "conservative leaders" who have "called for retreat."

"Surrender?" he asked. "Not on your life! . . . Thank God we have read the end of the Book. We know how this war comes out. Yes, we are fighting a spiritual war. We must fight it with grace, courtesy, and love, but also with determination and zeal."

At this point, I was confused. I had forgotten that under Kennedy's form of hyper-Calvinism, many things are preordained. So he's read the end of the Book? Great. My first thought was, "Then go home and wait for the inevitable. Who are you to be so presumptuous as to think you can help God speed things along? He'll do this thing in his own time." But did Kennedy have any intention of dismissing us all with orders to go home and wait for the end of the Book?

No such luck. Kennedy just kept droning on. It was to get better. He insisted that most Americans agree with him, claiming that the nation has been led astray by misleading polls. "Our nation should not be guided by polls," Kennedy said, a veiled reference to the fact that Clinton's job-approval rating had remained high despite the White House sex scandal. "This country has been deceived horrendously by false polling, and I think the American people need to wake up to that."

Kennedy asserted that public opinion firms routinely refuse to call residents of "eleven conservative states" and they screen people with leading questions, excluding conservatives. According to his somewhat creative logic, since eleven states represent 22 percent of America's fifty states, one must add 22 percent to the number of Americans who say they disapprove of Clinton, thus reversing the results.

Even if it were true that polling firms do this—and it's not—Kennedy's math still wouldn't add up. But in the Twilight Zone of the Religious Right, things don't have to be logical or make sense. They simply have to be said with force and wrapped around an attack on some enemy, and the next thing you know, it's time for yet another standing ovation.

Other Kennedy claims were equally florid. He painted a portrait of an America overrun by drugs, teenage pregnancy, abortion, rampant crime, unwed mothers, and divorce. He said he acknowledges that his opponents consider him controversial and warned the crowd to expect opposition as they prepare for battle.

I was surprised at what came next, however. Kennedy stopped talking and turned the emcee duties over to an associate. After that, he appeared only intermittently at the podium, offering brief introductions of some speakers.

It's not that Kennedy was invisible or anything. He signed books for his adoring public and greeted everyone as we entered the banquet hall for a gala dinner on Saturday night. But while the speakers blasted forth from the podium during the conference, he merely sat up there behind them on stage, perched on a huge chair that I can only describe as a type of throne. And, despite the invective booming out of the loud speakers and frequent blasts of martial music, I swear I saw him nodding off once or twice.

At the time of the event, Kennedy was sixty-nine, and perhaps he was getting a little tired. In fact, it may be a little late for Kennedy, soon to be in his seventh decade, to launch a successful national Religious Right group. But not to worry, because Kennedy has younger helpers.

His primary spokesperson these days is Janet Folger, who runs his Center for Reclaiming America, a fledgling Religious Right political group that has gay bashing as its primary objective. Once ensconced in Fort Lauderdale, Folger quickly made a name for herself by spearheading a national ad campaign featuring "ex-homosexuals," people who claim to have been gay before converting to fundamentalist Christianity.

The "ex-gay" movement is the Religious Right's attempt to be kinder and gentler to homosexuals. It took many years, but in the late 1990s many Religious Right leaders finally got it into their heads that many Americans were disgusted by their rhetoric on gays.

Polls show Americans divided and conflicted on many gay-related issues. They may disagree on issues like applying civil rights laws to gay people or allowing gay adoption of children, but polls also show that most Americans don't see the need to demonize gays. Many Americans have adopted a "live-and-let-live" attitude and believe that gays ought to be more or less left alone. At some point, some Religious Right leaders decided that toning down the rhetoric might not be a bad idea. Not all of them took the advice—you can still hear plenty of ugly rhetoric out there—but some decided to try new avenues.

Instead of just rebuking homosexuals, Folger decided that showcasing the "ex-gay" ministries would be more productive. These ministries—notably, Exodus International and Parents and Friends of Ex-Gays (P-FOX)—had been around for years, but no one paid much attention to them. Thanks to Folger's help, they got a national platform. She arranged for a series of full-page ads to run in newspapers across the nation. One ad featured Anne Paulk, a former lesbian who is now married and a mother. Another featured more than eight hundred "ex-gays" who had gathered for a conference in Seattle.

Folger told the crowd how she had worked to get a group photo of the "ex-gays" after she conceived the ad campaign. Things looked rocky for a time. Stuck on the wrong coast in Florida, Folger was having difficulty arranging the logistics for a picture. She couldn't even line up a photographer. Her contact in Seattle was discouraged, thinking maybe he could get her a photo with fifty people in it. But then she started praying, and, well, the rest of the story is familiar.

"It was God-sized!" Folger exclaimed, telling the crowd how eventually more than eight hundred "ex-gays" joined the photo shoot. She attributed this success directly to God. At this point, I had to wonder about the god Folger and her supporters worship. To me it has always seemed a most curious type of god: He's a god who drops everything to make sure some extremist gets a good photographer in Seattle. At times, the god of the Religious Right seems to be little more than a really efficient personal assistant. I don't doubt that Folger got a good photographer, but I suspect the Yellow Pages had more to do with it than the Almighty.

Despite all of her "love the sinner, hate the sin" rhetoric, when push comes to shove, Folger advocates extreme measures against gay people. On July 30, 1998, she debated gay journalist Andrew Sullivan on ABC's *Nightline*. During the debate, Sullivan asked Folger repeatedly if she supports laws that make homosexual activity a crime punishable by incarceration. Folger kept dodging the question, but finally host Diane Sawyer demanded she answer. Folger replied, "I guess if you're looking at sodomy laws, there are sodomy laws on the books that I very much support."[7]

Folger's views on gays are standard Religious Right boilerplate. And, like many of her peers in the Religious Right, Folger has little use for Christianity that falls outside of her own narrow sight range.

In Jerry Falwell's *National Liberty Journal* she blasted Americans United Executive Director Barry W. Lynn, an ordained minister in the United Church of Christ, for criticizing the House of Representatives after the House considered a resolution on June 19, 1999, calling on Americans to engage in a day of "prayer, fasting, and humiliation." In an Americans United Press release dated June 28, 1999, Lynn chided the House for wasting time on "pious platitudes and meaningless resolutions."

"When a minister makes these kinds of statements about an endorsement of prayer and humility, doesn't it make you glad you don't attend his church?" said Folger. "Let us not be dissuaded by a 'reverend' who holds God's Word meaningless."[8]

(I would assert that it is Folger and her associates who make God's word meaningless by tossing it around as just another political football and an issue to be used to tar an opponent during the next campaign.)

She may have severe views, but there's no denying that Folger is energetic and establishes a good rapport with the crowd. At the "Reclaiming America" conference, she was especially incensed by efforts to pass federal legislation increasing the penalties for "hate crimes," such as assaults on gays and lesbians. The drive took on heightened urgency in 1998 after Matthew Shepard, a young gay man in Wyoming, was severely beaten and tied to a fence in freezing weather. Shepherd later died of his injuries.

"The goal of this legislation is to try to silence us," Folger said. She asserted that if the law passed, it would be illegal to read the first chapter of the biblical book of Romans over the radio, an act she said is already illegal in Canada.

Folger also blasted the Supreme Court for striking down the display of the Ten Commandments in public schools. "We live in a country that does everything it can to keep its focus away from God," she asserted.[9]

I found this claim especially amusing in a country where even professional football players prostrate themselves after scoring a touchdown, Nativity scenes spring up on city hall lawns every December, and TV and radio preachers (like Folger's boss) rant at us from every other television and radio station on the dial. Ask any European you happen to meet and they will set you straight: Americans are obsessed with religion. It is literally everywhere.

"Christian" book stores proliferate, "What Would Jesus Do?" bracelets are a fashion item, half of the population is transfixed by books about angels, and every politician in earshot is eager to tell you how much he or she loves God. Yet the Religious Right claims that we live in a culture that tries to shut down religion? Religion in America is alive and well, thank you, and the fact that it has invaded our political system is further evidence of that vitality. If Folger really wants to see moribund religion, she ought to visit European nations. Many of them have established state churches, church taxes, and government support for religion. The only thing the churches lack are members. In European nations, it isn't uncommon for 30 or 40 percent of the population to flirt with nonbelief. In this country it's in the single digits. (And oh, by the way, about those poor children growing up in the "godless" public school system that works so hard to crush their beliefs: New polls show that 95 percent of them believe in God and eight out of ten pray regularly.)[10]

Not surprisingly, given her background, Folger blasted the legalization of abortion and physician-assisted suicide. Of the latter issue, Folger said, "That is something Satan really wants to be involved in." She added that the practice must be stopped because "some people don't accept Christ until their deathbed." Folger then waved around a large plastic bag that had an elastic band at the bottom, claiming it is an "exit bag" being sent down from Canada—by forces she did not name—so people in America can kill themselves. (I had to wonder if this Canada bashing was part of a new Religious Right strategy. First the Canadians are telling ministers they can't read

Romans on the radio, and now they're shipping down bags so we can kill ourselves. Maybe we had better take a closer look at what's in that "Canadian bacon" they've been sending down.)

Folger also blasted the constitutional doctrine of church-state separation as it applies to public schools. Playing fast and loose with the facts, she asserted that U.S. District Judge Ira DeMent in northern Alabama had "called out the prayer police to look for students praying" at DeKalb County public schools.

I was especially appalled by this gross distortion since I know a great deal about *Chandler* v. *James*, the case in question. It was filed by attorneys with Americans United, and I have written about it extensively. In *Chandler*, an Alabama public school was accused of sponsoring Christian religious worship in various ways, including encouraging prayer before school events, allowing outside groups to distribute Bibles to students, and sponsoring assemblies with sectarian content. Judge DeMent merely ordered an end to school-sponsored religious worship, pointing out in his decision that students may pray voluntarily on their own time. Given the scope of the abuses in DeKalb County, and their long-running nature, DeMent ordered that monitors periodically visit the schools to make sure teachers and administrators were not violating his order. The monitors were not "prayer police," and they did not attempt to stop individual students from praying on their own. The schools, in fact, actually had a hand in picking the monitors.

Religious Right groups always need someone to demonize—it's better for fund-raising—and Kennedy and Folger decided that Judge DeMent was the perfect target. The two were so angered by DeMent's ruling that they launched a petition drive to persuade Congress to impeach him. Folger told the approving crowd that so far sixty thousand names had been collected on petitions demanding DeMent's ouster. She did not point out that no member of the House of Representatives has agreed to sponsor an impeachment resolution or that it stands virtually no chance of passage. Federal judges, after all, can be impeached only for committing "high crimes and misdemeanors." The last time I checked, handing down a ruling that right-wing pressure groups don't like does not qualify.

The following day, Folger reappeared at a session called "The Assault on Christianity," which consisted mostly of clips of television shows and movies that Coral Ridge Ministries claims portray Christians in a negative light.

I was reminded of the utter lack of sense of humor that many Religious Right activists have. One of the clips shown was from *The Simpsons*, the Fox network's popular animated series. It depicted Bart Simpson trying to get out of trouble by insisting that he hadn't been misbehaving, he was in fact reading the Bible. To the Religious Right, this is an all-out war on Christianity.

Another sitcom clip depicted a flashy preacher who lined his pockets and chased women. The reason a stereotype like that is funny is that it has a kernel of truth in it. How many television preachers, after all, have fallen because of greed and/or lust?

Curiously, Folger seems to blame church-state separation for the entertainment industry's alleged anti-Christian bias. At the session, she distributed a sheet titled "Restoring the Christian Voice," which she claimed helps in "debunking the whole separation of church and state nonsense on which most of this rests."

Among other things, the sheet insists that church-state separation is not an American concept but rather appears in "the Constitution of the former Soviet Union." Folger added that Thomas Jefferson's views on the First Amendment are not important since "he had nothing to do with the Constitution."

Stay with me as I say this one more time: I am always amazed that as late as 1999, Religious Right propagandists are still engaging in Red-baiting. What's worse, they can't even get their story straight. Another speaker at the same conference, Benny Proffitt, told the crowd at a workshop on religion in public schools that church-state separation comes from the *Communist Manifesto*. If you're going to engage in a Red smear campaign, at least get the story right.

In fact, the *Communist Manifesto* says nothing about separation of church and state. (I did something Proffitt apparently can't be bothered to do: looked it up and read it.) As for the old Soviet Constitution, it might have. So what? That document also contained a guarantee of free speech and press. Does that make those concepts communistic? The Soviets told their people they had all sorts of freedoms—obviously modeled on the U.S. Bill of Rights—but never bothered to actually implement them.

Later during the session, Folger was joined by Jerry Newcombe, a Kennedy associate who has coauthored several books with the TV preacher. Newcombe asserted that Hollywood deliberately puts anti-Christian bias into TV shows and movies to promote a "godless culture." As an example, Newcombe said several recent movies have featured "Christian serial killers," a character Newcombe said is ironic since, according to a Time-Life book he read about serial murderers, there has never been a Christian serial killer. (In reality, Newcombe added, many serial killers are homosexuals.)

Newcombe chastised conferees for being "a part of the problem" by going to see movies without first finding out what they are about.

The session was wildly popular, drawing a standing-room-only crowd with some three hundred people turned away at the door. As it concluded, Folger passed out "life cards" listing companies that Coral Ridge Ministries has decided to boycott for alleged "anti-family" policies, including funding Planned Parenthood. The companies included Target department stores, Johnson & Johnson, American Express, and Levi Strauss. (General Mills has already apparently caved in to Coral Ridge's pressure, and the firm's name was blacked out on the card.)

Folger also emceed a curiously named "Homosexual Panel," which consisted not of homosexuals but of "ex-homosexuals" John and Anne Paulk, who gave their testimonies of how Jesus delivered them from the "gay lifestyle." The Paulks' comments were mostly about their personal experiences. They seemed sincere and refrained from overt gay bashing. That job was left to Robert H. Knight, director of cultural studies at the Family Research Council. (See more on Knight in chapter 7.) He didn't waste any time. Quipping, "I'm not a homophobe, by the way, although I play one on television," Knight asserted, "The end goal of gay activism is the criminalization of Christianity."

Despite his claims to the contrary, I believe the evidence shows that Knight is one of the nation's premier homophobes. He never hesitated to reach for the most lurid rhetoric about gays that he could find. He insisted, for example, that another goal of the homosexual rights movement is to legalize sex between adults and children and told the crowd that hate crimes legislation "is the precursor toward thought crimes."

After accusing gays of advocating pedophilia, Knight said, "It is about going after the kids, ultimately. It's about teaching them in schools that gay is OK, and they might be gay and if they've even had a single thought about it, you might as well try it, otherwise you may damage your self-esteem. . . . So they're coming into the schools rapidly now under the guise of AIDS education and tolerance education."

Although Knight urged the crowd "to show that we don't hate homosexuals," he went on to call abortion, pornography, and gay rights "an iron triangle," asserting that gay people are involved in promoting all three issues.

He also advised the crowd to examine the marchers at pro-choice rallies. "They are usually pretty big, heavyset women," he said, "who look like they've been over working Oktoberfest for the last six years. You know, there's six beer mugs in each arm. All right, it's a stereotype, but I swear looking at that footage, that's what you see—a lot of people who are angry, women who have shed their femininity and adopted a masculine outlook and are fiercely protective of abortion, which is the holy sacrament of feminism."

I kept waiting for Knight to say that some of his best friends are gay. He didn't let me down. After ridiculing gay people for fifteen minutes and accusing them of all manner of crimes, he actually said, "I know people who are gay. Some dear friends of mine are."

Knight's gay friends probably would not have felt too comfortable at the conference. Gay bashing was a constant theme. On Friday morning attendees were entertained by Debbie and Angie Winans, gospel singers who did a live rendition of their antigay song "Not Natural." In the conference exhibit hall, "ex-gay" ministries distributed material, and one group sponsored a display accusing Clinton of being a stooge of the gay rights movement.

I stopped at one booth run by an outfit called Americans for Truth about Homosexuality and picked up a booklet titled *The Homosexual Agenda: How the Gay Lobby is Targeting America's Children*, which is mostly a compilation of wild charges accusing gay groups of advocating pedophilia.

Knight's rhetoric may sound extreme, but it was tame compared to the invective against legal abortion unleashed by Dr. Laurence White, senior pastor of Our Savior Lutheran Church in Houston. Asserting that "America is in deadly peril," White insisted that the country will soon face judgment from God for nearly three decades of legal abortion. White several times compared legal abortion in America to Nazi Germany. He talked about visiting Germany with his two grown sons and their trip to a concentration camp. After the trip, he said, his sons urged him to increase his activism against abortion.

Nazi-era Germans, White asserted, kept religion and government separate "and their nation was destroyed. That retreat was facilitated by the lie of the absolute separation of church and state." (Actually, the Nazi government signed a concordat with the Vatican and sought to establish a "National Reich Church" designed to bring several Protestant denominations under total state control. The

Nazis sought to control religion, neuter its voice, and use it for their evil ends. That is not separation of church and state.[11])

Continued White, "My friends, it's happening again. It's happening here in our beloved America." Legal abortion, White added, "makes Hitler look like a humanitarian by comparison." He urged everyone to get involved in politics but added, "Our God is not the mascot of the Republican Party. . . . If the Republican Party cannot nominate a candidate with the courage to put an end to the slaughter, then we must look elsewhere for leadership."

The next day White led a workshop titled "Pulpits Aflame," during which he called church-state separation "the sharpest sword in the devil's arsenal, and it has immobilized churches all over the land."

Separation of religion and government, according to White, is among many "lies from the father of lies. The devil uses them to hinder and hamper the mandate of the church."

White then launched into a detailed discussion of Matt. 22, a New Testament passage that is frequently cited as being supportive of the separation of church and state. In the passage, Jesus is approached by Pharisees who ask him if it is proper to pay taxes to the ruling Romans.

Jesus knows this is a trap. If he says yes, the people, who chafe under Roman oppression, will turn against him. If he says no, the Roman authorities will label him a rabble-rouser and imprison him. So Jesus points to a silver coin and asks the Pharisees whose image is one the coin. When they reply, "Caesar's," he says, "Then render unto Caesar the things that are Caesar's and unto God the things that are God's."

White called this passage the "separationist's favorite text" but said it has been misinterpreted. According to his somewhat creative analysis, when Jesus asked whose image was on the coin, he was really reminding the Pharisees that even Caesar was created in God's image. Therefore the passage, White insisted, is really an affirmation of "God's sovereignty over all He has created. . . . There is nothing in this world that is not under God's control, and that includes you and me and every government on the face of this earth." White's analysis shows that if fundamentalists work hard enough, they can pretty much make the Bible say anything or support nearly any of their far-right political views.

White blasted Christian pastors, especially "cowed separation-of-church-and-state boys," who are wary of jumping into politics for fear of losing their tax exempt status. "We may lose our tax-exemptions," he said. "History may say the worst thing to happen to the Christian churches was tax exemption because it keeps us from speaking out."

Unlike Christian Coalition events, Kennedy's "Reclaiming America" did not feature a lot of speeches by elected officials. The only one to appear was House Majority Leader Dick Armey (R-Texas). Armey, who substituted at the last minute for conservative columnist Thomas, gave a rambling, low-key speech mostly about the importance of families. It included tepid calls for private school vouchers, tax cuts, and a space-based missile defense system. Having heard Armey speak at other venues, I was surprised at his weak delivery in Fort Lauderdale.

"This is a good country," said Armey, half mumbling, "and we are good people. It's our country. Let's take it back."

Although the program was not stacked with GOP all-stars, there was no mistaking the political sentiments of the crowd. They routinely hissed or booed whenever Clinton's name was mentioned, and cheered loudly when Knight talked about his desire to work for Gary Bauer in the White House. In the exhibit hall, one firm did brisk business selling hats, buttons, and shirts embossed with the names of GOP presidential hopefuls, as well as bumper stickers reading, "I Support Ken Starr" and "Proud Member of the Vast, Right-Wing Conspiracy." One bitter-sounding man told me, "Democracy is the worst form of government. If we had the rule of law, we wouldn't have to put up with this jerk in the White House."

Bauer was the only Republican presidential aspirant given podium time. During his remarks Friday night, Bauer, who at the time was taking a leave of absence from the Family Research Council to run for president, criticized Paul Weyrich, referring to him not by name but merely as "a conservative leader," for issuing a controversial memo, just before the conference started, asserting that the Religious Right had failed to change American culture and needed to create its own parallel institutions.

Charged Bauer, "The fact that this conference is being held in the wake of that memo is very important. If that memo is right, this conference is ludicrous. But none of us believe that. Dr. Kennedy doesn't believe that, and I don't believe that. Words like 'I give up' can't be in our vocabulary."

Bauer urged judges all over America to display the Ten Commandments in courtrooms and added, "We will either rediscover virtue or we will lose our liberty." He asserted that in modern-day America, adultery has become the norm, then, barely a minute later, praised Rep. Henry Hyde (R-Ill.) "and the other House managers who stood for our Constitution" during the House indictment of Clinton and then in his subsequent impeachment trial. (Bauer, of course, did not mention the evidence of Hyde's own adulterous affair that surfaced during the impeachment debate. Hyde's defense for his adultery was that it was a "youthful indiscretion." He was in his forties at the time it happened.)

But overall, Bauer's remarks were unexpectedly low-key. He drew the heaviest applause when he pledged to make opposing legal abortion the keystone of his presidential campaign. "I promise you this: On this issue, I will not be moved," he said. The remark drew a standing ovation.

Bauer was followed by right-wing radio talk show host Janet Parshall, who was recently named chief spokesperson for the Family Research Council to pick up some of Bauer's duties while he was out on the stump. Noting her D.C. location, Parshall said, "I am a war correspondent from Babylon. But I am not here to talk about politics; I am here to talk about principle. I do not work for a party. I serve a king, and I am not ashamed of my ambassadorship."

Parshall, who has an odd habit of referring to the audience as "beloved" every other minute, took the sharpest shots at Clinton of all the event speakers. Calling the Senate acquittal "a sham," Parshall asserted that the president "has lost the moral imperative to govern the nation" and insisted that if the people had risen up to demand "that this shameless man be removed from the White House, the Senate would have done it."

Describing Clinton as a liar and "an unstable man," Parshall said America is engaged in a "moral and spiritual battle" but insisted that the tide is turning toward the Religious Right. She cited as evidence a poll conducted by the liberal Center for Gender Equality, released shortly before the conference, which claimed that American women are adopting conservative ideas and that a majority now oppose legal abortion.

To rally the Religious Right's troops for battle, Parshall told a story about George Washington at the Battle of Trenton. Asked by soldiers what they should do if they ran out of bullets, Washington replied, "Then use your bayonets."

Said Parshall, "We must use our spiritual bayonets. We must use the bayonets, for the nation must be taken for the love of God." There was talk about love, but I could not help but think that bayonets are designed to gouge people to death, or at the very least maim them. It was one of the more gory military metaphors I heard during the event.

The following day was devoted to workshops. I attended three—White's "Pulpits Aflame," Folger's attack on Hollywood, and a third that was most revealing.

This session focused on public schools. Like many Religious Right figures, Kennedy can't seem to decide what to do about public education. The Religious Right alternates between calling public schools moral cesspools unfit for decent children and yearning to take over the schools and transform them into Christian fundamentalist parochial schools. That dichotomy was evident at "Reclaiming America."

At the last "breakout" session I attended, the speaker, Benny Proffitt, who ministers to young people, clearly favored the takeover approach. His session was dedicated to outlining an ambitious agenda for using public school students to spark a revival in America. It was a telling example of how the Religious Right seeks to reach a generation of young people even though the Supreme Court has banned mandatory programs of religious worship in public schools.

Proffitt is founder and president of First Priority of America, an organization with offices in Alpharetta, Georgia, and Nashville, Tennessee. His plan is simple: He urges churches to band together to coach junior high and high school students on how to form Christian clubs on campus under the federal Equal Access Act and then use the clubs as instruments for aggressive proselytism. The Equal Access Act is federal legislation that requires public secondary schools to allow students to form religious clubs if any clubs not directly related to the curriculum are already meeting. For example, if a high school has a scuba club but does not teach scuba, then the act is triggered, and students may form religious clubs. The law states that religious clubs are supposed to be student-run.

Under Proffitt's plan, local churches—need I say they must be ultraconservative in theology?—join forces to train students and fund their activities. Students then use the Equal Access Act to gain a foothold in the school. Students are instructed to spend time seeking converts and regularly report the number of conversions to First Priority.

Proffitt, a former public school teacher who resigned in 1979 after he was told to stop preaching to students, scorned the Supreme Court rulings of 1962 and 1963 that removed government-mandated prayer and religious worship from public schools. Unfortunately, his analysis of those cases and what the high court said in them was rife with errors.

"I saw first-hand God removed from the school system," said Proffitt. "I saw the destruction and devastation that had on a generation of young people."

He asserted that the 1962 ruling was especially offensive because the prayers challenged were Christian prayers, calling it "an attack on our Christian heritage." Proffitt should take some time to read carefully the court's ruling in *Engel* v. *Vitale*. If he did, he would learn that the prayer challenged was hardly "Christian." Rather, it was a "nondenominational" prayer written by the New York Board of Regents, the state school board.

I find it hard to believe that anyone in America wants to recite, or wants their children to recite, bland, "to-whom-it-may-concern" prayers composed by government bodies. It seems especially odd that religious fundamentalists, who claim to take their faith so seriously, would champion this watered-down pseudospirituality.

Proffitt added that a few years later the Supreme Court ordered "God removed from every public building in America." Here I simply couldn't figure out what he was referring to. There is no Supreme Court ruling requiring this. In 1980 the high court did strike down a Kentucky law requiring the posting of the Ten Commandments in public schools, but 1980 is not "a few years" from 1962, and the case was limited to public schools, not every government building.

Over the years, I have heard Religious Right leaders make the most outrageous statements about Supreme Court rulings. Some do this because of their ignorance, others do it deliberately to deceive their uninformed followers. Proffitt probably belongs in the former camp, as he seems to believe some rather strange things. His attack on the teaching of evolution in the public schools clearly demonstrated this. He asserted, "We wonder why they [students] carry guns and kill each other. Well, we've told them, 'You're nothing, you're a freak, you're an accident of nature. That's all.'"

According to Proffitt, America can be saved only if fundamentalism finds a way into the schools. "The only way we're going to change America is to raise an entire generation with the message of the Gospel," he said. He added that it's too late for "Generation X" to be saved but insisted that the next generation is ripe for the Gospel. Much is at stake, he said.

"If we miss this next generation, God will walk away from this nation completely. . . . If we don't think He will, we have our heads in the sand," Proffitt said. "If we're going to reach a generation, we've got to take the message to that place where the generation is—the schools."

Proffitt claims to have established First Priority clubs in three thousand schools spread over two hundred communities, but his scheme may have some legal pitfalls. The Equal Access Act, for example, states that "nonschool persons may not direct, conduct, control, or regularly attend activities of student groups."

But Proffitt is nonplussed. He told the crowd not to worry when church-state objections are raised. "There is no such thing as separation of church and state," he said. "It doesn't exist. There's only one document in history where that exists—the *Communist Manifesto*. We can't separate them because we are the church and the state."

Of course, the federal courts are still lagging behind Proffitt's insights and continue to strike down government-mandated religion in the public schools on the basis of the separation of church and state. Proffitt didn't explain how well his defense, "Your honor, it's from the *Communist Manifesto*" would go over in a courtroom. Not too well I'm afraid.

Continued Proffitt, "If we don't reach our young people, somebody will—the pornography world, the drug culture will. You ever heard of the Muslim Church [*sic*]? They've got a plan to reach America. Ever heard of Louis Farrakhan? He has raised $1 billion to build Muslim outreach centers on every college campus."

It's sometimes hard for me to refrain from laughing when I hear

Religious Right figures uttering statements that are, to be absolutely blunt, just plain stupid. The reference to the Muslim "church" was a real knee slapper, but the idea of Louis Farrakhan's Nation of Islam invading America's colleges campuses to win young people over to his peculiar strain of black Islam was too much.

During the question-and-answer session, I asked Proffitt about problems that might arise from attempts to convert Jewish and other non-Christian students. I explained to Proffitt that I live in the Washington, D.C., suburbs and said I wasn't sure how some Jewish parents would react when their kids get a heavy dose of Christian fundamentalist proselytism in the public schools.

Proffitt said he sure sympathized. He suggested that maybe the Jewish kids could form their own club. But then he quickly added that winning souls is the goal—and that means all souls. While he urged Christian young people to be "gentle and not use a hard sell," he added, "If we're going to fulfill the Great Commission, we've got to go and tell everyone. I really don't see a way around the Gospel message. The message is for the world."

A "Messianic Jew" in the audience agreed with Proffitt and said she was grateful for such evangelism, since it led her to Jesus and made her "zealous for the Lord." Proffitt nodded approvingly, but lest anyone get the wrong idea, quickly added, "I have a lot of Jewish friends and Messianic Jewish friends. I tell them, 'He's your Messiah. You introduced him to me.' "

Despite Proffitt's enthusiasm for First Priority clubs, not everyone was persuaded that his scheme is the way to go. One man in the audience called public schools "the counsel of the ungodly" (an expression from the New Testament). He said Christian children have no business being enrolled there because they are more likely to be "dragged down into the world" than to win souls. He also accused Proffitt of using children to do a job that belongs to adults.

Proffitt disagreed, pointing out that in Birmingham, Alabama, where First Priority clubs are popular, seven thousand students "came to Christ. It was done by the students themselves, and it can happen in every community in this country." He later added, "Satan thinks he owns our schools. He's got a fence around them. Jesus said the gates of hell cannot prevail against the church. We can take them down."

Proffitt was not the only conference speaker who focused on fusing religion and public education. During the main sessions, Phillip Johnson, a University of California at Berkeley law professor who has written several books attacking evolution, outlined an ambitious plan for toppling Darwinism.

Asserting that Darwin's theory is "based on awful science, just terrible," Johnson said the theory has "divided the people of God" and that means "the way is open for the agnostics to say, 'We need to put all of this aside.'"

Johnson calls his movement "The Wedge." The objective, he said, is to convince people that Darwinism is inherently atheistic, thus shifting the debate from creationism vs. evolution to the existence of God vs. the nonexistence of God.

From there people are introduced to "the truth" of the Bible and then "the question of sin" and finally "introduced to Jesus."

I found Johnson's comments most revealing. Creationists insist that their ideas are science, not religion, yet for them the study of creationism is little more than a vehicle for evangelism. If creationism is science, then why is the end goal of its study a conversion to fundamentalist Christianity? If it always comes back to the Bible and Jesus, then call it what it is: religion. It's not science.

"You must unify your own side and divide the other side," Johnson said. He added that he wants to temporarily suspend the debate between young-Earth creationists, who insist that the planet is only six thousand years old, and old-Earth creationists, who accept that the Earth is ancient. This debate, he said, can be resumed once Darwinism is overthrown.

Johnson, himself an old-Earth creationist, did not explain how the two camps would reconcile this tremendous gap. Old-Earthers concede that the planet is five billion years old; the young-Earthers insist this is heresy and say the planet is about six thousand years old. Once Darwinism is overthrown, perhaps they will compromise and agree that the Earth is 484 million years old. Or perhaps it can be five billion years old on Monday, Wednesday, and Friday and six thousand years old on Tuesday, Thursday, and Saturday. (Sunday would be a kind of neutral day with the Earth technically being five billion years old but frequently lying about it and claiming to be only six thousand years old.)

Actually, I'm pining for the day when the old-Earthers and the young-Earthers take off the gloves and go at it, because I know that the young-Earthers are dogmatic zealots who say any Earth age over six thousand years is "unbiblical." Get ready to duck whenever right-wingers start throwing that word around. Personally, I believe the young-Earthers will rip the old-Earthers to shreds, simply because they are meaner. Some of the young-Earthers are so crazy as to assert that fossils in the Earth that indicate an ancient planet were put there by Satan to trip us up. Let the games begin.

Johnson added that he is happy to be working with university professors, such as Michael Behe of Lehigh University in Pennsylvania, who are critical of aspects of Darwinism, even though they may not themselves be literal creationists. This strategy, he said, "enables us to get a foothold in the academic world and the academic journals. You have to prepare minds to hear the truth. You can't do it all at once."

Johnson was not the only conference speaker to attack evolution. Geoff Stevens, a ministerial student and former physics major at Kutztown University of Pennsylvania, told the crowd that evolution leads to abortion, homosexuality, and pornography. He blasted colleges for teaching it and took a shot at the late scientist and author Carl Sagan, telling the audience to much laughter, "[Sagan] used to be an evolutionist. He died a couple of years ago. I think he's a creationist now."

A third speaker, Dr. Buster Soaries, bragged about how he frequently flouts church-state rules in public schools. Soaries, senior pastor of First Baptist Church of Lincoln Gardens in Somerset, New Jersey, had recently been appointed New Jersey's secretary of state. He told the crowd he is often asked to speak in public schools about issues confronting teenagers.

"They always say to me, 'This is a public school. You can't talk about God,' as if there's some monitor around whose presence implies if you do, the ACLU will have you arrested," observed Soaries. "Every time, I say, 'I am going to speak in this school, and I am going to talk about God. . . .' If I got God in my flag, God on my money, God in my Declaration [of Independence], I don't have to keep God out of the schools!" His declaration was greeted with wild applause and a standing ovation.

Speakers like Soaries fill an important role for the Religious Right. Even though the crowd was overwhelmingly white, and even though only a handful of African Americans are involved in groups like the Christian Coalition and Kennedy's Center for Reclaiming America, these organizations must present the illusion of having minority support. It isn't hard to find a conservative African American who will come to the meetings and validate what the group stands for. This gives members a comfortable lie to cling to—that even minority communities support their mission. It's a necessary part of any well-assembled religio-political group.

But alas, Kennedy himself seems to be souring on efforts to rescue public education. He has flirted openly with Exodus 2000, a fringe movement led by far-right activists that calls on evangelical Christians to withdraw their children from public schools by the year 2000.

In September 1998 Kennedy interviewed E. Ray Moore Jr., executive director of Exodus 2000, on Coral Ridge Ministries' *Truths that Transform* radio show. Moore later issued a press statement asserting that Kennedy "is poised to become a leading voice among national Christian leaders on behalf of the separation/exodus theme."[12]

There was a short break after the workshops and before the concluding banquet. I took the opportunity to race outside and walk around the block, enjoying the warm Florida sun and reminding myself that soon I would be free from this asylum for good. There remained just one more task. It wouldn't be pleasant, but once it was done I was free to return to the secular world. The final event was a banquet. It featured Bill Bright, founder of Campus Crusade for Christ. But before Bright took to the podium, dinner-goers watched a tribute video to Kennedy, covering his career as a onetime dance instructor, his conversion to an ultraconservative strain of Presbyterianism and ascension to the head of Coral Ridge Ministries, as well as his decision to use television broadcasting to reach millions of Americans (1999 was the ministry's twenty-fifth anniversary).

By the time the banquet started, I was so tired of being asked questions by fellow attendees like, "How is your walk with the Lord?" and "Where do you go to church?" that I considered blowing my cover and announcing myself as an opponent of Kennedy's views. I managed to get through my chicken without incident, however, and soon Bright took to the podium.

Bright's comments were brief, as he seemed fatigued. That is perhaps explained by the fact that at the time, as he discussed in his remarks, Bright was periodically engaging in forty-day fasts to spur revival in America.

Echoing other event speakers, Bright began by asserting that the country is "morally and spiritually bankrupt." He added that the nation had drifted from its founding when the framers "dedicated this nation to our Lord." (Did I somehow miss that in the Constitution?)

The country, asserted Bright, enjoyed God's favor until fifty years ago when we experienced "those infamous decisions of the Supreme Court that began to change all of that. And this nation, in my opinion, is now under the discipline of God." Nazi Germany and Soviet Russia, he asserted, were destroyed because they rejected God. "Unless God divinely intervenes, we will follow the example of these nations," he said. "We can't shake our fists in the face of God and disregard his laws without feeling his discipline."

Continued Bright, "You have already been instructed in how to take [political] precincts for Christ. I urge you to get involved in elections . . . and help elect godly people to office. . . . The Supreme Court has led a great revolution to turn our country away from God, and they need to be replaced. That won't happen unless we elect godly people from the precinct to the White House."

Kennedy then stood up to invite us all to a "patriotic concert" upstairs in the main conference hall. I fled the banquet hall in terror. My belief is it's always dangerous to mix jingoistic "God and country" rhetoric with a heavy meal. Excusing myself to my dinner partners, I made a beeline for the door, hailed a cab, and hightailed it back to my hotel.

Once there, I called my wife to tell her I missed her and to say good night to the kids. As we talked, I was reminded of how difficult child-rearing is and how annoying it is to be regarded by Kennedy and his followers as antifamily, anti-Christian, and anti-American, someone bent on destroying all that is good, decent, and pure.

Later I tried to soothe my nerves with television. We don't have cable TV at home, and it was a real treat to have access to the Sci-Fi Channel and the Cartoon Channel, but my mind kept racing. I couldn't help it. Even after twelve years of tracking the Religious Right "up close and personal" I still find prolonged exposure to mean-spirited rhetoric and spiritual arrogance unsettling. I was glad when, early the next morning, I boarded a 727 for Washington's National Airport.

What does all of this mean? For church-state separationists, Kennedy's effort to make himself a national political force is troubling. The televangelist takes a hard line, and he's not ashamed of it. Unlike Robertson, Kennedy does not pretend to have Jewish or Roman Catholic support. At his gathering, "Christian" had one definition only: people who read the Bible as a manual for political activism and who see their interpretation of the scriptures as inspired, inerrant, and infallible. Everyone else, in the words of Parshall, are "the lost" and their worldview is "hellish."

To be blunt, I found this type of rhetoric the most offensive of all. At one point in her admittedly well-delivered screed, Parshall said, "Right outside these doors is a world with a ticket stamped 'Destination: Hell.' We don't just want to pass legislation. The idea is to win them to the cross. We must resolve to conquer or die."

Conquer or die? Isn't there another way? How about, "Go home and mind your own business"? Take your children to the church of your choice, teach them what you like about sex education and human origins, refrain from seeing movies that seem risqué, and turn off the TV when something you consider offensive comes on. Why not, "Worry about your own children, and I'll worry about mine"? If it comes down to "conquer or die," then chances are there is going to be a lot of dying before anybody conquers. We've seen and still see today the results of "conquer or die" in action. They were called the Crusades. They are called Northern Ireland. They are called the Balkans. Nothing good comes of these efforts. In other words, "Been there, done that." It's time to try something else.

So the secret is out. I find triumphalist rhetoric that implies that I am nothing more than a lost soul to be converted or crushed unappealing. Kennedy seeks to "reclaim America," which raises a key question: Who claims it now? Several speakers identified likely suspects—"pagans," "the liberal media," "secular humanists," "radical homosexuals," and "extreme separationists." The concept of "taking back" the country from such forces and calls for "spiritual warfare," mixed generously with violent military metaphors, were constant themes. What's so "Christian" about this?

To Kennedy, the "culture wars" are waging full throttle. And if his troops have their way, church-state separation and America's commitment to individual freedom may be the first casualties of that conflict.

As a postscript to this chapter, I should point out that when I registered for "Reclaiming America for Christ" I entered the D. James Kennedy database. Even before the event, I was being bombarded with lurid fund-raising letters, most of them attacking gay people or the ACLU. Months after the conference these letters continued to pour into my mailbox, sometimes two per week.

Kennedy may have a fledgling grassroots campaign and a tenuous grip on the national stage, but there's one thing he definitely does have: a well-polished fund-raising machine designed to hit all of the hot buttons of his flock and separate them from their money. Because of the nature of my work, I have ended up on a number of Religious Right mailing lists. But no organization has hit my mailbox with the ferocity of Kennedy's money-raising machine.

Say what you will about Kennedy, he has apparently taken at least one biblical passages to heart: "Ask and ye shall receive."

Coral Ridge Ministries
Leader: The Rev. D. James Kennedy
Budget: Coral Ridge Ministries, $24,555,110
         Coral Ridge Presbyterian Church, $16,586,074
Membership: The church has about ten thousand members.
    Thousands more watch Kennedy's Sunday morning television broadcasts.
Address: P.O. Box 1940, Fort Lauderdale, FL 33302-1940
Website: http://www.coralridge.org

NOTES

1. Joel Belz, "It Begins in the Pulpit," *World* (April 27, 1996).
2. D. James Kennedy and Jim Nelson Black, *Character & Destiny: A Nation In Search of Its Soul* (Grand Rapids, Mich.: Zondervan Publishing House, 1994), p. 247.
3. D. James Kennedy and Jerry Newcombe, *The Gates of Hell Shall*

Not Prevail: The Attack on Christianity and What You Need to Know to Combat It (Nashville: Thomas Nelson Publishers, 1996), p. 135.

4. Kennedy and Black, *Character & Destiny*, p. 76.

5. Kennedy and Newcombe, *The Gates of Hell Shall Not Prevail*, pp. 179–80.

6. Hanna Rosin, "The Moral Minority: Thomas Was Among the Right. Now They Find Him Wrong," *Washington Post*, March 18, 1999.

7. M. Jane Taylor, "Fallout Continues Over Anti-Gay Ads Appearing in Newspapers," *Washington Blade*, August 14, 1998.

8. "House Rejects National Day of Prayer Resolution," *National Liberty Journal* (August 1999).

9. Statements made by various speakers are taken from my notes and tape recordings of the conference.

10. Claudia Wallis, "The Kids Are Alright," *Time* (July 5, 1999).

11. William L. Shirer, *The Rise and Fall of the Third Reich: A History of Nazi Germany* (New York: Simon & Schuster, 1960), pp. 234–35.

12. Rob Boston, "Missionary Man," *Church & State* (April 1999).

Chapter 2

ROAD TO VICTORY OR HIGHWAY TO HELL?

Getting Carsick with the Christian Coalition

When I began working at Americans United, there was no Christian Coalition. At that time, November of 1987, Pat Robertson's presidential campaign was in full swing. It didn't take long for it to collapse, and by spring Robertson was effectively out of the race after a disappointing performance in Super Tuesday, the first round of multi-state primaries.

There's a corny old saying, "When life hands you a lemon, make lemonade." Handed a lemon by the American voters, Robertson made gallons of the stuff. Robertson made the best of his defeat by forming the Christian Coalition, an organization that has greatly increased his political power and made him an inside player in national Republican politics.

Early in his campaign, Robertson announced that he would not run unless three million people signed petitions asking him to do so. This turned out to be a shrewd political move. This list gave Robertson a lucrative base to tap into for funding during the campaign, and afterward the people who had signed were solicited to join the Christian Coalition. Plus, Robertson had outside help in forming his Coalition. The organization was launched in part with $64,000 in seed money from the National Republican Senatorial Committee in October of 1990.[1]

In 1996, I wrote a book about Pat Robertson titled *The Most Dangerous Man in America? Pat Robertson and the Rise of the Christian Coalition.* Even as the book came off of the presses, I knew that it would probably need to be updated at some point. This seems to be as good a time as any. Thus, my purpose in this chapter is not to survey Robertson's entire career and the activities of the Coalition since it was founded. I already did that, and I direct readers interested in that type of information to *The Most Dangerous Man in America?*[2] This chapter will examine some of the Coalition's more recent activities with special emphasis on the group's annual "Road to Victory" conference.

As part of my ongoing research about the Christian Coalition, I attend the organization's "Road to Victory" conference every year. (The event has occurred annually since 1991.) These days it is usually held in mid-September in Washington, D.C., although the 1997 event was held in Atlanta.

The first two "Road to Victory" events were not held in Washington. They were held in Virginia Beach, which is the Coalition's backyard. They were also not open to the media. No matter. It was not difficult to get people inside who later reported on what went on. A freelance writer covered both events for the journal *Church & State.* Perhaps because he knew the meetings were being infiltrated, Robertson opened up the third "Road to Victory," the first one to occur in the nation's capital, to the media; all subsequent "Road to Victory" conferences have been open—to an extent.

There are always meetings and events at "Road to Victory" that are not open to the media or are "invitation only." Likewise, state caucus meetings are often closed to reporters. Again, it's not difficult to get people inside these meetings; I have been to several. One can hear some very interesting things at these smaller gatherings. In fact, these "meetings within the meeting" are essential for anyone who really wants to know what's going on at the Christian Coalition. Back in the days when the Coalition was operating as a tax-exempt entity and insisted it did not endorse candidates, I heard Coalition officials endorse several candidates or allow candidates themselves to appear and make what amounted to campaign speeches.

The breakout sessions, which examine specific political and social issues of interest to the coalition, and state caucus meetings (where state Coalition groups meet separately) attract smaller crowds, obviously. The main "Road to Victory" can attract as many as four thousand attendees. These events take place in huge halls. Giant screens project the images of the speakers who address the crowd from a huge elevated dais. Speakers are introduced with dancing spotlights and blaring music.

The format is simple: On day one, attendees listen to a revolving parade of speakers. Most are limited to twenty minutes. It's one after the other with few breaks. Many of them speak on the same topics, and thematic overlap is not uncommon. There's a banquet at the end of the second day, at which Robertson speaks, and day two is filled with the state meetings and smaller breakout sessions.

There is absolutely no venue for audience participation during the main sessions. Breakout speakers and panelists may or may not leave time for questions and comments. The themes stressed both days are Religious Right standards: demands for mandatory prayer in public schools, attacks on evolution, gay bashing, assaults on legal abortion, assaults on feminism, sessions recommending the end of public education, and so on. Thrown into this mix are tips on how to organize politically; how to manipulate computers, e-mail, and the World Wide Web to communicate and do research; and advice for dealing with the secular media.

Christian Coalition gatherings have a heavy partisan flavor. They are essentially Republican Party rallies. In election years, it's not uncommon for Robertson to invite GOP presidential candidates but no Democratic hopefuls. On rare occasions, a token conservative Democrat is added to a panel or given fifteen minutes to speak, but by and large, the "Road to Victory" is for Republicans only.

Much has changed at the Christian Coalition since I wrote *The Most Dangerous Man in America?* Ralph Reed, the whiz-kid executive director hired by Robertson to launch the organization, departed in September of 1997 and started a political consulting firm near Atlanta. But more interestingly, in June of 1999 the group was denied tax-exempt status by the Internal Revenue Service. The fallout from this startling development remains unclear as I write this book.

Bear with me while I give a brief primer on nonprofit tax law: The Christian Coalition was permitted to operate for nearly nine years as a tax-exempt group under IRS classification 501(c)(4) while the federal tax agency considered the organization's application for permanent status. Classification 501(c)(4) groups pay no federal tax, but donations to them are not tax deductible for the donor. This is different from 501(c)(3) organizations, donations to which are fully tax deductible. Groups that are 501(c)(3) include houses of worship, charities, and scientific and educational organizations.

Organizations classified as 501(c)(4) are permitted to engage in some partisan politicking, as long as it does not constitute the brunt of their activities. Anything over 50 percent is generally considered a violation. Those groups designated 501(c)(3) are absolutely barred from engaging in any partisan activities.

Americans United argued for years that the Christian Coalition was operating in violation of the 501(c)(4) rules. We maintained that the group was clearly 100 percent political, that is was essentially a far-right political action committee dedicated to getting the most conservative Republicans possible elected to public office.

We frequently sent material to the IRS to build this case. The problem was, we were only able to give the IRS pieces of the puzzle. It was up to the tax agency to put it all together. Once they did that, and examined the "big picture," we felt certain that the

Coalition would be denied tax exemption. Still, we were worried. It would take a savvy IRS agent with the time and ability to put everything together to see why we were right.

All of that became unnecessary in September of 1997, when Robertson delivered a highly partisan speech that laid out all of the Christian Coalition's political goals. In light of this speech, there could be little doubt that the Coalition viewed itself as an appendage of the Republican Party. Robertson never intended for these comments to become public, but they did—and they were a smoking gun.

Addressing a closed-door meeting of Christian Coalition state leaders during the "Road to Victory" conference, which that year was taking place in Atlanta, Robertson outlined a game plan to help the GOP retain control of Congress and for electing a conservative Republican to the White House in 2000.

Robertson didn't even bother to try to pretend that his scheme was nonpartisan. He spoke exclusively of marshalling forces to elect Republicans. The key, he said, was getting the conservative vote lined up behind one GOP presidential hopeful and propelling that person to victory.

"You know, the principle of warfare that has been used forever by those who wish to beat another enemy is, you know, divide and conquer," he said. Referring to the ancient Chinese warrior Sun Tzu, author of *The Art of War*, Robertson went on to say, "If you can split their forces, that was Sun Tzu's maxim, you know. Whenever possible avoid what he calls a juncture of forces. Don't ever let your enemy join together. So always get yourself in the middle to keep them split. And that technique we can use on others, but it's been used very effectively on us."[3]

Then Robertson got to the meat of things: "Now, we'll be coming in, in the next year or so, into a presidential primary. And so, we're nice people and we think this is just, 'we'll do what we want to do.' So this one likes this candidate, this one likes that candidate, and this one likes the other candidate. And so we have absolutely no effectiveness when the primary comes. None whatso-ever. Because we have split our vote among four or five people and so the other guy wins. And we have had a couple of so-called mod-erates. And moderates lose. You know, they lose. And we've had two major losers, and I don't want any more losers. I want a winner." (The "two major losers" reference is to the 1992 and 1996 Repub-lican presidential nominees, George Bush and Robert Dole.)

The Coalition, Robertson said, could have the power to elect the next president. "We're not a bunch of ingenues anymore, we're a sea-soned group of warriors," he told the crowd. "And we have to know what we're dealing with. We can't be swayed by rhetoric. . . . I told Don Hodel [then Christian Coalition president] when he joined us, I said, 'My dear friend, I want to hold out to you the possibility of selecting the next president of the United States because I think that's what we have in this organization.' And I believe we can indeed."

It got worse. Robertson went on to compare his Coalition to infamous political machines in history, including Tammany Hall. For those of you who have forgotten your history, Tammany Hall was a nineteenth-century Democratic political machine in New York state run by the notorious William Marcy "Boss" Tweed. In a nutshell, the machine bought the votes of immigrants, factory workers, poor people, and others by arranging small favors for them—perhaps finding someone a job or getting him a meeting with an influential public official. Tweed used these votes to elect cronies to the New York legislature and push through favorable leg-islation—favorable to Tweed and his associates, that is. Historians are in virtual agreement that the Tweed ring was one of the most cor-rupt, if not *the* most corrupt, machine ever to curse American pol-itics. (Historians estimate that Tweed and his crowd stole somewhere between $2 million and $20 million in taxpayer dollars during the ring's tenure.[4]) Such is Robertson's political model.

Referring to the Tweed ring and other political machines of bygone days, Robertson described them as a good deal more benign than they actually were. "They had an identified core of people who had bought into the values, whatever they were, and they worked the election and brought people out to vote," he said. "The other people were diffuse and fragmented, and they lost and the people that had the core won. I mean, this isn't complicated, but this is what we've got to do."

Robertson knew full well what he was saying was not strictly aboveboard. Several times he remarked that his comments were "in the family" and at one point quipped, "If there's any press here, would you please shoot yourself? Leave. Do something." Later he added, "This is getting more sensitive, but I think you ought to hear me. This is in the family."

Robertson promised to issue some sort of statement to let Coalition members know which GOP candidate he favored. He said it would not be a Coalition statement but would come from him personally as a "free American citizen." He went on to ridicule prominent Democratic hopefuls, calling Vice President Al Gore "Ozone Al" and asserting that House Minority Leader Richard Gephardt, who at that time was toying with the idea of seeking the Democratic nomination, was "probably worse, in the pocket of the labor unions, and we don't need somebody like that."

His Coalition, Robertson went on to boast, had helped the Republicans take control of Congress in 1994 and keep it in 1996. He asserted that he wanted more influence in the Republican Party, saying, "We're still not totally like we should be. And we also said by the year 2000 we'd have the presidency and that's to me the next goal. We can hold the Congress, get some more good people into the Congress and into the governors' mansions and then focus on the White House."

Robertson was obviously not aware of it, but his remarks were being recorded on an audiotape. Americans United obtained a copy of the tape and promptly turned it over to the IRS and the Federal Election Commission.

In addition, Americans United made copies of the tape for the media and held a press briefing in Washington on September 19. Stories about the tape's explosive comments appeared the next day in the *New York Times* and the *Washington Post* and were picked up for national distribution by the Associated Press, the Knight-Ridder newspaper chain, CNN, and other media outlets. The story appeared in virtually every major American newspaper, often on page one. It was big news because, as one reporter put it, the tape's explosive contents were "Robertson raw."

Coalition leaders tried to defend Robertson's comments as mere personal observations. It didn't fly. It was obvious from the comments on the tape that Robertson was issuing marching orders to his troops for partisan warfare. The tape, Americans United pointed out, was a smoking gun, the final piece of the puzzle that proved beyond a doubt that the Coalition is a highly partisan political hardball operation—hardly the type of group deserving of tax-exempt status.

I have no way of knowing if the tape played a large role in the IRS's decision to deny the Christian Coalition tax-exempt status. But I can't help but think that it did. The IRS file on the matter is not a public document, so we'll never know for sure. But I suspect if there were any doubts in the minds of the IRS staff about the partisan nature of the Christian Coalition, that tape put them to rest. Its contents were explosive.

At Americans United, we sometimes wonder if our efforts to expose Robertson as an extremist and unmask the Coalition as a hardball political operation have caught his attention. Considering what happened after the Coalition was denied tax exemption by the IRS, I believe we can safely assume that our efforts are doing the trick.

On July 2, 1999, less than one month after the IRS acted against the Coalition, six right-wing Republican senators wrote to Attorney General Janet Reno and demanded that she launch a *criminal* investigation of Americans United for allegedly trying to intimidate religious voters.

The six senators—Jesse Helms of North Carolina, Jeff Sessions of Alabama, Paul Coverdell of Georgia, Sam Brownback of Kansas, Don Nickles of Oklahoma, and Strom Thurmond of South Carolina—based the charge on the fact that Americans United has since 1996 issued memos to churches warning them that distributing Christian Coalition voter guides in churches could get them in tax trouble, since the guides are slanted to favor certain candidates.

Remember what I said earlier about 501(c)(3) organizations not being permitted to engage in partisan politics? This category includes churches and other houses of worship. They simply cannot endorse candidates or distribute partisan campaign literature. Yet the Christian Coalition was running around telling churches all over America that its "voter guides" were appropriate for distribution in churches. Americans United disagreed and thought churches deserves to hear both sides of the story.

Americans United's campaign is geared toward educating *houses of worship*. The memos are sent via e-mail and U.S. mail and are posted on our World Wide Web site (**www.au.org**). The memo is purely informational and is designed to make churches aware of the tax ramifications of intervening in partisan politics. It is in no way intended to intimidate any individual from voting.

Helms, Sessions, Coverdell, Brownback, Nickles, and Thurmond acted just days after Robertson met with Coverdell, Nickles, and Senate Majority Leader Trent Lott to outline strategy for reenergizing Christian fundamentalist voters for the 2000 elections. Reports are that Robertson was clearly distressed that the Coalition's loss of tax-exempt status would affect its ability to help Republicans. It is American United belief that this campaign to intimidate us might have been cooked up then.

(Shortly before all of this happened, Robertson had been unleashing regular rants against Americans United and its Executive Director, the Rev. Barry W. Lynn. On two different occasions on his nationally televised program, the *700 Club*, Robertson asserted that Lynn is such an extreme separationist he believes that if a church catches on fire, a municipal fire department should not be permitted to put it out. This is, of course, nonsense. Lynn believes no such thing. Robertson made it up out of whole cloth. To use an old-fashioned term, it's a bald-faced lie.)

After the Coalition was denied tax-exempt status, many people contacted Americans United to ask, "What took so long?" I can't answer that question, but I do know that on at least one previous occasion, the tax agency may have been on the verge of denying the Coalition's application.

During his closed-door remarks in Atlanta, Robertson let loose this interesting tidbit: He claimed that the IRS had been on the verge of denying the Coalition tax-exempt status some years before. The tape recording has him reporting that the tax agency sent "a great big, Valkyrie-like woman" to audit the group and claimed she showed up wearing a National Organization for Women belt buckle. The agent, Robertson said, recommended that the organization be denied tax-exempt status, a decision that was either not carried out or delayed for some reason. Later, Robertson said, the agent left the IRS and moved to Pennsylvania where she "opened up a lesbian bookstore."

In light of the fact that the Coalition was permitted to operate as tax exempt for an unprecedented nine years and that the IRS clearly bent over backwards to thoroughly examine the Coalition's application, it is absurd to charge, as Coalition supporters have done, that the IRS acted out of malice or out of some type of political vendetta. The fact is, the Christian Coalition never deserved to have a tax exemption in the first place. That the group was permitted to operate as if it had one for nine years is scandalous enough.

Coverage of Robertson's reckless remarks dominated the news for several days in late September of 1997. The rest of the "Road to Victory" that year received less coverage. That's a shame because I was there and found it to be the usual collection of right-wing extremists, rife with outrageous statements worthy of coverage.

I really do believe that most Americans just don't get it when it comes to the Religious Right. They persist in believing that the movement either has little power or isn't so bad after all. Spending some time at the "Road to Victory" debunks both of those assertions.

When it comes to extremism and just plain off-the-wall comments, no one at "Road to Victory" can hold a candle to Robertson. Listening to him rant, I often wonder how it's possible that a man who often seems unstable and holds such bizarre views has managed to make so much money.

(Although I should point out that Robertson's big mouth did sink one potentially lucrative business deal in 1999. The Bank of Scotland backed out of a deal to work with Robertson to bring telephone banking to the United States after protestors in Scotland boycotted the bank. Americans United worked with Scottish media to document Robertson's track record of extremism. It didn't help matters much when, in the middle of the controversy, on May 18, 1999, Robertson aired a segment on his *700 Club* calling Scotland a "rather dark land" under the sway of militant homosexuals.)

During a September 12 appreciation dinner for Ralph Reed at the 1997 "Road to Victory," Robertson reeled off a string of comments that I believe would shock the average American. At that time, court bashing was much in vogue among the Religious Right, and Robertson cut loose with a verbal assault on the federal courts.

"Today, we are witnessing judicial activism so intense and so radical that it begins to call into question the very legitimacy of the judicial system."[5] (The irony is most federal judges working today were appointed by Republican presidents—Ronald Reagan and George Bush.)

Robertson went on to attack not only legal abortion but the Supreme Court's ruling in 1965 in the case *Griswold* v. *Connecticut*. In that case, the high court ruled that states could not enforce laws that banned the sale of contraceptive devices to anyone—even married couples. This was a major expansion of Robertson's extreme antiabortion views, yet it was not reported outside of the pages of the journal *Church & State*.

Many Americans have qualms about legal abortion, many oppose it outright. But very, very few are so extreme as to assert that states should be able to deny *married couples* the right to access family planning. Robertson wrapped up his talk by demanding that the World Wide Web be censored.

Ralph Reed's comments were less politically charged but just as extreme. He pretended to be modest, telling the crowd that he hadn't built the Christian Coalition, "God built the Christian Coalition. . . . God built this house. And it's my prayer and it's my desire not that the honor for what He did would come to me nor to any other person. I want all of it to go to the only one who deserves it, and that's the Lord Jesus Christ."

At this point I was struggling to keep down the rich dessert I had just eaten. I've heard God given the credit (or the blame) for lots of things over the years, but there's no way you can pin the Christian Coalition on him. Personally, I thought Reed's comments boarded on blasphemy, and I was glad I was near the back of the hall, figuring people near the speakers' platform might get scorched if some lightning bolts were suddenly hurled down.

Robertson also played a tribute video featuring an all-GOP lineup praising Reed. Featured speakers included Senate Majority Leader Trent Lott and then–Speaker of the House Newt Gingrich. Several of the politicians thanked Reed for bringing more Republicans into the Congress—an odd accomplishment for an organization that at the time insisted it was nonpartisan.

One Republican politician, Gov. David Beasley of South Carolina, came in person to praise Reed. During his remarks, Beasley compared Reed to Jesus Christ, telling the Coalition head not to worry when he is attacked by his enemies because, "Remember, they nailed he who was perfect to a tree."

During the general conference sessions, a parade of GOP presidential wannabees trekked to the podium, among them former Tennessee Gov. Lamar Alexander, Missouri's U.S. Sen. John Ashcroft (who later decided to skip the race), and millionaire publisher Steve Forbes.

Watching Forbes grovel before the Christian Coalition was especially appalling, although not without its amusements. During the 1996 race, Forbes refused to stake out a firm position on abortion and dismissed the Christian Coalition as a group that "does not speak for most Christians." (At one point he also called Robertson a "toothy flake.")[6] Suddenly, a little over a year later, Forbes was Mr. Pro-Life and spent nearly all of his time blasting late-term abortions in a speech laced with biblical references. (Whoever wrote it for him really knew what this crowd wanted to hear.) All was forgiven; the crowd gave Forbes a standing ovation, and he walked—need I say stiffly?—off the stage.

The following year, 1998, the "Road to Victory" was back in Washington but just as extreme. One of the featured speakers was Charlton Heston, actor and National Rifle Association president. At a September 19 banquet, Heston offered up a stock speech he had been giving to conservative groups for months. Oddly enough, no one had taken the time to notice that it featured racially charged rhetoric, and the Coalition crowd certainly didn't care. They treated Heston as if he were Moses himself, not just a guy who once played Moses.

"Heaven help the God-fearing, law-abiding Caucasian middle class," Heston said. "Protestant or even worse evangelical Christian, Midwest or Southern or even worse rural, apparently straight or even worse admitted heterosexual, gun-owning or even worse NRA card–carrying average working stiff, or even worst of all, male working stiff. Because not only don't you count, you're a downright obstacle to social progress."

Continued Heston, "That's why sabers are rattling in America's mild-mannered living rooms. Americans are ready to fight for the true booty of the cultural war—their values. They want them back.

They want the America they built. They want an America where you can pray without feeling naive, love without feeling kinky, sing without profanity, be white without feeling guilty, own a gun without stigma, shout amen without apology, and prosper without being blamed."[7]

Although it was hard to top Heston's tirade, Robertson did his best. His remarks were a weird mix of apocalyptic doom and triumphalism—boilerplate Robertson in many ways. At one point, he warned that terrorist groups need only one quart of anthrax spores to kill three million people. This and the possibility of nuclear weapons falling into the hands of unstable dictators seemed to be occupying too much of his mind at the time. But it could all be avoided, Robertson insisted, if the nation would just return to faith in God. (Familiar with public opinion polls showing that 95 percent of Americans profess belief in God, I had to wonder what nation he was talking about.)

The rest of Robertson's remarks explored standard-issue Religious Right obsessions: strident attacks on the ACLU, legal abortion, the school prayer decisions, and President Clinton. After eight years of "Road to Victory" rants, it appeared that Robertson had little new to say.

"We can change iniquitous legislation," Robertson fulminated, "and with a new president who thinks in biblical terms, we may have two more Supreme Court justices who overturn *Roe* v. *Wade* and some of these awful decisions. Believe me, America is a prize worth having."

Don Hodel, who had yet to be kicked out as Coalition president, displayed a 1988 copy of *U.S. News & World Report* trumpeting Robertson's "hidden army" that was working to take over the Republican Party. "Ladies and gentlemen, you're the hidden army," he said. "And let me say, it is more than the Republican Party that is our target. Ladies and gentlemen, it is the United States of America; we are determined to change our culture."

It's hard to tell which was worse: Heston's race-baiting or Robertson's off-the-wall extremism. It's always a contest to determine the hands-down most offensive speaker at a "Road to Victory" conference. Since Robertson speaks every year, all other contenders have tough competition.

That doesn't keep them from trying. Over the years I've heard William Bennett, who hasn't had a real job since the Bush administration—except for rewriting Aesop's Fables and pawning them off on a gullible public as brilliant insights—scold the entire nation for various and sundry perceived defects (mostly for failing to agree with William Bennett on political matters). I've endured the mad ramblings of Robert Bork, the failed Supreme Court candidate, whose views are so far outside the judicial mainstream that every time he opens his mouth I'm thankful for all of those liberal groups that kept this dangerous man off our nation's highest court and confined him forever (I hope) to the right-wing's rubber chicken circuit.

I've listened to Pat Buchanan rant and rave and say mean-spirited, untrue things about America, running down our nation and being hailed as a hero for it. I've endured the pathetic bombast of Star Parker, a black antiwelfare activist who screams, says nothing of substance or value, ends up blaming the poor for their own predicament, and wins applause from an audience that is 99 percent white.

I've listened to gay bashers, pseudohistorians, antifeminists, propagandists who have nothing better to do than tell lies about our public schools, and simple-minded folks who blame all of our nation's problems on one Supreme Court ruling. (It's either the decision banning mandatory prayer in schools or the one legalizing abortion; take your pick.)

Some speakers appear at "Road to Victory" year after year. For several years running I was forced to endure the tirades of David Barton, a Texas man who makes his living rewriting history and asserting, against all available evidence, that the United States was founded by fundamentalist Christians for fundamentalist Christians and that separation of church and state is a "myth." (See more on Barton in chapter 8.)

These are all bad, but the worst thing I've had to endure during the "Road to Victory" is the annual address by Rabbi Daniel Lapin, a Washington State rabbi who is the Christian Coalition's token Jewish supporter.

Lapin, a South African expatriate, runs Toward Tradition, a Jewish group that fronts for the Christian Right. I will never claim to understand the motivations of such people. To me, it is self-evident that forcing young children to take part in Christian worship in public schools is not a positive development for the Jewish community. To me it is obvious why American Jews should be wary of a TV preacher who once wrote an entire book based on anti-Semitic sources that dredged up hoary conspiracy theories about international bankers engineering world wars. To me it's perfectly understandable that many Jews get nervous when right-wingers start talking about "reclaiming America for Christ" or remaking America as a "Christian nation."

Yet Lapin persists. His support is minimal, his delivery is unimpressive, and his ideas weren't original when Jerry Falwell first spouted them in the mid-1970s. Yet he persists.

Robertson clings to Lapin, even though the man is frequently incoherent, and his speeches are crude and offensive. Robertson needs him to claim Jewish support. Lapin needs Robertson or else he would be completely obscure instead of just irrelevant. The relationship is parasitic and unhealthy.

Listening to Lapin rave, even for a mere twenty minutes, is almost too much to bear. Worse than that, it is the ultimate waste of perfectly good time that could be spent doing virtually anything else. When Lapin finally shuts up, one is acutely aware that the time just spent listening to him is *gone*, irrevocably gone. It will never be back, and it has been squandered. The thought is utterly depressing—every time.

A friend once showed me a site on the World Wide Web that was essentially a huge entertainment database. You could, for example, plug in the name of an old television show and find out when it aired, who played in the cast, what the episodes were titled, and more. That night at home I looked up the site. Before I knew it, an hour had passed. I was dismayed and frankly a little embarrassed. The time had been wasted, and all I had learned was the name of the actor who played the character "Huggy Bear" on the old detective show *Starsky and Hutch*. Yet I consider that time better spent than any of the occasions I have had to listen to Rabbi Lapin.

After a day of main speakers like Lapin and others who pass for right-wing pundits, "Road to Victory" attendees are turned loose to attend state caucuses and breakout sessions. The 1998 breakout sessions featured the usual collection of right-wing flummery. My favorite comment came from Patrick Fagan, a Heritage Foundation "scholar" who participated on a panel dealing with parental rights. A member of the audience asked Fagan what should be done about "immoral" material in public libraries. A nonplussed Fagan said the solution is simple: Check the material out and refuse to return it. Refuse to pay any fines.[8]

How novel. Now, there is one drawback: Where I come from, checking books out of the library and refusing to either return them or pay for replacements is called "stealing." My parents taught me not to do it. I teach the same thing to my kids. I understand most major religions teach that, too. You have to stretch the definition of "pro-family" quite far to get it to encompass stealing. Some would say it can't be done.

Energy and enthusiasm appeared high at the 1998 "Road to Victory," but apparently there was turmoil just beneath the surface. Four months after the 1998 trip down the "Road to Victory," Coalition president Hodel was forced to take an exit ramp. Molly Clatworthy, a Coalition spokesperson, told the Associated Press, "Don has decided to retire, effective immediately." This is rarely the type of statement you want to read about yourself in the newspaper.

The situation looked suspicious. Sure enough, the real story soon leaked out. On February 10, 1999, the *Washington Times*, an ultra-conservative daily owned by the Rev. Sun Myung Moon of the Unification Church, reported that Hodel had been forced out. Hodel had apparently been a victim of Robertson's ever-changing moods.

Oddly enough, it was Robertson's inability to make up his mind over what should be done with President Clinton that led to Hodel's downfall. During the 1998 "Road to Victory," Robertson had demanded that Clinton be impeached over his affair with White House intern Monica Lewinsky. This was the tough-talking line attendees expected. It went over well. But once impeachment got underway and it became obvious that the American public had little stomach for it, Robertson switched sides and told his *700 Club* audience that the matter should be dropped, as there were not enough votes for impeachment in the Senate. The next day, newspapers reported that Robertson, a major conservative leader, had said it was time to drop impeachment. This was big news, because until Robertson commented, all prominent conservatives were marching in lockstep to the impeachment beat.

Robertson's comments, the *Times* reported, led Hodel to believe that the Coalition "was not consistently putting principle over politics." Hodel reportedly had the temerity to send Robertson a memo proposing that Robertson step aside as chairman of the Coalition board. Although Robertson described Hodel as an old friend on more than one occasion, I have to wonder how well Hodel really knew the TV preacher. Anyone even remotely familiar with Robertson and his mercurial temperament should have realized that a memo like that would not go over well.

Sure enough, in reply, said the paper, Robertson "sent a tersely worded letter accepting a resignation Mr. Hodel had not offered."[9]

Six months later, in the wake of the IRS's decision to deny the Coalition tax-exempt status, Robertson struck again. This time he demoted Randy Tate, a former one-term congressman from Washington state who had been named Reed's replacement as executive director. Tate, who didn't even begin to fill Reed's shoes, was named an "executive vice president" and sent to Washington, D.C., to oversee Coalition lobbying efforts. Robertson announced he would become president of the Christian Coaltion and would personally direct the group's daily operations.

By this time there had been a veritable exodus of top staff from the Coalition. Chuck Cunningham, national operations director, left the group and returned to his former employer, the National Rifle Association. Spokesman Arne Owens resigned, as did other senior staffers.

Mary Jacoby, the *St. Petersburg Times* reporter who broke the story about the IRS's decision to deny the Coalition tax-exempt status, also noted in her story that the group was in disarray. Active chapters had plummeted from twenty-five to six, and the organization's budget was off sharply. Robertson had to pump in $1 million of his own money one year to keep the group afloat.[10]

The Coalition had been struggling with financial problems and a stagnant membership for years. Although the group's leaders frequently claimed a membership of nearly 2 million, Americans United used postal records to prove that Coalition membership was less than half a million.

The problems had apparently been mounting for a few years. In December of 1997, the organization undertook a major restructuring. One-fifth of its 110-member staff was fired just before Christmas. Among the casualties was the Coalition's slick, four-color magazine *Christian American*. It was replaced with a low-tech, four-page newsletter.[11]

The Coalition also dumped its Samaritan Project, an outreach effort to African Americans headed by the Rev. Earl Jackson. Reed had announced the Samaritan Project with much hype at a Washington press conference just eleven months earlier. At the time, Reed described the project as the Coalition's top legislative priority.

The Samaritan Project sought to lure blacks into the Republican Party by promoting private school vouchers and government funding of "faith-based social services." It was a flop and never garnered significant black support. At the press conference announcing the venture, however, Reed did manage to drum up a few African American pastors to attend. One of them, the Rev. Lawrence Haygood of Tuskegee, Alabama, compared Reed to Martin Luther King Jr. and remarked, "We in the black community have looked for a leader in a black form. But he did not show up in a black form. He has come in a white form, in the image of Ralph Reed."[12]

Critics pointed out that the Coalition had no track record of supporting civil rights or working in the best interests of the African American community. In fact, the organization in 1990 took credit for the reelection of Sen. Jesse Helms (R–N.C.), who based his campaign on thinly veiled racial appeals. Helms narrowly defeated former Charlotte mayor Harvey Gantt, an African American.

Robertson also served as an apologist for the former apartheid regime in South Africa and once appeared on state-run television there to criticize American blacks for supporting boycotts against the country.[13]

The organization's problems continued to mount. In the fall of 1997, Judy Liebert, who had served as the Coalition's chief financial officer, began releasing interesting information about the organization's internal operations. Liebert had been fired in 1996 after six years with the Coalition, saying she was disillusioned with its tactics. She was let go after telling federal investigators that a direct-mail vendor with close ties to Reed was overcharging the organization. Her claims triggered a federal grand jury investigation.[14]

Liebert also told the Norfolk/Virginia Beach *Virginian-Pilot* newspaper about a pattern of partisan activity and intervention in political campaigns at the Coalition. In one case, she asserted, the Coalition sent out letters endorsing a Republican in a Virginia legislative race. The letters were mailed on plain paper, with no indication they had come from the Coalition. A staffer told Liebert she had been ordered to erase copies of the letter from Coalition computers.[15] (Coalition officials denied the charges.)

Linda Lourey, an accountant who worked under Liebert, backed up some of her claims. "Basically, everybody reported to Ralph," Lourey told the newspaper. "You didn't have a normal corporate structure. He would hire people and give them a title, but the title meant absolutely nothing. There was responsibility but no authority."[16]

In 1999, after Tate's demotion and the IRS's decision to deny the Coalition tax-exempt status, another shake-up occurred. The Coalition was split into two organizations—Christian Coalition International, which is to be a for-profit entity run like a corporation, and Christian Coalition of America, which will operate through a 501(c)(4) status already held by the Christian Coalition of Texas.

To us at Americans United, it looked like a shell game. If the IRS denied the Christian Coalition 501(c)(4) status because some of its activities were inappropriate under that status, the group cannot simply continue those same activities through an already constituted 501(c)(4) group. It seems obvious to me that the IRS has more work and investigating to do. Speaking for Americans United, I know that we will remain on the case as well.

Another change at the Coalition was designed to revitalize the group's flagging grassroots presence. Roberta Combs, a Christian Coalition organizer from South Carolina, was brought in to head up this task. Unfortunately for the Coalition, the aggressive Combs rubbed some staffers the wrong way. They nicknamed her "Hurricane Roberta" and, according to the *Hill*, a Capitol Hill weekly, many of them quickly grew weary of her pushy style.

The Coalition, the *Hill* reported, is "an organization that for months has been split with internal tensions that have been exhibited in cloak-and-dagger power plays both sinister and ridiculous."[17]

On August 2, 1999, *New York Times* religion reporter Laurie

Goodstein did an in-depth piece that indicated just how serious the Coalition's problems had become. The group, Goodstein reported, is saddled with a $2.5 million debt because many of its small donors jumped ship after Reed resigned. In addition, a rash of resignations at the state level left the Coalition with viable state chapters in just seven states—South Carolina, Georgia, Florida, Texas, Massachusetts, Oklahoma, and Washington.

Former employees told Goodstein stories about temp workers being hired to give the Coalition's offices the appearance of activity when TV crews came by to conduct interviews and of staff members who "leapfrogged ahead of the reporters to fill empty offices and telephones." (Mike Russell, a Coalition spokesman, admitted that temp workers had been hired but said this was done at the request of TV reporters who wanted a busier atmosphere for the cameras. He denied that "leapfrogging" had occurred.)[18]

Goodstein also confirmed something that Americans United has known for a long time—that the Coalition's membership is nowhere near two million. Many of the names on its list, she noted, are "one-time donors, bad addresses and people who once signed a petition or called an 800 number. . . ."

Coalition claims to have distributed forty million voter guides in 1998 were also wildly inflated. Apparently, many of those guides never made it into the hands of voters. "We never distributed forty million guides," said Dave Welch, the Coalition's former national field director. "State affiliates took stacks of them to recycling centers after the election. A lot of churches just put a pile of them on the back table. I never considered effective distribution anything short of inserting them into church bulletins, but in a very few churches did that actually happen."[19]

The Christian Coalition is trying to reorganize. Staffers told Goodstein that the group hopes to have coordinators in all fifty states by the 2000 elections and planned to hold a series of "God and Country" rallies featuring Robertson to boost momentum.

"I would say we've lost some momentum," Russell admitted. "But the grassroots of the organization are still there. It's just a question now of getting back out and reenergizing the existing network."[20]

The day after that story ran, the Coalition won a minor victory in federal court when U.S. District Court Joyce Hens Green dismissed the bulk of a lawsuit against the group that had been filed by the Federal Election Commission in 1996.

The FEC charged that the Coalition had improperly coordinated its activities with Republican campaigns. Reading federal election law exceedingly narrowly, Green rejected the FEC's claims, saying the group had not engaged in "express advocacy" by telling people who to vote for on its voter guides. Green conceded that the guides are stacked in favor of GOP candidates but said that was not enough to violate federal election law.[21]

The Coalition immediately issued a press release proclaiming that a federal court had declared its voter guides "nonpartisan." The decision said nothing of the kind. In fact, Judge Green specifically points out the partisan nature of the Coalition's guides and many of its activities in her decision. Her opinion, in fact, is a veritable recounting of the partisan nature of the Coalition and discusses in detail how the Christian Coalition worked hand in glove with assorted GOP campaigns.

Judge Green did rule for the FEC in two instances. She found that the Coalition violated federal election law by endorsing House Speaker Newt Gingrich in 1994 and improperly sharing the group's mailing list with Senate candidate Oliver North that same year. The Coalition was assessed a "civil penalty" for these transgressions.

Judge Green's decision was a mere footnote to the IRS's earlier ruling denying the group tax-exempt status. Federal tax law is a lot tighter than federal election law. Federal tax law states that churches and nonprofit groups may not engage in any partisan politicking. Despite the FEC's loss, churches are still forbidden to distribute partisan campaign materials—like Christian Coalition voter guides.

The FEC victory was a mere respite for the Coalition. Its problems continued to mount as 1999 came to a close. Even as Robertson was crowing about the unprecedented influence the organization would have on the 2000 elections, the exodus of top staff continued. In late November 1999, Tate jumped ship. His resignation left the Coalition with virtually no experienced senior staff. At the same time, it was reported that a direct-mail firm that had helped the Coalition raise more than $7 million was suing the group for $386,000, saying it had not been paid for its work since the previous spring.[22]

Does all of this mean the Christian Coalition is on the ropes? I doubt it. It's not uncommon for advocacy organizations to have periods of feast or famine. Some groups do crash and burn, but only after sustained periods of hardship. The Christian Coalition isn't close to that yet. The group's ups and downs are to be expected. Any organization that survives nine years will see staff turnover and even a certain amount of internal turmoil. It's inevitable.

In the Christian Coalition's case, there is an additional wild card: Pat Robertson. The volatile TV preacher is prone to say whatever is on his mind at any given moment. When he pops off in this manner on national television, the repercussions can be serious. When Robertson told his television audience that impeachment proceedings against Clinton were a waste of time and ought to be dropped, for example, he seemed surprised at the uproar it caused. Apparently, many supporters and staff members left the group after that outburst. It is often left to Robertson's staff to try to perform damage control. I suppose there are some people who would thrive working under these conditions, but most, I suspect, would just find it frustrating. An unpredictable leader cannot create a stable organization.

So while the Coalition is in turmoil, it would be premature or wishful thinking to write the group off. Robertson is a millionaire many times over and can easily prop up the organization during lean times—as he has done already, in fact. The Coalition is entrenched in the Republican Party in many states. These people cannot simply be removed overnight. I believe the Coalition will remain a force in American politics for many years to come. Of course its power will wax and wane. It will have victories and defeats. This is to be expected from any group that's in the game for the long haul.

With the Christian Coalition in such turmoil, I knew that the 1999 "Road to Victory" would be an event I could not miss. Sure enough, the 1999 event, held October 1–2, had an air of despair around it. For starters, attendance was off. Coalition officials claimed that thirty-five hundred people attended, but I would say the crowd was more like two thousand to twenty-five hundred. Entire wings of the ballroom sat empty during the main sessions. Also, in previous years, the Christian Coalition has booked the Washington Hilton solid. This year, the hotel had enough space left over to book two other major events at the same time.

I attended a number of state caucuses and "breakout" sessions, as did other members of the Americans United staff. In virtually all of them, we heard Coalition supporters grumbling about collapsing chapters, laid-off staff, and dwindling resources. At the Pennsylvania caucus, the session leader frankly admitted that the state chapter was rebuilding. At the Michigan meeting, attendees complained that nothing was happening these days. Americans United staffers heard similar complaints in state meetings for South Carolina, Iowa, Louisiana, New York, and others.

One of our staff members agreed to attend a caucus meeting for Coalition members in New Hampshire and Vermont. We thought this might be an interesting meeting since New Hampshire holds the nation's first primary. Perhaps there would be some partisan political content. But the meeting turned out to be not so fascinating, chiefly because our staffer was the only person who showed up for it.

Nevertheless, nearly every major Republican presidential hopeful trekked to the 1999 "Road to Victory" to woo the Coalition. (Notable exceptions were Arizona Sen. John McCain, whom the Coalition despises because he dares to support campaign finance reform, and Pat Buchanan, who at the time was flirting with a third-party bid that later became a reality when the fiery commentator announced that he would seek the nomination of the Reform Party.) Robertson, however, undercut most of the candidates by making it clear that he is supporting Texas Gov. George W. Bush. During a press conference held after the Friday morning sessions, Robertson dismissed the chances of candidates like Gary Bauer and Steve Forbes and said Elizabeth Dole would make a better vice president. He stated repeatedly that Bush was acceptable to him and opined that he believes the Texas governor would be a good president.

As usual, the conference was little more than a Republican Party rally. During his remarks, Reed got up and told a bunch of jokes about Clinton and Gore, celebrated the fact that the Coalition has helped to kick certain Democrats out of office since 1990, applauded the election of various Republicans, and then, with a straight face, told the crowd the group must always remain nonpartisan.

And, also as usual, an overwhelming—at time suffocating—air of meanness hung over the event like a thick cloud of smog smothering Los Angeles on a bad day. I'm always amazed at how a "Christian" group can be so vile and mean-spirited. These folks need to take off their trendy "WWJD" bracelets for a minute and ask themselves if Jesus would use their type of rhetoric.

At every "Road to Victory," there is always at least one speaker whose hateful rhetoric goes way over the top. In 1999 that role was played by Bishop Earl Jackson, one of the Coalition's small band of black conservatives. Jackson ran the group's Samaritan Project for ten months before the Coalition decided it wasn't really interested in helping the poor after all. Nevertheless, he remains in the group's orbit, and the Coalition trots him out every year in a desperate attempt to show that the group has support in a minority community when it clearly does not.

Jackson's performance at the 1999 meeting consisted mainly of hollering vile invective for fifteen or twenty minutes, much to the delight of the crowd. Shouting virtually his entire speech, Jackson called for no compromise with "them"—"them" being identified as the usual suspects for Religious Right rage, chiefly the liberal establishment, popular culture, Hollywood, the media, and so on.

Jackson told the crowd not to even bother talking with those who disagree. "The fact of the matter is that Jesus did not come to compromise with the devil, he came to destroy the words of the devil." Jackson said. "Now people will say, 'Well now, Bishop Jackson, that sounds awfully harsh. . . .' Let me tell you something, if they are going to stand with the devil, then they must fall with the devil."

Quoting Bible verses that promise that anyone who goes against the word of God will be "crushed to powder," Jackson continued, "We are the believers who have the right to say that what we believe is going to prevail, we don't care what the liberals and what the media have to say about it. . . . I will not be satisfied until every Christian in America realizes that we need to be standing together. We are at war! We are at war!"

It's always important, when one is a Religious Right figure delivering a rant like this, to throw in a line about loving your enemies. After all, Jesus did recommends that, and one would not want to appear to be a extremist by going against Jesus' advice. Jackson did employ the necessary line, but I was not persuaded. The rest of what he said was too severe. It's hard for me to imagine loving someone yet still thinking it's a good idea to crush that person to powder.

I also thought that Jackson's use of war metaphors cast further doubt on the depth of his love for those who oppose him politically. Armies that engage one another in battle are not normally filled with love for each other. In fact, it's standard practice, through propaganda and constant agitation, for a nation to demonize the country it goes to war with. Wars are not about love; they are about destruction and vanquishing your foes utterly. And that's exactly what Jackson called for.

(Just before the 1999 "Road to Victory," I saw a clever editorial cartoon by Joel Pett of the *Lexington Herald-Leader* in Kentucky. It depicted a man and a woman leaving a church. The man was saying, "Just between us, I hate the sinners as much as I hate the sins!" In my opinion, that is the Christian Coalition in a nutshell).

Jackson may have ratcheted up the rhetoric because Rabbi Lapin wasn't at the 1999 event. "Christian nation" advocate David Barton, who is not mean, merely vapid, did resurface in 1999, but he spoke so fast it was hard to determine exactly what he was saying. The gist of it seemed to be that some national leaders during the colonial period were Christians, therefore we should not have a separation of church and state.

The other highlight of the 1999 "Road to Victory"—or low point, depending on your perspective—was Robertson's kickoff speech. It was essentially divided into two parts. Part two was a standard-issue Religious Right tirade blasting public education, legal abortion, gay people, and so forth. Ho hum.

But part one was bizarre. During it, Robertson, alternating between a toothy grin and a dark scowl, laid out a grim scenario for the coming new millennium. Too much of the world, he said, lives in poverty and hopelessness, surrounded by squalor, filth, and disease. Three times he mentioned his concern over people in the Third World being menaced by "intestinal parasites." At the same time, Robertson added, the world is threatened by unstable dictators and biological weapons of mass destruction.

In today's world, Robertson said, 25 percent of the people hold 85 percent of the wealth. The Christian Coalition in the next millennium, he asserted, "must respond to the agonizing cry of suffering that is reaching our ears." He called for programs to help the world's poor become self-sufficient and told the crowd about a trip he made to the Philippines, during which he arranged for families living on garbage heaps to receive low-interest loans so they could start small businesses.

Robertson asserted that these poorest of the poor could sell food or perhaps cloth. It was unclear to me, however, how their neighbors, who also presumably live on garbage heaps, would be able to afford these items. Nevertheless, Robertson assured us the program was a great success.

The crowd seemed unsure how to react to Robertson's "end world hunger" rant. Although he denied he was advocating any new programs, his rhetoric at times had an oddly left-wing, internationalist feel to it—strictly taboo for this crowd. For instance, the TV preacher noted that the United States, as the world's wealthiest country, could afford to establish new international programs. Crowd reaction to this proposal was muffled at best, and it garnered only polite applause. Perhaps sensing the crowd's lukewarm response, Robertson soon shifted to the second half of his remarks—the red meat—and all was well with the world again.

I can't fully explain Robertson's sudden interest in erradicating intestinal parasites and world poverty—and to be frank, I doubt his sincerity—but some of the impetus for it may have come from Robertson's wife Adelia, usually known as "Dede." Dede Robertson gave a rambling speech Saturday morning at the 1999 "Road to Victory"—the first time she ever addressed the event—during which she mostly bashed public education but also bemoaned the fact that "everyone is more interested in maintaining the status quo and a full billfold. No one is interested in our children."

Dede Robertson talked about visiting Appalachia, where she saw "children with no shoes." Her solution to poverty is twofold: more private sector involvement and "we've got to stop electing people who are for big government." She also called for an infusion of fundamentalist Christianity in government, saying, "This country was founded on the principles of the Bible, not the principles of the Koran or any other book."

I should point out here that the Robertsons are multimillionaires. It's as if Robertson and his wife woke up one day from their lives of privilege and suddenly realized there are poor people in the world. Their answer is an injection of that good old bootstrap capitalism. That may or may not be a viable solution, but I think it's mostly irrelevant anyway, as I doubt the Robertsons have any real intention of alleviating world hunger.

I have good cause for this skepticism: We've been down this road before. On January 30, 1997, former Christian Coalition director Ralph Reed held a press conference in Washington to announce that the Coalition would spend the year lobbying in Congress on behalf of the poor. Ten months after the effort, the infamous Samaritan Project was shut down, having done virtually nothing except demand vouchers.

This time, I think Robertson's antipoverty rant was designed to impress members of an international delegation he had brought in for the conference. Many of these people came from poor Latin American nations, and Robertson's promise might have seemed impressive to them. Given his track record, I don't expect Robertson to fill many empty bellies, cover many unshod feet, or kill many intestinal parasites.

Of the presidential candidates who spoke during the 1999 event, most were unimpressive. Bush gave a standard stump speech with a few mild references to abortion thrown in. Gary Bauer and Steve Forbes were a little more strident, both promising to appoint only "pro-life" justices to the Supreme Court. (Bauer went even further, saying all of his appointees to every government department, and presumably all his ambassadors, will be antiabortion.) Dole delivered stock campaign remarks, and not very well I might add. She called for an end to abortion and a moment of silence and displaying the Ten Commandments in public schools. (Not long after the event, Dole dropped out of the race.)

Utah Sen. Orrin Hatch provided the most entertainment. Hatch spent much of his time talking about the importance of appointing right-wingers to the Supreme Court, but for some reason he decided to wrap up with a weird apocalyptic tangent.

Hatch warned the crowd that the end of the world may be soon at hand. Although the nation appears prosperous and is at peace, Hatch said, problems lurk just below the surface. He cited Hal Lindsey's book, *The Late Great Planet Earth*, a best-seller in 1970 but now largely discredited, that warned of a coming apocalypse. Lindsey, Hatch said, wrote that signs of the end include strange weather, rapid technological advances, rampant homosexuality, gluttony, and a preoccupation with sex.

"Sound familiar?" Hatch asked.

Senate Majority Leader Trent Lott spoke and basically begged the crowd to elect more Republicans to the Senate. Lott took care to include several gratuitous references to Sen. Ted Kennedy (D–Mass.) in his speech so the crowd could boo.

House Speaker Dennis Hastert was also on hand. Hastert's remarks were very dull, amounting to a dry recitation on taxes and health care reform. He never once mentioned abortion, school prayer, or federal funding of the arts. I found myself missing Newt Gingrich who, when he was Speaker of the House, appeared at "Road to Victory" every year and knew how to please the Christian Coalition crowd.

Gingrich had been listed as a speaker on early "Road to Victory '99" promotional materials but mysteriously vanished at some point along the way. Oddly enough, Gingrich dropped off the program at about the same time that reports surfaced in the media that he had dumped his second wife to take up with a much younger woman with whom he had been having an ongoing relationship. During the conference, several speakers heaped abuse on Clinton for his extramarital dalliances. Not one took Gingrich to task for doing the same thing. (Conservative columnist Cal Thomas, who is anathema to the Coalition these days for daring to express the apostate view that partisan politics does not belong in houses of worship, had the best line about the former Speaker. Just days before the "Road to Victory" event, Thomas, speaking at a panel discussion on religion and politics hosted by Americans United, quipped, "How are you going to impose family values on the country when you won't even impose them on yourself?"

I left the 1999 "Road to Victory" feeling like I do every year after the event: in need of a nice, long shower. I also couldn't help but feel a little optimistic. After eight years of attending these gatherings, I had for the first time seen and heard real evidence that the organization was in trouble. I didn't believe the Christian Coalition would collapse next week, but clearly the group had experienced some setbacks. Maybe things would get worse for the Coalition and it would, someday, go the way of the Moral Marjority. It was a big dream perhaps, but one well worth having.

At "Road to Victory" conferences I have had the opportunity to attend state caucus meetings and sit in on more intimate gatherings where state or local leaders outline strategy and discusse activities. This is always interesting because it has allowed me to see how the Coalition operates at the grassroots. But I was curious to learn more. What was missing, from my perspective, was how the Coalition operates when it's not cruising along the "Road to Victory." In other words, how do Coalition chapters really function?

I had an opportunity to find out for myself early in 1998. Since I have attended so many "Road to Victory" conferences, I'm on the group's mailing and telephone lists. I never fail to get a phone call on primary and general election days, reminding me to vote. But the notice I got in early 1998 was something different: It was an invitation to help form a local chapter of the Christian Coalition in Montgomery County, Maryland, my adopted home.

By way of a little background, I should say that I am not a native Marylander. I was born and raised in central Pennsylvania and moved to Maryland's Washington, D.C., suburbs in January of 1986, almost two years before I started working at Americans United. My hometown in Pennsylvania, where my mother and several of my siblings still live, is conservative; there's very little racial or religious diversity. Most people are Roman Catholics or Protestants of one denomination or another.

Montgomery County is worlds removed from that. It's upscale and socially progressive. The county leans Democratic, and although it is currently represented in Congress by a Republican, she is one of the most liberal members of that party in the House. In short, it does not appear to be fertile ground for Christian Coalition organizing. Naturally, I had to find out what was going on.

The initial formation meeting was held in a Protestant church in a community known as Germantown. I had expected I would be just another face in a crowd of thirty or forty and figured it would be easy to blend in with the background and lay low, which is my habit when engaging in "deep cover." But when I walked in the door of the church meeting room, I had to rapidly shift strategies because only eight people had showed up.

The organizer of our chapter was an affable middle-aged man I'll call "Alex." (The names have been changed to protect not the innocent but the guilty, or at least those who ought to feel guilty.) I could see from the beginning that Alex would have a hard time taking Montgomery County for Pat Robertson. His army consisted of a diverse collection of individuals drawn from the county's anemic antiabortion movement (including one gentleman who would not stop talking) and one spy. But every revolution has to start somewhere, so we set to the task.

The first order of business was to name an interim board of directors. Since we were a small, intimate group, we decided to name ourselves the temporary board. Thus, I hold the distinction of being perhaps the only employee of Americans United for Separation of Church and State to have held a directors seat—albeit briefly—on the board of a Christian Coalition chapter.

Then the fun started. Mostly people just complained about their misfortune to live in a county cursed with a Democratic majority. One elderly gentleman, I'll call him "Stu," spat out that the school board and county council were all "secular humanists." See, I was learning things already. Up to that point, I had assumed that most local politicians were Christians or Jews. Stu also asserted that school board elections in the county were "rigged by the teachers' unions." The purpose of this evil plot, he explained, was to make sure that sex education, the teaching of evolution, and humanism remained dominant in our county's public schools.

At one point, I'm not sure why, someone brought up global warming. This met with a general sigh of dismay from the crowd. One woman piped up, "It's not happening! All the top scientists say it's not." She assured us we could trust her on this because, "I have a science degree."

Eventually we had formulated a type of action plan: We would put out a voters guide for state legislative races. We would talk about what issues to include in the guide next time. As Alex put it, "The problem is knowing who to vote for. . . . That's where the Christian Coalition comes in."

That was a shocking statement. The Coalition's party line at that time was that its voter guides were "nonpartisan" and designed merely to educate voters, not persuade them to vote for one candidate over another.

Someone asked Alex why we didn't include school board candidates on the guide. His face fell as he replied, "I was told there was nobody worthwhile running. They are all proabortion and pro–sex education. . . . Montgomery County is not easy, but that's no reason why we should not try."

Then Alex announced that we had a special visitor. Lisa, the director of the state Christian Coalition, had come all the way from her home near Cumberland to pump us up.

Lisa began by telling an inspirational story about how "Christians" in Garrett County, a rural enclave in far western Maryland, had taken over the school board. Before that happened, she said, only two members of the seven-member board "were Christians."

I've been through Garrett County. Culturally, it has a lot in common with West Virginia—*very* rural. I considered asking Lisa what religion those five other board members were—Buddhists, perhaps? Maybe Hindus?

But I didn't get the opportunity because Lisa had launched into an explanation of how we were to achieve our goals through neighborhood voter identification and turnout on election day. Lots of people don't vote, she said, but if the right kind of people vote, our kind of folks can win. Our job was to visit our neighbors, scope out the right-wingers, get them registered, and, if we had to, drive them ourselves to the polls on election day.

I was taken aback. I knew that this "voter ID" election strategy was yesterday's news. The Christian Coalition used to use it but had abandoned it in favor of a church-based model that called for aggressive distribution of voter guides the Sunday before election days. I was depressed. How were we ever going to capture the county for Pat with this ancient, discredited model? Sadly I concluded that I, the spy, knew more about organizing a Christian Coalition chapter than the anointed leaders of the group.

Lisa concluded with some dire warnings. "I believe America as we know it is not going to exist in fifteen or twenty years from now if we don't act," she said. "Our government has started to take away our freedoms, so gradually we haven't noticed it. The United States is giving up sovereignty to the UN right and left. I'm not ready to let the decisions of our government be made by an international community."

It would have been nice to stick around and chat over coffee and cookies. I especially wanted Stu to flesh out that rigged election thing for me and see if he could provide proof that the school board was all secular humanists so I could show my neighbors, but I had already wasted two hours on a Saturday morning when I could have been home with the kids, so I took my leave.

Unfortunately, I missed the next meeting. I had a conflict, as I had agreed months earlier to speak before a meeting of Planned Parenthood in Washington. I really wanted to call up Alex and say, "Sorry, Alex, but I can't make the meeting this month. I'm addressing Planned Parenthood downtown. Can you call me later and fill me in?"

Instead, I remained mum and went to the local Coalition meeting the following month. Stu had big news: He had decided to run for the Maryland House of Delegates! We were all happy for him. I don't live in Stu's district, so I was especially happy.

Someone asked Stu what issues he would stress during the campaign. He replied, "The first thing I'm going to do is shut off these butlers to the gay people."

Several of us just looked at him. Butlers to the gay people! Whatever could he mean? We prodded a little, and the answer came out: Stu was referring to some type of local government program that sent home health care professionals into the homes of terminally ill people who had serious cases of AIDS.

As Stu spoke, an unshaven man next to me nodded approvingly. He was active in the local antiabortion movement and to me always looked like he had a glint of fanaticism in his eyes. I did not know whether to feel sorry for them both or simply be enraged.

We also had visits from a few politicians that Saturday. Two Republican hopefuls dropped by. One man was seeking to become state's attorney, and a woman had filed for a seat on the county council. They talked openly about winning our support and getting endorsements. Again, I found this odd behavior for a "nonpartisan" group.

The gentleman seeking to become state's attorney was especially enthusiastic about the proposed voter guide. Four or five well phrased questions, he asserted, would tell us "who's with us and who's not."

The woman seeking the at-large council seat was not shy about asking us for financial support. She gave each of us an envelope with a short note inside. I have reproduced it here, quirky punctuation and capitalization and all:

"I am asking for your support. I know we both share the same *Christian* beliefs in a very difficult environment but with your support I can become a really viable candidate in this coming elections. I know I can win, but I can not do it without you. Please pretty please, Support me."

It was a heartfelt plea delivered to at least thirteen people, but it was not enough. Neither of these hopefuls were successful in winning election to public office.

I missed a few more meetings but got back to one that summer. There I learned that the Maryland Christian Coalition was in turmoil. Lisa had resigned, and we were adrift! I was appalled. Who would save Maryland from the coming UN takeover? How could Lisa abandon us at this critical time?

Also, I had been receiving regular e-mail updates from Lisa at the Maryland headquarters. They warned me about militant homosexual activists bent on destroying my family, more stuff about United Nations takeovers of the country, the latest schemes of the "radical feminists," the usual kind of thing. I found them very helpful and knew I would certainly miss them.

Alex tried to paste a good face on the news. Locally, we were doing fine. Thirteen people had come out for this meeting, and our voter guide was almost completed.

More months passed. Election day came and went. About a week before election day, I received the local Coalition voter guide in the mail—highly irregular. They are supposed to be distributed in churches. Anyway, Stu had somehow managed to win the Republican nomination for House of Delegates. The district he wanted to represent is so heavy with Democrats that he may not have had an opponent. In any case, Stu's "no butlers for the gay people" platform failed to excite the voters. On election day, three candidates out a field of six won election to represent Stu's district. Stu was not among them. In fact, he came in dead last, capturing 6 percent of the vote.

It's easy to poke fun at the Christian Coalition in my county. They had an uphill struggle all the time. But I know from experience that chapters in other parts of the country are much better organized and more effective. In South Carolina, where Roberta Combs used to reside, Coalition chapters essentially doubled as local units of the GOP. Moderates who refused to play ball were forced out. Also, I've had plenty of calls over the years from people all over the country who do battle with Christian Coalition chapters on a host of issues, from library censorship and creationism to antiabortion drives and antigay initiatives. I wish all Coalition chapters were as ineffective as the one in Montgomery County, but I know that's not the case.

I want to conclude this chapter with a warning: Don't buy into the view that circulates periodically that the Christian Coalition (or the larger Religious Right movement, for that matter) is dead or dying. In the twelve years I have worked at Americans United, I have seen the Religious Right's obituary written many times, always prematurely.

It's true that right-wing newspaper columnist Cal Thomas and Free Congress Foundation★ head Paul Weyrich have called for fundamentalist Christians to step out of politics. My response to that is: so what? Thomas is a columnist, not the leader of a national organization, and as I was writing this book, he had already been effectively shunned for his views. Weyrich helped form the Moral Majority but is a peripheral figure these days. Besides, he's not a fundamentalist Protestant, he's an Eastern Rite Catholic. Few in the Religious Right are likely to heed his call.

The nation's leading Religious Right leaders have already rejected Thomas's and Weyrich's views. Having tasted some political power, men like Pat Robertson, James Dobson, and D. James Kennedy are not likely to voluntarily give it up. I'm surprised that anyone would believe that.

Stories that the Religious Right is dead surface periodically in the media and have the potential to do great damage. They mislead people. They cause some activists to become less active. They lead some folks

---

★The Free Congress Foundation is a far-right "think tank" headquartered in Washington. Free Congress promotes conservative economic policies but has always taken a strong interest in social issues, such as abortion and gay rights, as well.

to let their guard down. They lull others into a false sense of complacency. This is just what the Religious Right wants. Don't fall for it.

I heard Robertson speak at a "Road to Victory" conference in 1995 about the great strides the Christian Coalition had made in taking over the Republican Party in the states. A magazine had reported that the Coalition was dominant in about half of the state GOP units and had a significant presence in many others. Robertson said that was great but that more work remained to be done because "I like 100 percent."[23]

It's wishful thinking to believe that Robertson will simply decide to go away. It's wishful thinking to believe that his Christian Coalition will collapse overnight. It's wishful thinking to believe that the Religious Right will simply fade from view. Robertson wants 100 percent. He has stated his views up front. His agenda is no longer a secret. His ambitions and those of his Christian Coalition have been laid out for the American people to see. He will work toward them until the very day he draws his last breath.

Christian Coalition
Leader: Marion G. "Pat" Robertson
Budget: Varies from $17 million to $25 million annually
**Membership: Claims two million; actual membership is
    much less, perhaps 450,000 or lower.**
Address: 1801-L Sara Drive, Chesapeake, VA 23320★
Website: http://www.cc.org

NOTES

1. Michael Isikoff, "Christian Coalition Steps Boldly into Politics," *Washington Post*, September 10, 1992.

★At press time, the Coalition was planning to move its offices, but hadn't established a new address.

2. Robert Boston, *The Most Dangerous Man in America? Pat Robertson and the Rise of the Christian Coalition* (Amherst, N.Y.: Prometheus Books, 1996).

3. Rob Boston and Joseph L. Conn, "Boss Pat," *Church & State* (October 1997).

4. Nathan Miller, *Stealing From America: A History of Corruption from Jamestown to Reagan* (New York: Paragon House, 1992), pp.210–21.

5. Ibid.

6. Boston and Conn, "Boss Pat."

7. Joseph L. Conn, "God, Guns and the GOP," *Church & State* (November 1998).

8. Ibid.

9. Ralph Z. Hallow, "Hodel Resigns as President of Christian Coalition," *Washington Times*, February 10, 1999.

10. Mary Jacoby, "Christian Coalition Denied Tax Exemption," *St. Petersburg Times*, June 10, 1999.

11. Joseph L. Conn, "Leaner and Meaner," *Church & State* (February 1998).

12. Rob Boston, "Ralph Reed's War on Poverty: Hope or Hype?" *Church & State* (March 1997).

13. Boston, *The Most Dangerous Man in America?* pp. 165–66.

14. Bill Sizemore, "Don't Ask, Don't Tell," *Church & State* (October 1997).

15. Ibid.

16. Bill Sizemore, "Fired Official Is a Key Player in Christian Coalition Troubles," *Virginian-Pilot*, July 27, 1997.

17. Robert Schlesinger, "Christian Coalition Struggles to Overcome Its Internal Divisions," *The Hill*, June 23, 1999.

18. Laurie Goodstein, "Coalition's Woes May Hinder Goals Of Christian Right," *New York Times*, August 2, 1999.

19. Ibid.

20. Ibid.

21. *Federal Election Commission v. The Christian Coalition*, 96-1781, U.S. District Court for the District of Columbia.

22. Liz Szabo, "Christian Coalition Beseiged by Financial and Leadership Woes," *Virginian-Pilot*, December 2, 1999.

23. Joseph L. Conn, "Power Trip," *Church & State* (October 1995).

Chapter 3

JERRY FALWELL

From Moral Majoritarian to Marginal Moaner

The first thing I have to say about Jerry Falwell is blunt and unkind but true: Jerry Falwell is washed up. He's a has-been, yesterday's news. He continues to lurk about the periphery of the Religious Right, but he's a mere curiosity these days, something like a carnival exhibit—the amazing petrified Religious Right leader.

Actually, the best analogy to make about Jerry Falwell in the opening days of the twenty-first century is this: He's like one of those old hard-rock bands that hasn't had a hit since the Carter administration. Sometimes you come across them playing county fairs or tumble-down nightclubs in the bad end of town. Usually, the only original member left is the bass player. You might go to see them out of curiosity, but you wouldn't buy their new self-produced CD. This is not to say that Jerry Falwell isn't still annoying. He is. He still appears on television and talk radio shows. When the producers of these shows can't get anyone else to come on to parrot the Religious Right line, they know there is always Jerry Falwell. Americans United Executive Director Barry W. Lynn has had several run-ins with Falwell on television programs over the past few years. I even took him on one day on Fox News Channel in 1998.

My purpose here is not to recount the long career of Jerry Falwell. Others have done that. But since he's still out there, and isn't likely to go away anytime soon, I want to share some information and reflections about Americans United's dealings with Falwell over the years.

Falwell is still worth knowing about, even if he is a mere historical curiosity. After all, Falwell was pivotal to the rise of the Religious Right. Falwell, an obscure Baptist preacher from Lynchburg, Virginia, paved the way for Pat Robertson, James Dobson, D. James Kennedy, and a host of other Religious Right leaders that plague our land today. I cannot say definitely that Robertson et al. would not exist were it not for Falwell, but his experience in forming the Moral Majority certainly made it easier for the groups that came later. Falwell blazed the trail; others fixed it up and made it smooth. The modern Religious Right owes that debt to Falwell. In my view, he has much to answer for.

Ironically, Falwell was at first a mere puppet in the hands of other right-wingers. By now the story of the formation of the Moral Majority is well known: Two conservative activists, Paul Weyrich and Howard Phillips, traveled to Lynchburg and persuaded Falwell to form the Moral Majority. Falwell didn't even come up with the name; it was Weyrich's idea.

These far-right activists were looking for a minister to act as a mouthpiece. Falwell had been fingered as a likely candidate by Ed McAteer, a right-wing activist and former salesman who had had a long friendship with Falwell.

The idea that Weyrich, Phillips, McAteer, and others cooked up was to find a way to convince evangelical Christians to support Republican candidates. Many evangelicals had historically been Democrats. Many had voted for Jimmy Carter in 1976. Weyrich and company wanted to find a way to bring them into the GOP. Having a minister form an organization that focused exclusively on issues like abortion, gay rights, and school prayer seemed the perfect solution.

I remember quite clearly Falwell's rise to national prominence in the late 1970s. I was a high school student at the time, and I recall asking a friend of mine, "Who is this guy?" Suddenly Falwell seemed to be everywhere, and the name "Moral Majority" was in the papers constantly. (I also recall seeing what remains to this day one of my favorite bumper stickers: "The Moral Majority Is Neither.")

In hindsight, it's now obvious that the Moral Majority was a paper tiger. Falwell had an impressive mailing list and his bombast made good copy and led to many TV appearances, but he had nothing like a true grassroots movement. The Moral Majority claimed large numbers of chapters, but many of them, it now seems, existed only on paper. But at the time, it looked like a real, formidable grassroots operation that just might take the nation by storm.

Instead, here's what really happened: The group became increasingly less influential as the 1980s dragged on and Ronald Reagan left office. In the summer of 1989, Falwell shut down the Moral Majority. By then, its staff had dwindled to twelve. Many Americans were probably surprised to learn that it still existed. One conservative political commentator told the media that the disbanding of the Moral Majority would make no difference in the political landscape. He was right.

Robertson, Dobson, Gary Bauer, and other Religious Right leaders undoubtedly learned from Falwell's mistakes. Falwell seemed to believe that he could change America from the top down. After helping elect Reagan president in 1980, Falwell sat back and waited for all that he wanted to be handed to him.

But the real world of politics stymied Falwell's dreams. Reagan introduced a school prayer amendment, but it failed in the Senate. Reagan criticized legal abortion, but his first appointment to the Supreme Court, Sandra Day O'Connor, voted to keep the procedure legal. Reagan pushed for tuition tax credits for private education, but Congress refused to go along.

More savvy Religious Right leaders saw that the way to bring about real change is from the bottom up. Accordingly, they focused on local politics as well as state and federal races. James Dobson's Focus on the Family, for example, maintains allied organizations in many state capitals. Ralph Reed of the Christian Coalition used to talk about school board seats being more important than congressional seats.

Some of this was hyperbole. Reed obviously put a lot of work and time into changing the composition of Congress. But he trained his activists not to forget what was going on in their own political backyards as well.

After the demise of the Moral Majority, many in the nation's media forgot about Falwell. Americans United kept an eye on him. Falwell said he wanted to build up Liberty University, the fundamentalist Christian school he runs in Lynchburg. He promised to step away from politics and focus on the university. For a few years he did that.

Falwell's desire to focus on Liberty University drew him into a protracted battle with Americans United in 1990. The case started when Americans United got wind of Falwell's efforts to obtain $60 million in tax-free industrial development bonds from the city of Lynchburg. Falwell wanted to use the bonds to underwrite new construction at the school and consolidate its debt.

But there was one problem: Liberty University had always been soaked with fundamentalist Christianity. Applicants were required to submit a paper detailing their "personal testimony for the Lord Jesus Christ" as well as a letter of recommendation from their pastor. Once attending the school, students had to go to church services three times a week and take courses in creationism.

Faculty and staff at the school were required to join Falwell's Thomas Road Baptist Church and tithe 10 percent to it. Classes began with prayer, and students were required to participate in "Christian service" in order to graduate.[1]

The separation of church and state means that government may not get into the business of funding religious enterprises. Churches and all of their sectarian projects must be funded with voluntary contributions, not money coerced from the taxpayer. Falwell's university, it seemed obvious, was much too religious to qualify for even indirect state aid through bond financing.

Falwell quickly made a series of cosmetic changes to the school. Suddenly mandatory church services were "convocations." "Christian service" became "community service." Creationism was shuttled off to the philosophy department and became an elective course. Applicants no longer had to explain their relationship with Christ.

The irony of the situation was not lost on many: Falwell had founded the school as a haven for fundamentalist Christian students who did not want a secular education. Yet here he was secularizing the school for a few of Caesar's coins.

When the authority agreed to issue the bonds, Americans United helped local residents file suit. The lead plaintiffs were Nick Habel, a retired Baptist minister, and city residents Haynie Kabler and Jeff Somers. A local judge ruled in favor of Liberty, but the plaintiffs appealed. When the case reached the Supreme Court of Virginia, the ruling was unanimous: Liberty was too "pervasively sectarian" to qualify for the bonds.

A lot of interesting information came out during the court action. For example, although a draft copy of a student handbook containing the revised, less sectarian policies was introduced at trial, it turned out that no copies were ever printed or distributed to prospective students. Instead, Liberty continued to rely on an old handbook that contained all of the old policies. Asked about the discrepancy, a Falwell spokesman said the school had held off printing the new handbooks to save money. Americans United had suspected all along that the proposed "changes" at Liberty were mere verbiage that would never be implemented. It appeared we were correct.[2]

After the courtroom defeat, Falwell attempted to obtain taxable bonds from a private company, but the firm backed out of the deal. The following year, Falwell attempted to turn the school's financial woes into gold by mailing out a fund-raising letter implying that the university could go bankrupt without more support.

The letter, dated December 18, 1991, said, "Our attorneys have given me permission to advise you that Liberty University could be forced to file for Chapter 11 bankruptcy in the next few days. They also gave me permission to tell you why this tragic thing is imminent. . . . There is still time to save this Christian university from bankruptcy."

Two weeks later, a reporter with the Lynchburg *News & Advance* called the school to follow up on this alarming development. Falwell replied, "We never had any intention of filing for bankruptcy. We have not implied anywhere any imminence of bankruptcy. We said that could be an alternative."[3]

In 1992 Falwell engaged in more doublespeak in a separate controversy over state aid to Liberty students. Americans United had challenged the ability of Liberty students to receive aid under a Virginia program called the Tuition Assistance Grants Program. To qualify for the program, Falwell again agreed to secularize Liberty, including ending the requirement that students attend religious services three times per week.

Even as he was agreeing to these changes, Falwell continued to appear on his *Old Time Gospel Hour* television program and insist that Liberty's goal was to train "champions for Christ." I know, as I taped many of these programs. He also said, "We require church attendance Sunday morning, Sunday night, and Wednesday night of all students."

An American United attorney and I attended a meeting of the Virginia State Council of Higher Education on December 10, 1992. During that meeting, Liberty officials admitted that church attendance was still required except in a few cases, such as a student having a job with hours that conflicted with the services. Asked if the school would expel a student who flatly refused to attend religious services, university President A. Pierre Guillermin dodged the question by replying that students like that would probably realize they were not compatible with Liberty and leave the school voluntarily.

After the fiasco over the bonds, Falwell decided to lay low for a couple of years trying to get the school's financial house in order. The school was finally bailed out in 1998 when Art Williams, a millionaire insurance magnate, gave Liberty $70 million.[4]

Even while striving to keep Liberty from going belly-up, Falwell was plotting to reenter the political scene. He resurfaced in 1993 with a claim that he was considering reactivating the Moral Majority. I believe he thought the time was right for him to reemerge on the national stage. After all, a Democrat was occupying the White House. Shortly after the election of Bill Clinton, Falwell mailed out fund-raising letters nationwide asking people to vote yes or no on whether he should restart the Moral Majority. He also asked people to donate money to his efforts.

Falwell refused to disclose the results of the vote, or how much money the appeal raised. He did not restart the Moral Majority and later told *USA Today* he would never run a group by that name again. Instead, Falwell announced the formation of a group called the Liberty Alliance. Falwell bragged that it would organize conservative pastors all over America, but this new group soon became inactive.

Early in 1994 Falwell announced the formation of yet another new group, this one called Mission America. Falwell said the group would have no staff or budget, and its primary activity would be to publish a newspaper called the *Liberty Flame*, now called the *National Liberty Journal.* However, the journal's masthead states that it is published by Falwell's Thomas Road Baptist Church, and on Falwell's website (www.falwell.com) there is no mention of Mission America. Instead, Falwell claims to be doing public policy work though the Liberty Alliance. At this writing, it is unclear whether Mission America is actually doing anything, or even if it still exists.

But Falwell's main activity during the years 1994 and 1995 was hawking a scurrilous anti-Clinton video called *The Clinton Chronicles* through infomercials on national television. Though he apparently had a hand in its creation, Falwell did not produce the tape personally. That task was done by Pat Matrisciana, a California Religious Right activist and head of an anti-Clinton group called Citizens for Honest Government.[5]

The tape was loaded with unsubstantiated charges against Clinton. It accused him of everything from engineering the killings of political enemies to being a cocaine addict. No solid proof was offered for any of the charges. *Salon* magazine, an online publication, reported in 1998 that in one case, a figure who appeared on tape in silhouette and who was identified as an "investigative reporter" whose life had been placed in danger by looking into Clinton's activities was actually Matrisciana.

"Obviously I'm not an investigative reporter," Matrisciana told *Salon*. "And I doubt our lives were actually in any danger. That was Jerry's idea to do that. . . . He thought that would be dramatic." *Salon* also reported that Falwell gave Matrisciana $200,000 to underwrite the cost of producing *The Clinton Chronicles*. (Falwell had raised the funds through yet another direct mail appeal.)[6]

The Clinton Chronicles is so outrageous that even other conservatives criticized Falwell for distributing the tape. Among them was national scold William Bennett, who, in a rare bout with the virtues he claims to champion, told reporters he didn't think Falwell should be involved in such business.

All along, Falwell continued to mail fund-raising letters begging what was left of his supporters to keep him afloat. I've seen some of these letters. They are truly pathetic, even by right-wing direct mail standards. In early 1994 he sent out a letter attacking Bob Hattoy, a former White House advisor whom Falwell accused of turning sensitive government material over to "subversive homosexual groups." Falwell begged for money to "restore dignity to the White House and the Oval Office."

There was one problem with the letter: Hattoy had long been moved out of the White House and shifted to the Interior Department, where he was put to work on the issue of grazing fees for ranchers who keep cattle on federally owned land.

Meanwhile, Falwell sought to boost his bottom line by cozying up to the Rev. Sun Myung Moon, founder of the Unification Church. Moon's *Unification News* reported on Falwell's July 26, 1994, appearance at a church event in Washington, D.C. Falwell spoke at the inaugural meeting of the Youth Federation for World Peace, a Unification group. He was featured in a front-page photo along with Moon and his wife.

Falwell never disclosed how much he was paid to appear at the Moon event, but Moon has paid other national figures fees in the six figures to speak. Nor did Falwell say if he agreed with Moon's theology, which holds that Moon is the messiah, sent to complete the failed mission of Jesus Christ. Somehow I doubt it. The following year, Falwell spoke at two other Moon events, one which took place in Uruguay.

On November 23, 1997, the *Washington Post* reported on another Moon-Falwell financial connection. A Moon group called the Women's Federation for World Peace gave $3.5 million to a group called the Christian Heritage Foundation, which later used the money to buy some of Liberty's debt. A Moon official told the foundation that the money was for "Falwell's people." The *Post* also reported that a Moon publishing group had lent Falwell $400,000 at 6 percent interest in 1996 for use in propping up Liberty.[7]

Falwell denied he had ever solicited money from Moon and said he was not aware of the Moon connection when he accepted the loan.

In April of 1996 Falwell appeared at a "Washington for Jesus" rally in the nation's capital, where he led a mock trial of America for engaging in seven deadly sins: persecution of the church, homosexuality, abortion, racism, addictions, occultism, and HIV/AIDS. (The acronym spells PHARAOH. These right-wingers are so clever.)

"We come today," said Falwell, "to declare this nation guilty of violating God's law and to call this nation to repentance to forsake her sins and to acknowledge Christ Jesus as Lord."[8]

Following the event, Falwell announced that he would hold a series of "God Save America" rallies at cities around the nation because America "is perilously close to experiencing God's judgment" and has entered a "post-Christian era." (Has anyone told this to the 85 percent of Americans who tell pollsters they are Christians?) The rallies, if they ever occurred, attracted little attention.

In the summer of 1997 Falwell announced a new venture to elect conservative Christians to public office. In a *Falwell Fax* dated June 13, 1997, Falwell explained how he had mobilized local churches to help Mark Earley win the GOP primary in the Virginia attorney general's race. Falwell said Earley won because individual pastors across the state urged their congregants to vote for him. "I am more convinced than ever that conservative Christians can accomplish similar victories across our nation by conducting similar campaigns," Falwell wrote.

One pastor, Dr. George Sweet of Atlantic Shores Baptist Church in Virginia Beach (the church Earley attended at the time), sent a mailing in early June of 1997 to more than two thousand Virginia pastors outlining Earley's views and asking them to "tell their congregations the records of the four candidates."

Falwell claimed that Sweet had not told anyone who to vote for, but Sweet's letter is quite clear in this regard and reads, "I am asking you to join me in not only voting for Mark Earley on June 10th, but to also join me in sharing with your congregation how you personally plan to vote."

Elsewhere in the missive Sweet wrote, "[Earley] has courageously stood up for us—please stand up now for him. I am enclosing the kind of personal endorsement I will give Mark this Sunday, June 8th. *Please join me and stand up on June 8th, share your personal endorsement of Mark Earley, and encourage your members to go to the polls on June 10th.*"

Federal tax law prohibits churches and other nonprofit groups from endorsing candidates for public office. Falwell may have thought he had found a way around that rule by asking pastors to issue "personal" endorsements, but to us at Americans United it still smelled bad. We reported Falwell and Sweet to the Internal Revenue Service on July 2, 1997, and asked the federal tax agency to investigate the matter.

Later that same year, Falwell made yet another effort to regain the national spotlight. He launched a new campaign to get some attention by attacking an ABC television show called *Ellen*. Falwell was incensed when the sitcom's producers announced that its lead character would "come out" as a lesbian on national TV. The move would make *Ellen* the first network program with a gay lead character.

Falwell called on conservative Christians to boycott the show's advertisers. He also began referring to the show's star, comedian Ellen DeGeneres, who is gay in real life, as "Ellen degenerate."

Falwell's attack on *Ellen* was not successful. The "coming out" episode was highly rated. The show did fail to keep an audience, however, and was eventually cancelled. TV critics said that this had more to do with a failure by its writers to develop interesting and funny plots than Falwell's complaints.

That same year a motion picture was released, *The People vs. Larry Flynt*, which chronicled Falwell's lawsuit against pornographer Flynt, publisher of *Hustler* and other X-rated magazines. Falwell sued *Hustler* in 1984 after the magazine ran an ad parody implying that Falwell had had an incestuous relationship with his mother in an outhouse. The case went all the way to the U.S. Supreme Court, where Flynt prevailed. Release of the film led to a new round of media appearances for Falwell, some of them done alongside Flynt. Still, few Americans seemed to care, or more importantly, know, that Jerry Falwell was back.

The media's renewed interest in Falwell was short-lived, but in a few instances, he debated members of the Americans United staff. On April 7, 1998, I found myself up against him on Fox News Channel. We were slated to discuss morality in America.

I knew Falwell would bash public education; he always does. I had come prepared. In 1979 Falwell wrote a book called *America Can Be Saved!* where he called for the end of public schools.

"One day, I hope in the next ten years, I trust that we will have more Christian day schools than there are public schools," Falwell wrote in the book. "I hope I live to see the day when, as in the early days of our country, we won't have any public schools. The churches will have taken them over again and Christians will be running them. What a happy day that will be!"[9]

Sure enough, once on air Falwell wasted no time in lighting into public education. (He is nothing if not predictable.) I fired back with the quote from the book. Falwell employed a rather surprising defense: He denied he had ever written the book!

"That book was discredited years ago," he said. "It was printed by someone without our permission. We did not print that book. Someone like you did that. . . . I had nothing to do with it. I had no voice in it."

Americans United does not own a complete copy of *America Can Be Saved!*, just photocopies of some pages. To get to the truth of the matter, I called the book's publisher, Sword of the Lord Publishers in Murfreesboro, Tennessee. The business manager at Sword of the Lord pulled the file on the book. He confirmed that it was produced with Falwell's full cooperation. The tome was in fact a compilation of sermons by Falwell that had appeared in the organization's *Sword of the Lord* evangelistic publication.

Sword of the Lord Publishing printed 15,213 copies of the book on April 30, 1979. The business manager was kind enough to fax me a copy of Falwell's Introduction to the book. It reads in part, "Eleven revival messages are included in this book. Each one was either preached in a Sword of the Lord Conference on revival or printed in *Sword of the Lord* magazine. I wanted them to be published in book form by the Sword of the Lord because this paper . . . has done more to promote revival and holy living in America during the last 40 years than any other single organization."

I should point out that Falwell broke with the Sword of the Lord organization some years ago after a dispute over doctrinal matters. Still, his cooperation with the production of the book seems clear. If his views have since changed, he should say that instead of spinning a wild tale of how an entire book was printed and distributed bearing his name without his permission.

Two months after our bout on Fox News Channel, Falwell changed his story about the book yet again. Confronted with the quote on June 18, 1998, by Americans United Director of Communications Joe Conn on CBS Radio's *Gil Gross Show,* Falwell said, "That book was written twenty-five years ago by Sword of the Lord Publishers. . . . And they, allegedly, from hearing one of my sermons, published my sermons. We had no editing, no proofing whatsoever."

But this new explanation doesn't wash either. It conflicts sharply with what Falwell wrote in 1979 in the book's Introduction. In 1979 Falwell specifically stated that *he wanted* the sermons produced by Sword of the Lord. Nineteen years later, he expects us to believe that Sword of the Lord issued them without his permission in some type of guerrilla publishing operation. (I imagine there's a law against that sort of thing.) It's obvious what is going on here: Falwell is embarrassed by the book's contents and would like to cover it up. He should not be allowed to get away with it.

(By the way, I remain on the lookout for an intact copy of *America Can Be Saved!* The first person to send me one will win a free lifetime subscription to *Church & State.*)

Like a lot of Religious Right leaders, Falwell has a history of making extreme statements and then trying to modify them when they become public. On January 14, 1999, he told a group of pastors at a conference in Kingsport, Tennessee, that the Antichrist is probably walking the earth today and is Jewish.

"Is he alive and here today?" asked Falwell. "Probably. Because when he appears during the Tribulation period, he will be a full-grown counterfeit of Christ. Of course he'll be Jewish. Of course he'll pretend to be Christ. And if, in fact, the Lord is coming soon, and he'll be an adult at the presentation of himself, he must be alive somewhere today."[10]

Several Jewish groups took umbrage at the statement. Abraham H. Foxman of the Anti-Defamation League accused Falwell of promoting anti-Semitism.

But Falwell remained nonplussed. In a clarifying statement, he wrote, "This belief is 2,000 years old and has no anti-Semitic roots. This is simply historic and prophetic orthodox Christian doctrine that most theologians, Christian and non-Christian, have understood for two millennia."[11]

Less than a month later Falwell was in the news again, this time for the now-famous "Tinky Winky incident." It all started when the February 1999 issue of the *National Liberty Journal* ran an unbylined article attacking *Teletubbies*, a popular PBS children's television show imported from England, that features four colorful characters who cavort in a sunny land of make believe.

One of the Teletubbies is named Tinky Winky. He is purple, has a triangle-shaped antenna on his head, and sometimes carries a red bag. Falwell's newspaper was suspicious. Something wasn't right.

"Parents Alert . . . Tinky Winky Comes Out of the Closet" screamed the headline over the article. It warned that Tinky Winky "has been the subject of debate since the series premiered in England in 1997. The character, whose voice is obviously that of a boy, has been found carrying a purse in many episodes and has become a favorite character among gay groups worldwide."

Continued the article, "Now, further evidence that the creators of the series intend for Tinky Winky to be a gay role model have [*sic*] surfaced. He is purple—the gay pride color; and his antenna is shaped like a triangle—the gay pride symbol. . . . These subtle depictions are no doubt intentional and parents are warned to be alert to these elements of the series."[10]

Falwell's attack on Tinky Winky was picked up by the Associated Press. It appeared in newspapers all over America. Late-night talk show hosts and editorial cartoonists had a field day. Columnists let loose with predictable jokes about Falwell investigating Fred Flintstone and Barney Rubble. Another pointed out that Bugs Bunny seems awfully fond of drag.

Now it can be told: Americans United had a hand in bringing this story to light. Our Director of Communications, Joe Conn, reads a lot of Religious Right publications. He first spotted the *National Liberty Journal's* attack on Tinky Winky. He showed it to me. We started musing on whether it might make an a quirky news story for a reporter somewhere. Joe began making calls. It took a few days, but eventually he planted the story with an Associated Press reporter in Richmond. The rest, as they say, is history.

Since the story didn't have anything to do with separation of church and state, some of Americans United's opponents criticized us for leaking it. Our motivation was to help people understand that Falwell holds extreme and unusual views on a variety of subjects. We wanted people, the next time they heard Falwell attack public education or church-state separation, to stop and think, "Wait a minute—isn't this the same guy who thinks one of the Teletubbies is gay? Perhaps he's not a reliable source of information."

The March issue of the *National Liberty Journal* contained an article by Falwell titled, "I Didn't 'Out' Tinky Winky." In the piece, Falwell said he had never seen *Teletubbies* and that the original piece criticizing the character had been written by J. M. Smith, the newspaper's editor. But Falwell endorsed Smith's conclusions, writing, "As a Christian, I believe that role-modeling the gay lifestyle is damaging to children."[13]

Smith ran an article in the same issue headlined "Tinky Winky Is the Tip of the Iceberg," which accused Hollywood of promoting "a vast homosexual influence in popular sitcoms and dramas. . . . Considering the dramatic influx of homosexual themes in modern television, it should come as no surprise that there might appear gay subtexts in a few TV shows—even shows designed for children."[14]

Until Smith and Falwell spoke publicly, many of my colleagues at Americans United had never seen *Teletubbies*. I had a leg up on them there. At the time the controversy broke, my son Paul was about eighteen months old. Paul was often—how shall I say this nicely?—a "busy" child. One morning I noticed him staring at the TV with great intensity. *Teletubbies* was on. My wife and I would occasionally let him watch the show in the mornings. At one point, he took to pointing at the screen and crying out, "Laa Laa! Po!"—two of Tinky Winky's friends. (Dipsy is the third.)

It was kind of creepy seeing a television show cast a spell over a child that young, but, watching *Teletubbies* myself, I had to admit that it had a weird kind of charm.

A few months after the controversy blew over, I took Paul to a toy store to buy him a *Teletubbies* doll. All four were in stock. I set one of each in front of him and told him to take his pick. He examined them all with great care, then, with a deliberate look in his eyes, reached straight out and plucked Laa Laa, the yellow Teletubby with the curly Q on his head, from the shelf. Falwell, I suppose, would approve. (Although the possibility remains that Laa Laa, who is after all yellow, might be sending out subtle messages to our children as well, indoctrinating them into the "coward lifestyle.")

This is the part of the book where I'm supposed to wrap up by expressing my outrage over Falwell and explaining what a threat he is to American values and democracy. I don't believe I need to get into all of that. Falwell has left a long track record of deceit, dissembling, and mean-spirited character assassination. He is a discredit to the values of the God he claims to serve. His record is so spotted that it speaks for itself. I don't have to discredit Falwell; he has done that himself.

The American people know this. That's why most of them consider Falwell either irrelevant or a buffoon. Even the people of Virginia, Falwell's home state, keep him at arm's length. A 1995 Mason-

Dixon poll of Virginians found only 10 percent giving Falwell a favorable rating. A whopping 52 percent said they had an unfavorable impression of him.

Scripture tells us that a prophet will be scorned in his own land. That may explain why the American people have rejected Falwell. Personally, I think there's simpler explanation: The guy is annoying.

Liberty Alliance/*National Liberty Journal*
Leader: The Rev. Jerry Falwell
Budget: $5.8 million (1996 figure)
Membership: Falwell claims the group is not a membership organization.
Address: Route 7, Box 172, Forest, VA 24551
Website: http://www.falwell.com

NOTES

1. Joseph L. Conn, "Don't Buy Liberty Bonds," *Church & State* (March 1990).

2. Rob Boston, "Victory In Virginia," *Church & State* (February 1991).

3. Jan Vertefeuille, "No Bankruptcy Threat at Liberty, Falwell Says," Religious News Service, January 15, 1992.

4. "An Education in Giving," Associated Press dispatch, February 4, 1998.

5. Murray Waas, "The Falwell Connection," *Salon* (March 11, 1998).

6. Ibid.

7. Marc Fisher and Jeff Leen, "A Church in Flux Is Flush with Cash," *Washington Post*, November 23, 1997.

8. "Churches Should Shun Politicization, Says Ex-Moral Majority Pastor," *Church & State* (June 1996)

9. Jerry Falwell, *America Can Be Saved!* (Murfreesboro, Tenn.: Sword of the Lord Publishers, 1979), pp. 52–53.

10. Sonja Barisic, "Falwell Says Antichrist Probably on Earth Now," Associated Press dispatch, January 16, 1999.

11. Larry Witham, "Falwell Angers Jews with Antichrist Talk," *Washington Times*, January 20, 1999.

12. "Parents Alert: Tinky Winky Comes Out of the Closet," *National Liberty Journal* (February 1999).

13. Jerry Falwell, "I Didn't 'Out' Tinky Winky," *National Liberty Journal* (March 1999).

14. J. M. Smith, "Tinky Winky Is the Tip of the Iceberg," *National Liberty Journal* (March 1999).

Chapter 4

MEN BEHAVING POLITELY

A Weekend with the Promise Keepers

T he first thing I noticed about the Promise Keepers is that they are resourceful. When I walked into Robert F. Kennedy Stadium on a warm June night in 1997, I saw that nearly all of the women's rooms had been converted into men's rooms through the simple device of a piece of paper slapped over the "WO."

The Promise Keepers knew they would have no fear of running into women in those restrooms. Women, after all, are not supposed to attend Promise Keeper rallies. They are permitted to volunteer and work concessions, but they aren't supposed to be in the stadium when the testosterone for Jesus starts to flow; somebody could get hurt.

It was a muggy night. I was a few minutes late, and as I walked toward the stadium following hundreds of other men, I heard the sound of forty thousand voices singing "Rock of Ages." I know it wasn't supposed to sound creepy, but it just did. Those deep, rugged voices had taken a spiritual and made it sound like a battle anthem.

As I drew near the stadium, I was taken aback by a man walking around with a large sign reading, "Is Oral Sex Kosher?" who was accosting men as they entered with a flier. I accepted one but can't say I found it enlightening. It didn't make a whole lot of sense, but his answer seemed to be "no."

As I walked through the turnstiles, I realized I had come unarmed. Just about every man there had a huge bag or backpack—the better to carry a large Bible in. I had only a pen and small note-book. I have two Bibles at home, but I hadn't remembered to bring either one. The first is one of those "Good News for Modern Man" type things that were popular in the 1970s. It's written in the ver-nacular of those times, so you have the apostles saying things like, "You bet," and "Right on, Jesus." (Okay, I'm exaggerating.) Worse yet, it's a Douay (Roman Catholic) Version!

The other is a standard King James Version that a Gideon handed to me some years ago. It has all of the "whereases" and "begats" in it, but it wouldn't do me any good tonight, as it was crammed into a bookcase at home. I decided to soldier on. Promise Keepers are friendly, and I knew that if I needed to see a Bible, a neighbor would share his.

Once seated, I surveyed the crowd. Promise Keepers men wear what amounts to a uniform: shorts with a polo or T-shirt, low-cut white socks and sneakers, and a baseball cap. Writing or images on the T-shirt are optional, but if any are there, they should not feature a foul-mouthed pro wrestler or a satanic rock band. They should say something nice about Jesus. A backpack for carrying a water bottle, snacks, and the enormous Bible are essential.

At the time I attended the stadium rally, Promise Keepers had been much in the news. Many people didn't seem to know what to make of the group. Some saw it as merely another revival move-ment. Others were sure Promise Keepers would become the new wave of the Religious Right.

Promise Keepers was founded by Bill McCartney, a former foot-ball coach at the University of Colorado, in 1991. As its website (**www.promisekeepers.org**) tells it, McCartney was driving back from a Fellowship of Christian Athletes meeting with a friend one night, and the two got to talking about a plan to fill a football stadium with conservative Christian men. Some time after that, McCartney met with seventy-one of his male associates to plan what would become the first Promise Keepers rally. The event took place at the University of Colorado's basketball arena in July of 1991 and attracted forty-two hundred men.

The group has clearly come a long way since then. At RFK stadium we had ten times as many participants.

Being at a Promise Keepers event is like stepping into some sort of weird parallel universe where men actually have feelings. You see men doing things there that men just don't do very often—at least not in front of other men. Men cry, hug each other, huddle together in small groups, confess their wicked deeds to one another, and sing raucous religious hymns while swaying to a gospel-approved beat. Men of different races and generations join hands, trying to make connections that have always eluded them.

The crowd, mostly middle-aged and white, had a decidedly upscale, yuppie feel to it. I imagine most of them were from middle or upper management, and I tried to visualize them taking their new selves, full of love and the spirit of the Lord, into the cutthroat world of office politics.

But I don't imagine many of them did that. I got the strong impression, after the first night even, that backsliding is a major problem for the Promise Keepers. In fact, I came to believe that a better name for the group might be "Promise Makers." It's a lot easier to make a promise, after all, than it is to keep it. And I think it would be a safe guess to say that a lot of the Promise Keepers haven't mastered the latter as well as the former.

Several speakers touched on this theme of backsliding, some overtly, some subtly. At one point, we were even shown a video featuring a fictionalized account of a group of men who had attended a Promise Keepers rally. The men got pumped up by the event but afterwards slipped back into their old habits. One guy couldn't stay out of strip clubs; another was into gambling, and a third bickered with his wife.

It's easy to see how this backsliding could happen in the real world. The atmosphere of the stadium rallies is electric. You really can feel a type of energy moving through the place. Men let down their guard and stop perceiving strangers as rivals or potential threats. The attendees are friendly. Several struck up spontaneous conversations with me and invited me to join in their activities. It's almost as if the men say collectively, "The women aren't around—let's quit being jerks!"

Furthermore, Promise Keepers events are deliberately structured to provoke a strong emotional response. The rallies take place in football stadiums, places where men usually meet for combat, albeit staged combat. Promise Keepers lures men in with the promise of the superficial male bonding found through shared interest in sports, the type of bonding that's deemed "safe" for men, then turns that on its head. Instead of grunting, drinking beer, and rooting for teams, men are forced to confront their misdeeds and examine their lives and actions. If they decide they come up short, the only place they can turn for comfort and support is other men—sometimes total strangers.

It's high-energy. That's why men hug, dance, cry, and laugh with joy. To me, it seemed as if some of the men were intoxicated—not on alcohol or drugs but on good feelings, love, "the spirit," whatever you want to call it.

But just as the effects of liquor wear off, so do the effects of a Promise Keepers emotional blast. I got the strong impression that once men left the safe confines of the stadium and returned to their workaday lives and family responsibilities, they just couldn't keep that level of energy and enthusiasm going. It's bound to fade. And when that starts, they pick up old habits again.

The Promise Keepers answer to this phenomenon is "accountability groups." Men are urged to band together in small groups of four or five to meet regularly. The idea is to keep a little of that enthusiasm going and to support one another when those old bad habits come back with their temptations.

I remained on the Promise Keepers mailing list after the event. The idea of accountability groups was constantly stressed in the group's newsletter and other materials. Newsletter articles frequently recounted how hundreds of groups were getting started all over the country, of commitmentss men made to the Promise Keepers way. I have no way of knowing if many of these groups collapsed after two or three meetings or if they are still going strong. But clearly, small-group formation was an important Promise Keepers goal.

A few months after the rally I attended, McCartney seemed to take things a step farther by advocating "shepherding," a controversial practice during which a small group of people turn almost complete control of their lives over to a spiritual leader.

Appearing on Pat Robertson's *700 Club* on September 30, 1997, McCartney talked about Promise Keepers's upcoming "Stand in the Gap" rally in Washington, D.C., and said, "I see every guy leaving out of there and coming under the authority of a local shepherd. And then I see the shepherds networking . . . and we can start to make a difference as men."

At the "Stand in the Gap" rally, which took place on October 4, 1997, McCartney exhorted his followers, "Can't no guy leave out of here as a lone ranger." He urged men to "return home and submit to the authority of a local shepherd."

These are controversial practices, and I have no way of knowing how many men have willingly submitted to shepherds. Still, I have no reason to doubt Promise Keepers' sincerity. If the anecdotes from the newsletter are to be believed, the organization has succeeded in helping some men break free of destructive behaviors or reconnect with their wives. The group has undoubtedly made some men better husbands and fathers.

What concerns me is the Promise Keepers' assumption, common among Religious Right groups, that its way of doing things is the natural or correct way—because it's the "biblical" way. McCartney's stand on "shepherding," for example, is drawn from a passage in Paul's letter to the Hebrews, which reads, "Obey them that have the rule over you and submit yourselves" (Heb. 13:17).

Obviously a passage like this is open to many interpretations, and theologians disagree among themselves as to its exact meaning. To McCartney it obviously refers to shepherding, case closed. At "Stand in the Gap" he said, "It's a clear mandate. It's not optional."

Promise Keepers is also controversial in part because of its stance on women. In recent years the organization has tried to soften its view of how women are to be treated in a marriage, but the bottom line is the same: Men rule, women serve. A woman is to submit to her husband as the church should submit to God. What's worse, Promise Keepers argue that when they do this, they're really doing the woman a favor.

This model may make sense for some families. There are women out there who want to live in this type of arrangement. I have no problem with that. But other families are structured in different ways. Many couples, for example, believe in a power-sharing arrangement of equal partners. Promise Keepers rarely denigrate this model—at least overtly—but they make it clear it's not how things are supposed to be.

Why not? Mostly because someone has decided the Bible says differently. It always comes down to this: The Bible tells me so. Yet even among Religious Right organizations and conservative denominations, the Bible says different things. Passages are interpreted in different ways. Passages that seem obtuse or inconvenient are ignored. Even the Christian Reconstructionists, who seek a society based on a literal reading of the Old Testament, disagree among themselves on what certain passages mean.

So, in a nutshell, it isn't "the Bible tells me so" at all. It's "some guy said the Bible tells me so." Who is that guy? For most Promise Keepers that guy is Bill McCartney. What are McCartney's qualifications to interpret the Bible? Well, McCartney was a football coach.

McCartney is not a theologian, a pastor, or a religious leader. He has never attended a seminary. A onetime Roman Catholic, McCartney now attends a Pentecostal church, Boulder Valley Christian Fellowship, whose pastor, James Ryle, frequently speaks at Promise Keepers rallies. As McCartney himself told NBC's *Meet the Press* on October 5, 1997, "I depend on my pastor to help define the word of God for me. I haven't studied. I haven't been to seminary. I'm very much at risk, if you will. I need to stay under constant monitoring."

McCartney addressed the crowd on Friday night. I found his remarks to be an unnerving blend of moral certainty and fanaticism. I had gone to the Promise Keepers expecting to be shocked and possibly disturbed by what I heard. For the most part that did not happen, with one very big exception—when Coach McCartney took the stage.

This is not to say that I found the Promise Keepers as a movement scary. I know that as a good church-state separationist, I'm supposed to find the Promise Keepers scary. But to be honest, they just weren't all that frightening. I'd rather hang out with the Promise Keepers than the Christian Coalition any day. When attending Christian Coalition events, I often got the impression that some group members, if they knew who I am and what I believe, would be more than happy to tie me to a stake and light some brush underneath it. Promise Keepers devotees would most likely just hug me a lot and urge me to confess my sins to a guy nearby named Ray.

But, while the Promise Keepers en masse failed to scare me, McCartney as an individual did. McCartney's speech wasn't so much an address as a rant. His face was frequently twisted and contorted, and, leering down at the crowd from a giant video screen, he frequently looked like a madman. I may not be explaining it well, but the whole aura had a *1984* feel to it. Remember the "two-minute hate"? McCartney's talk was like a forty-minute hate.

Think of McCartney like this: Most families have at least one member who has gone off the deep end religiously. I still remember a (now ex-) brother-in-law of mine waving a Bible at my mother over Sunday dinner, explaining why she, as a Roman Catholic, was going to end up in Hell. (This in a large way explains why he's an *ex*-brother-in-law.) He had found religion and became simply intolerable, burning with all the manic zeal of a new convert. McCartney reminded me of the annoying relative who won't stop preaching about Jesus, even at the family reunion or summer picnic. He's always on.

McCartney said he was thankful for previous revival efforts in America but then faulted them because 85 percent were led "by ladies." This time, that just wasn't going to cut it. God, he said, was calling men to lead the nation to repentance—and, from what he said, the Almighty is losing patience with us.

"Our God has been mocked, our God has been put down," McCartney said. "He's calling on his men to make a difference, not only in this nation but in the entire world."

McCartney outlined a strategy with four prongs to save the nation: home, church, community, and stadium. And when he said stadium, he wasn't talking football.

At home, he said, godly men are to talk to their children about Jesus constantly, over and over again. "We've been led to believe we oppress kids if we talk about Jesus," he said. "I can't find that in the Word. We're supposed to be talking about Jesus all day long and all night long."

As a parent, I have to say I thought McCartney's strategy left a lot to be desired. I've learned over the years that one sure way to get a kid to put a bean up his nose is to tell him constantly, "Hey, don't put that bean up your nose." Of course parents work hard at passing their values on to their sons and daughters, but if you overdo it, look out when the teen rebellion years hit.

Church and community, McCartney said, are the places to bring revival by finding men, especially layabout pastors who may not be with the program, and forming small groups. Then everyone just sort of heads off to the stadium for the nearest PK rally where they all get to "yield, surrender, obey. . . . Serving the Lord is a privilege."

All of this was interesting, but I was waiting for the good stuff. McCartney didn't let me down. I knew we backsliding men were sooner or later in for a good whopping for our nasty behavior; I wasn't disappointed.

According to McCartney, Promise Keepers' own research shows that 62 percent of all group members say sexual sin is their biggest problem. In case anyone didn't get it, the coach listed them off for us: lust, pornography, adultery, fornication, homosexuality. (Personally, I thought he was being a little hard on us with the lust thing. Even Jimmy Carter wrestled with lust.)

"Many of us have been dabbling in stuff we have no business looking at," the coach said. Fortunately, there was an easy answer: Coach advised us that if we got sexually aroused while watching television, turn it off. Walk out of movies if they get racy.

"The only sex you can have is with your wife," McCartney said. "If you're single, get married. There is no other sex."

McCartney made it clear that if America fell, it would be the fault of us men for allowing ourselves to get distracted by the fleshpots of popular culture—or perhaps something even more nefarious. "The men of God in this nation are not going to be defeated from the outside," he said. "It will be because of betrayal if we go down."

Now it was getting creepy. Betrayal? By whom? The backsliding guy next to me? The one I'm supposed to be reaching out to and asking to join my accountability group? I didn't much like the undercurrent of suspicion coach was planting in us. It didn't seem helpful.

McCartney harangued on the topic of sexual sin for quite a long time. After a while, it began to seem like an unhealthy obsession. It's obviously a topic near to his heart. He topped things off with an odd request: He exhorted every man in the audience to find a stranger nearby and confess to one another all of our sexual sins.

I looked around. Crowd psychology is a tricky thing. I speak before groups myself (although not to forty-five hundred at a pop), and I know that there are moments when, as a speaker, you either take a crowd with you or start to lose them. Coach was starting to lose us. Some guys were wandering around, finding partners, staring at the concrete stadium floor and mumbling. But many more had a different idea.

Suddenly thousands of men started heading for the exits. After all, it was late, it was Friday night, and coach was clearly winding up. We had picked up the gist of what he was saying. Message received. One could stick around for one more round of "Amazing Grace," but perhaps it made more sense to get to the subway a little early. Why not beat the crowds?

On the train back out to the suburbs, I was surrounded by men wearing green wristbands, our "tickets" to the Promise Keepers rally. One sixty-something gentleman had taken McCartney's advice to heart and was attempting to witness to a teenage boy who, despite the heat, was wearing a black leather jacket. The young man also had hair that was a tough-to-pin-down shade of yellowish-green and enough ear- and nose-rings to set off an airport security device. He didn't seem convinced.

Day two, Saturday, featured a financial seminar. Promise Keepers are concerned about sex, but they're also worried about money. Ron Blue, our financial consultant, informed us that two thousand Bible verses mention money—more than any other topic. Intoned Blue, "The Bible has the answer to financial security."

I wondered about that. The Bible was written before credit cards, direct deposit, home mortgages, or IRAs. What could it tell us? Unfortunately, Blue's recipe for financial security turned out to be rather simplistic: Spend less than you earn. Credit cards, he said, allow us to fund a lifestyle "God does not allow." I didn't really need the Bible to tell me that.

But Blue added a biblical spin: The money that men blow paying interest on credit cards, Blue said, really belongs to God. It's "kingdom money" and by turning it over to banks we were cheating God. For shame! That would have to stop. The credit cards, he said, should go into a trash can, or better, yet, a hot oven. He advised us to pay off our debts and then join an accountability group.

Getting one million men out of debt, Blue said, would free up $12 billion for "kingdom work." I don't know where he got the figures, but it sounded impressive. Blue then warned us not to buy anything on credit except a home. A mortgage is okay but nothing else is.

I've heard Pat Robertson give the same advice. To me, it always seemed nonsensical. We all know there is too much consumer debt in America, but it does not follow that *all* consumer debt is bad. Some things are worth assuming a reasonable, manageable amount of debt for.

I surveyed the crowd, looked at all of those middle managers. It had cost me $65 to get in. I suspected that most of the guys here had done what I did: paid for it with a credit card. To many of these men, I don't imagine it was big financial hit to plop down that entrance fee. (Promise Keepers later dropped all admissions fees. More on this in a bit.)

The night before, however, I had talked to some guys from a working-class neighborhood in Baltimore. I didn't ask them how they paid the gate fee, but I suspect they had either taken up a special collection at church or received a reduced admission fee. To these guys, $65 didn't just mean skipping next Saturday's visit to the golf course or a week of eating fast food lunches instead of chowing down at fancy restaurants near the office. It was real money. I had to wonder how these men felt about Blue's advice.

It's easy to advise people to pay cash for everything when you yourself have the cash to pay for everything. Robertson is a multi-millionaire, and I suspect Blue does all right as well. However, most of the rest of us are not rich. I grew up in a working-class home. My father was a housepainter. I know that working-class folks rarely have $20,000 lying around for a new car or even $5,000 for a used model. No car means no private transportation, which can mean no work. Under these circumstances, is financing a car really such a bad idea? If you can meet the monthly payment in your budget, and you are not overextending yourself financially, is it really against God's plan to buy a car with a commercial loan offering a decent interest rate? I hope not, as I've never paid a lump sum of cash for a car in my life. Like just about everyone else, I finance them. Does that make me a bad person? Am I poking God in the eye every time I make a car payment?

And what about financing an education? How many people can afford to pay $15,000 or $20,000 per year or more for a college education and its related expenses up front? Education loans are usually available at low interest. Is it such a bad thing to assume some debt to educate yourself or give your offspring a leg up? Many financial advisors say it's not, pointing out that on average, people with college degrees make higher salaries. The debt is worth it in the long run. Some of Blue's advice, I came to believe, was way too simplistic.

Blue concluded with a strong pitch to buy his book, which was, conveniently, available in a resources tent on site. The message seemed to be, "Yes, melt your credit cards, but *after* you've bought my book."

Blue was only the beginning of a long line of speakers who suddenly turned into pitchmen. Day two definitely had the feel of an intermittent Promise Keepers infomercial. During the day, we were exhorted to avail ourselves of various Promise Keepers "resources"— never products, always "resources." They were all for sale in that tent.

A Promise Keepers daily planner would help us keep track of all of our appointments and provide a daily Bible verse. There was even a PK Bible. (One speaker said of the tent, "You need to stop there. Be blessed by the resources provided for you.")

I cruised the tent. The Promise Keepers logo had been slapped onto just about everything imaginable: T-shirts, cups, mugs, key-chains, pens, and hats. There were rows and rows of videos, books, CDs, and audiocassettes. VISA and MasterCard were cheerfully accepted. Better get that credit card out of the oven!

The next speaker told us all about accountability groups—how to form them and how to keep them going. If at all possible, we were to form groups that day, before we left. The men you had come with were the place to start.

Unfortunately, during his remarks an annoying, intermittent drippy sky turned into a downpour. RFK Stadium isn't domed. Soon we were all thoroughly soaked. A few guys danced around in the rain, as if it were some type of cleansing shower sent down by Jesus to wash away their sins. The metaphor may have worked for a while, but it quickly got tiresome. Rain was dripping off my nose and onto my sneakers. I can't say I liked it. Soon lightning bolts were crashing down from an angry sky. The video monitor flickered once or twice. The rain wasn't charming anymore; it was merely making us miserable. I left, wondering why God had chosen to smite his servants with this foul weather.

A lot of people asked me about the Promise Keepers event. They were naturally curious. Many of them wanted to know if the rally had been political. I had to disappoint them. The RFK event was almost totally apolitical. No politicians appeared on stage to speak. No one was told to vote for or against certain candidates. No one criticized national leaders. In fact, prayers were led for then–Washington Mayor Marion Barry, Congress, and President Bill Clinton.

This is not to say all was sweetness and light. Some Promise

Keepers had come into town early to spruce up sagging D.C. public schools. At first I thought it was a nice gesture, since some schools got a coat of paint and other repairs that they otherwise might not have received. But one Promise Keepers staffer, Gen. Alonzo Short, told us that there was a second agenda.

"Whereas the Supreme Court may have taken prayer out of our schools," he intoned, "you painted, fixed, and cleaned up, and I'm sure you consecrated those schools. D.C. schools will never be the same." That seemed like a cheap shot. The Supreme Court removed mandatory prayer and Christian worship from public schools, not voluntary religious exercises. Why promote that old canard?

Also, there was very little of the "subjugation of women" line at this meeting. I did not interpret this to mean that Promise Keepers have dropped this as a tenet of belief. Rather, I think they were simply tired of taking heat for it and decided to tone down the rhetoric.

But this is not to say that all Promise Keepers rallies are free from political talk. At one 1996 rally, TV preacher John Hagee blasted legal abortion, civil rights, and our secular government. He criticized the separation of church and state, called for official prayer in public schools, and urged parents to file lawsuits over religious issues in public schools.[1]

At a rally in Charlotte in June of 1996, evangelical activist and ex–Watergate figure Chuck Colson delivered a speech that amounted to a declaration of war against church–state separation and secular government. Blasting modern culture, Colson asserted that the only way to reverse things is through politics. He then praised Robin Hayes, then the Republican candidate for governor, saying, "Thank God men like this are in politics."

Colson concluded with a call for all "Christians" to join forces, saying, "We're in a culture war, and we can't afford to be divided. If we march together at abortion clinics, we do so as brothers and sisters."[2]

I never made it back to another Promise Keepers rally, but to this day I remain on the group's mailing list (I have a "constituent number"!) and keep tabs on them through the media and occasional visits to their website.

The most dramatic development concerning the Promise Keepers occurred in March of 1998, when Promise Keepers officials announced that the entire 345-member staff in Colorado Springs would be laid off. The organization had sponsored a huge, free rally called "Stand in the Gap" in Washington, D.C., in October of 1997. The costs associated with this rally were higher than anticipated, and this, coupled with the decision to drop admission fees to the stadium events, depleted the group's budget. The organization said it would rely on volunteer staff.

Some newspaper editorial writers and columnists saluted Promise Keepers for taking this bold leap of faith. In reality, it was little more than a media stunt. When word got out that Promise Keepers was in trouble, millions of men nationwide made pledges of financial support. The coffers were replenished, and soon the staff was recalled.

I feel certain that the leaders of Promise Keepers did not make a blind leap of faith and trust the outcome to God. They knew what the outcome would be. The group merely made a shift from being an organization funded by gate fees to one funded through fund-raising mail. Along with the Promise Keepers newsletter, I get regular pitches for money. (But, to give Promise Keepers some credit, the group always tells men to pay the bills at home and support the churches they attend before sending anything to Promise Keepers.) In other words, Promise Keepers had decided to raise its budget the way most Religious Right groups do—through direct mail.

I have also been uninterested in all of talk about whether the Promise Keepers will "go political." Promise Keepers' leaders say the group is not about politics, but a survey of the organization's members conducted by the *Washington Post* during the "Stand in the Gap" rally showed that the overwhelming majority of attendees are registered Republicans who consider themselves conservative. They expressed concern over the standard Religious Right issues— Promise Keepers oppose legal abortion and gay rights and support prayer in schools, vouchers, and the like.[3] Additionally, most come from a demographic group that traditionally has a high voter turnout. Promise Keepers don't have to "go political." They already are. Promise Keepers does not have to tell men what to think about social issues. The men already agree. It's in that sense that Promise Keepers meetings are apolitical.

I will grant that my exposure to Promise Keepers was limited. I don't claim to be an expert after attending a two-day stadium rally and reading some newsletters. But I do know something of the psychology of men, since I am one. To me, Promise Keepers seemed to be as much about men desperately seeking to find an acceptable way to express themselves emotionally as it did religion. Society expects men to be strong and reserved emotionally. Promise Keepers gives men a forum to drop that persona for a while in an atmosphere that is completely nonthreatening because other men are doing it, too. It's a place where no other man will laugh at you for crying or question your virility for talking about your feelings.

And, of course, we must accept the fact that some men feel displaced or threatened by the rise of the women's equality movement. I have always found this stance ironic, given that men still run most major corporations, still fill most of the ranks of middle and upper management, still account for most national politicians, and still make more money than women do for performing comparable jobs. But for these threatened men, Promise Keepers is surely a haven. For some men, Promise Keepers provides the perfect excuse to assert authority at home—it's in the Bible. The thinking may be that women may not "know their place" in the office anymore, but by God they'll know it at home.

It's no use for Promise Keepers to pretend that this is not a controversial stand. It is. I can understand completely why some women's groups have expressed concern over Promise Keepers' "men should rule the household" theology. As I stated earlier, some women may voluntarily choose to live in households like this. When it is brought into a home against a woman's will, it is going to cause discord and dissention. The Promise Keepers stance seems to assume that the woman's place in the home and the church is a second-class role. Those can be fighting words. That's why some organizations, notably Equal Partners in Faith, a group that formed to respond to the Promise Keepers' antifeminist theology, speak out against the Promise Keepers.

As of this writing, Promise Keepers seemed to be on the decline. In late July of 1999 McCartney said in an interview in Denver that he was distressed that more minorities are not involved in Promise Keepers. "It is tragic, heart-rending, and crushing that we haven't made more headway" in attracting minorities, McCartney said. "You look around this year and see what the percentage of people of color is. I'm hoping to be surprised, but I'm not optimistic."[4]

Promise Keepers watchers noted that attendance at the 1998 rallies was off, sharply in some cases, and events in 1999 did not show great recovery. This did not surprise me. Historically, many evangelical movements begin with what is to outsiders a startling burst of enthusiasm and what appears to be explosive growth. But this level of energy is difficult to sustain. Sooner or later, growth tapers off. Some participants lose interest, and the number of "converts" slows down. Promise Keepers is likely to be on the American scene for a long time, but I don't see them becoming the Religious Right's shock troops. They don't need to be. The Religious Right already has those troops—through groups like the Christian Coalition and the Family Research Council.

In the meantime, Promise Keepers will probably keep doing what they do best, as capsulized by a T-shirt I saw one participant wearing: "Real Men Sing Real Loud."

Promise Keepers
Leader: Bill McCartney
Budget: $41 million
Membership: More than two million men have attended
  Promise Keepers rallies since 1991.
Address: P.O. Box 103001, Denver, CO 80250-3001
Website: http://www.promisekeepers.org

NOTES

1. "TV Preacher Hagee Attacks Separation At Promise Keepers Rally," *Church & State* (October 1996).

2. L. Dean Allen III, "Breaking Down The Wall?" *Church & State* (January 1997).

3. "Promise Keepers Poll," *Washington Post*, October 11, 1997.

4. Religion News Service dispatch printed in the *Washington Post*, July 31, 1999.

Chapter 5

A JONES TO BASH THE PRESIDENT?

John Whitehead and the Rutherford Institute

L ate in 1997, an obscure attorney in Charlottesville, Virginia, named John W. Whitehead suddenly, if briefly, became the darling of the nation's media. For a few months, it seemed as if Whitehead was everywhere. the *Washington Post* and the *New York Times* ran in-depth profiles on him. Writers for glossy national magazines trekked to Charlottesville to interview him. CBS News's popular newsmagazine *60 Minutes* did a piece.

Whitehead captured the media spotlight when, early in October of 1997, he agreed to represent Paula Jones, the Arkansas woman who was suing President Bill Clinton for alleged sexual harassment. When he took on the case, Whitehead inadvertently became a player in the impeachment of the president that was about to unfold. Once Whitehead's Rutherford Institute accepted Jones as a client, its attorneys began receiving tips about other women who claimed to have had sexual liaisons with the president. This eventually led Independent Counsel Kenneth Starr to Monica Lewinsky.

At one point, according to the *New York Times*, Rutherford attorneys received a call from a "nervous young woman" who reported that a woman named Monica had had sex with Clinton in the White House. Later, the anonymous tipster called back and provided Monica's last name: Lewinsky. Donovan Campbell, a member of the Rutherford Institute's board of directors, contacted Linda Tripp, the former White House employee and Lewinsky confidant. Tripp secretly recorded conversations she had with Lewinsky about Clinton and turned everything over to Starr. The rest, as the cliché goes, is history.

For me, seeing Whitehead on the news nearly every night during this period of the Lewinsky–Clinton saga was jarring. To most Americans, Whitehead was a total nonentity. But I had been tracking Whitehead's career at the Rutherford Institute for a long time—since 1988. I had previously interviewed Whitehead and profiled him in *Church & State*. I had written about the Institute's cases and followed them through state and federal courts. I couldn't help but wonder how this man, whose primary interest was bashing the separation of church and state and criticizing the Supreme Court for its rulings in this area, got in the middle of the Clinton–Lewinsky affair.

Whitehead seemed an odd choice to be handling Jones's case. Put bluntly, he simply had no track record in sexual harassment suits. In fact, until he agreed to represent Jones, Whitehead earned his daily bread running the Institute as a rather pedestrian Religious Right legal aid group. He fought for more religious activities in the public schools and attacked the separation of church and state. He insisted that rampant secularism was bringing down religion in the United States and frequently criticized the American Civil Liberties Union.

Before Pat Robertson formed the American Center for Law and Justice, Whitehead ran what was probably the nation's largest and most active Religious Right legal group. To this day, Whitehead chafes at being identified with this camp. He doesn't like to be lumped in with the Religious Right. I will concede that Whitehead's views have changed over the years (more on this in a bit) and that lately he has taken some stands that put some distance between him and other Religious Right leaders like Jerry Falwell and Pat Robertson.

But only on some issues. Whitehead remains a critic of church-state separation, and at the legal seminars he runs for attorneys, attendees are taught that church-state separation was not the intention of the founders.

In the early days of the Institute, when I first started monitoring the organization, Whitehead's jargon and arguments were boilerplate Religious Right rhetoric: The founders never intended for there to be a separation of church and state, church-state separation is all too often hostile toward religion, the United States was founded to be a "Christian nation," and it was the founders' intention to allow the states to promote Christianity. I had seen these arguments many times. Nothing Whitehead was asserting seemed different from what Robertson and other Religious Right leaders said.

In some ways, Whitehead was even more extreme. In my opinion, his first book, *The Separation Illusion: A Lawyer Examines the First Amendment* (1977), flirts with Christian Reconstructionism, the far-right philosophy that holds that the United States's laws should be based on the harsh legal code of the Old Testament, which ought to be read literally (i.e., blasphemers, adulterers, "incorrigible" teenagers, and the "unchaste" get the death penalty). I am not saying that Whitehead ever was or is now a Reconstructionist. (And he says he has moved far from their camp.) Clearly his views have changed over the years. But his first book and other early ones he penned appear to have been obviously influenced by that philosophy. It's also worth noting that *The Separation Illusion* contains a foreword by Rousas John Rushdoony, the dean of the Christian Reconstructionist movement, and that Rushdoony served on the first board of the directors of the Rutherford Institute. A relationship did exist.

The Separation Illusion contains some rather extreme rhetoric. Whitehead calls public schools "satanic imitations of the true God's institutional church" and criticizes "our Jewish neighbors" for advocating the end of mandatory Christian worship in public schools. He warns that a "youth führer" is waiting in the wings to lead America's young people astray and frets that Congress may pass legislation requiring youngsters to attend youth camps "in the same manner as the Hitler youth were."[1]

The book is long out of print, and I was able to track it down only by using a web-based service that scans used book stores nationwide for used and out-of-print volumes. To be fair to Whitehead, his Institute does not market the book today. When I asked him about it during an interview in 1998, he said he had not read it in a long time and said he would probably not agree with all of it today.

So who is John Wayne Whitehead? What is the Rutherford Institute? To begin with, the Institute takes its name from a seventeenth-century Scottish minister, Samuel Rutherford, who argued in his book *Lex Rex* that God's law takes precedence over a king's law. Whitehead founded the group in 1982, running it out of his home. When I first got wind of the group, it was headquartered in Manassas, Virginia. Later Whitehead moved the Institute to Charlottesville, home of the University of Virginia.

The Rutherford Institute had humble beginnings but managed to prosper. By 1998 the group had an annual budget of nearly $4 million and a staff of forty. Whitehead, making $192,000 yearly, lives with his wife and five children on a ten-acre farm near Culpeper, Virginia. The organization has three satellite offices and has even started branches overseas.

In a nutshell, Whitehead's group believes that the separation of church and state has been taken too far. He asserts that government neutrality toward religion has become government hostility toward religion. Whitehead believes that government can endorse or promote religion in certain circumstances. Rutherford attorneys seek a reversal in the Supreme Court's church-state jurisprudence. They want the courts to substantially lower or knock down entirely the "wall of separation between church and state" that Thomas Jefferson spoke of.

And what about Whitehead? His journey to the Rutherford Institute has apparently been a long, strange trip. In media interviews he granted after taking on the Jones case, Whitehead talked about his immersion in the drug culture of the 1960s and his early dabblings with socialism. A native of Arkansas, Whitehead knew Clinton while a college student and once interviewed him for a school newspaper.

Whitehead told *60 Minutes* that he converted to fundamentalist Christianity in the mid-1970s after reading Hal Lindsey's book *The Late Great Planet Earth*. I did a double-take when I heard that. The book, first published in 1970, was all the rage when I was a kid. I read it, but even as a child of tender years I saw it for what it was: pure, unmitigated tripe. Time proved me right. Lindsey achieved fame and fortune by taking the prophetic writings of the book of Revelation and attempting to align them with contemporary events. Thus, the Roman Empire was to rise again though a European confederacy, and an Arab-African alliance, working with the Soviet Union, was to invade Israel. Lindsey once predicted that the Second Coming of Jesus would occur in 1988.

He also expected the "Rapture," whereby all good Christians are magically swept up into Heaven in one fell swoop, to occur in 1981. Between 1981 and 1988 there was supposed to have been a world war pitting a European confederacy against the Soviet Union. According to Lindsey's scenario, this conflict would go nuclear and kill one-third of the world's population until Jesus came back to stop it all.[2]

Christian and conservative and armed with a law degree, Whitehead grew disenchanted with the practice of secular law and decided to start his own firm.

In 1978, Whitehead, along with John Conlan, a former Republican U.S. senator from Arizona, wrote what many Religious Right leaders consider a seminal article in the *Texas Tech Law Review*. The article, "The Establishment of the Religion of Secular Humanism and Its First Amendment Implications," argued that "secular humanism," which the Religious Right defines as a type of nontheistic religion, was the de facto established religion of government.

But much has transpired in the twenty years since that article was written. Whitehead had started the Rutherford Institute and watched its budget expand fourfold. Now, with the Jones case, Whitehead seemed on the verge of gaining a national reputation. With so much going on, I thought it was time to check in again with John Whitehead.

My interview with Whitehead took place on a sunny February day in 1998 at the nondescript offices of the Rutherford Institute. The group is located in an anonymous strip mall off U.S. Route 29, just a few miles north of Charlottesville. The Rutherford Institute is located above a gynecologist's office and marked only by a small sign at the entrance to the parking lot. No one can accuse Whitehead of opulence.

I had come hoping I could figure out exactly what Whitehead was up to in accepting the Jones case. At first, I assumed that Whitehead was simply interested in tapping into the lucrative Clinton-bashing stream, which had proved fruitful for other right-wing groups. Yet Whitehead continued to insist in media interviews that this was not the case. He even went out of his way in some public statements to say that Clinton was not a bad president and praised some of his initiatives on religious liberty.

Something wasn't right. It didn't seem to make sense. I had been reading Rutherford Institute materials long enough to know that the group was no friend of Clinton's. In a June 1995 column for his *Rutherford* magazine, for example, Whitehead wrote: "Some say Clinton is hopelessly indecisive and unsure what he wishes to accomplish during his presidency. Even a short inventory of Clinton's waffling, gaffes, and poor judgment raises serious questions

The Moral Majority may be long gone, but Jerry Falwell still makes news. Most recently, he provided fodder for late-night talk show hosts when his *National Liberty Journal* outed Teletubby® Tinky Winky®. (Joe Conn/*Church & State*)

Pat Robertson's Christian Coalition is the most recognizable of the Religious Right organizations. It is also the most politically influential—partisan politicking cost the Coalition its tax-exempt status. (*The Photographers*)

A highlight of D. James Kennedy's 1999 "Reclaiming America for Christ" conference was the emphasis on the "ex-gay" ministries, an example of what the Religious Right considers a "kinder and gentler" approach to homosexuals. (Joe Conn/*Church & State*)

Headed by child psychologist James Dobson, Focus on the Family poses as a family ministry. But Dobson's efforts to become a major player in conservative politics involve more than just promoting "family values." (Bart Bartholomew/*The New York Times*)

Enthusiasm for Bill McCartney's Promise Keepers may be waning: Since the huge 1997 "Stand in the Gap" rally in Washington, D.C., attendance at the group's rallies has declined sharply. (Troy Wayrynen/*The Columbian* [Vancouver, Wash.])

John W. Whitehead hasn't lost his sense of humor, even though his Rutherford Institute has lost supporters since it represented Paula Jones in her 1997 sexual harassment case against President Clinton. (Rob Boston/*Church & State*)

David Barton, founder of the WallBuilders, travels around the United States pushing his revisionist history about the "Christian roots" of the country. (Joe Conn/*Church & State*)

Despite its innocuous-sounding name, Gary Bauer's Family Research Council is an openly political organization representing far-right views. The FRC spends most of its time promoting ultraconservative policies on abortion, gay rights, and censorship. (Jennifer Warburg)

William Donohue and the Catholic League for Religious and Civil Rights work to intimidate opponents of the Catholic Church's political goals—especially when those goals coincide with the League's far-right perspective. (Rick Reinhard)

Gay bashing is the medium of choice for the Traditional Values Coalition's Louis Sheldon, a California-based minister who is working hard to establish a national presence. (Joe Conn/*Church & State*)

Born-again Christian evangelist William Murray claims that his atheist mother, Madalyn Murray O'Hair, filed her famous lawsuit against school prayer on orders from Soviet Russia. (Joe Conn/*Church & State*)

Robert Simonds's Citizens for Excellence in Education uses local school board elections in its attempt to take over the public schools for fundamentalist Christianity. (*Church & State*) about the President of the United States."[3] The column went on to criticize Clinton for his stands on gays in the military, his antiwar protests during the Vietnam era, and his marital infidelity.

An earlier issue of *Rutherford*, from April of 1994, was even harder on the president and leveled what can only be considered as a hysterical charge. "We have every indication that Clinton is quietly constructing a despotic government and a new society of intolerance to traditional values," wrote Karen Augustine, then the journal's editor. "So why don't we do something? The American people must recognize that Bill Clinton is a wolf in sheep's clothing. . . . What more will it take to propel us into action? Now is not the time for silence. We must fight for what we believe."[4]

The cover of the April 1994 magazine depicted a garish montage of Clinton with demonic-looking red eyes. The type beneath him read, "Bill Clinton's Agenda For Change." Articles inside accused Clinton of favoring an unfettered right to abortion and special rights for homosexuals and of "trashing traditional values and advocating a new definition of life, death, and the family," as well as wanting "to create an entirely new society controlled by a massive government."[5]

But in the post-Jones era, Whitehead began singing a different tune. Clinton, he told the Associated Press in November of 1997, had been "a decent president." Whitehead even said he would have voted for Clinton were the president not pro-choice on abortion.

I traveled to Charlottesville in part to find out if this remarkable reversal of opinion was genuine. Whitehead insisted that it was, but some critics had their doubts and believed his claims were an attempt to portray himself as a moderate now that national attention was focused on the Institute.

It was gracious of Whitehead to grant me an interview. The Rutherford Institute and Americans United had not always been on good terms. We had been critical of the group's views in the past. Yet when I called for an interview, Whitehead's staff not only arranged it but insisted I come down to Charlottesville for a personal meeting. I was more than happy to take advantage of the opportunity. Once there, I was well received and treated with every courtesy.

One of the first things Whitehead told me is that he is not part of the "Clinton haters," far-right activists who dogged Clinton ever since his first presidential campaign in 1992. Whitehead denied having a financial motive to taking on the Jones case and added that money had not been pouring in to the Institute since he accepted the case; in fact, he said he had lost support.

Whitehead said he took Jones's case in part because he believes her story and that he believes women should be free from sexual harassment. But he went on to praise Clinton's religious liberty initiatives and said they have helped make the country more open to religious expression. He even went so far as to tell the *Washington Post*, "Clinton has done more for religious liberty than any other recent president."[6]

I found this curious, since I knew that Whitehead had earlier actually criticized several Clinton religious freedom initiatives. The Institute did not back the Religious Freedom Restoration Act of 1993, legislation fashioned by Congress with wide bipartisan support that was designed to shore up religious freedom rights in the wake of a 1990 Supreme Court ruling that many observers believed limited religious liberty. When Clinton released a directive on religious activity in public schools in July of 1995, the Institute immediately went on the warpath. Whitehead issued a two-page memo, which he mailed to school districts around the country, calling the directive "misleading" and asserting that "in some instances case law fails to support some of its asserted principles."

The Institution took this action even though the directive was noncontroversial and merely summarized the religious liberty rights of public school students. The document was based on a pamphlet drawn up by a coalition of groups earlier in 1995. The coalition was diverse and contained organizations that promote the separation of church and state as well as conservative groups. The directive represented an effort to find common ground by groups that often do not see eye to eye on these matters. Not only did the Institute not join this laudable effort, they attacked it.

One year after the directive was issued, the Institute went so far as to hold a press conference at the National Press Club in Washington, D.C., to attack the guidelines again. Unfortunately for the Institute, only three people showed up: me and two interns from conservative organizations.

And, as I mentioned earlier, research I had conducted at Americans United detailed a track record of Institute attacks on Clinton, some of them quite strident. That infamous April 1994 issue of *Rutherford* contained an article in which Whitehead referred to Clinton's proposed health care reforms as "the new Fascism" and wrote, "The Clintons will now decide who can provide medical care for our children, what the care will be, and when it will be provided. If a parent attempts to go against their decision, he or she may be sent to jail. Thus, this latest 'health care' provision is simply another insult to our God-given right to care for and nurture our children." (The article was accompanied by a photo of a group of Nazis, wearing swastika armbands, underneath a banner with the presidential seal and the words "Health Security.")[7]

The same magazine also contained an interview with far-right conservative operative Paul Weyrich, who criticized Clinton, and included comments by right-wing columnist Cal Thomas, a former Institute board member, who opined that he would give Clinton's presidency "a D or D minus." Thomas also lambasted Mrs. Clinton for "her legions of feminists and homosexuals that are populating and multiplying in this administration in ways I have never seen before."[8]

About a year later, in June of 1995, *Rutherford* ran a cover story on "The Clinton Chronicles," a scurrilous videotape that levels a number of unsubstantiated charges against Clinton. Although by this time the tape had been criticized even by conservatives like William Bennett, the article suggested there might be something to its reckless accusations. It concludes that "the allegations on the tape are disturbing" and criticized the mainstream media for not taking them more seriously.[9]

The Clinton Chronicles was produced by Citizens for Honest Government, a virulently anti-Clinton outfit fond of conspiracy theories, and was hawked by Jerry Falwell on his *Old-Time Gospel Hour* throughout 1994 and 1995. Among other things, the tape asserts that Clinton is a drug addict, that he arranged murders in Arkansas, and that he was part of drug-smuggling ring that operated out of Mena, Arkansas. No proof is offered for any of these allegations.

In addition, Whitehead's Institute mailed a series of fund-raising letters critical of Clinton's policies in 1994. Whitehead did concede to me that the tone of these letters may have been a little strident, but he defends the mailings as reflecting legitimate concerns that the group had at that time. In a June 1994 appeal for funds, Whitehead asserted, "Clearly, the President's domestic social policies are encouraging our popular culture to tell youngsters, 'Forget what you're learning at home—religious beliefs and principles have no place in our society.' Youngsters are confused and need answers." Clinton was attacked for his "open promotion of homosexuality, abortion, promiscuity, and sexual experimentation among our young people." Elsewhere, the letter accuses Clinton of advocating "sweeping, anti-religion policies."

As recently as January of 1997, Whitehead wrote to supporters to urge them not to be discouraged in the wake of Clinton's reelection. "Now that Bill Clinton has been reelected and is about to be sworn in as our nation's 53rd [sic] President, many people are disheartened and disillusioned," says the letter. "But this is not the time to become discouraged and give up."

Shots at Clinton are scattered throughout the letter. One asserts that the president has been "disturbingly effective in silencing and weakening the pro-life movement" and suggests that Clinton's support for legal abortion could lead to "euthanasia for the aged and the killing of those considered not fit to live."

I asked Whitehead about these articles and letters. In light of them, I said, wouldn't it be reasonable to conclude that the Institute is no fan of Clinton and that may explain why it was helping Jones? Whitehead's main defense against the charge of Clinton bashing is, he told me, that he believes Clinton changed and became a better president during his second term.

"I looked at Clinton," said Whitehead, "and I saw him doing things that were positive, and I changed about the man, because I judged him on his acts. I'm not political. I judged the man on how he's performing in office. Before God I can stand and say, 'I would say the guy's doing a good job.' If I were not involved in this Paula Jones case and didn't know more intimately some of things I know involving the case, I'd probably have a higher opinion of the man. That's the truth."

During our interview, Whitehead seemed sincere. And certainly it would be difficult to argue, in light of how the case turned out, that he actually came out ahead by handling the Jones case. Whitehead told me that his donors and supporters reacted negatively to the Institute's decision to help Jones, and the group took a financial hit. (It probably didn't help that Jones was using the case to raise money for her own purposes and seemed reluctant to share those funds with the Institute.) Eventually, the Institute dropped the case entirely.

I am certainly in no position to know what was in Whitehead's heart when he first took on the case. I very much doubt, however, that he ever thought it would cause him to lose money and support. I remain convinced that he thought it would be, if not a gold mine, then a silver one.

The Institute certainly tried to use the Jones case to raise cash.

Shortly after agreeing to enter the case, the Institute sent out a letter, signed by Jones on pink stationery, appealing for funds. Religious Right groups take on inflammatory cases for a few reasons: to raise money, to win media appearances, and to find new support. Whitehead may have thought the Jones case would deliver all three. It did propel him into the media spotlight for a while, but apparently the case failed to translate into much new support or big bucks from Clinton haters.

I was also a little reluctant to accept Whitehead's claim that suddenly Clinton was OK in his book, because I knew that Whitehead and the Institute had a record of making extreme statements about America and then later trying to step back from them when it seemed convenient, or when the statements became public and proved embarrassing. Perhaps they were doing the same thing in Clinton's case.

A good case in point is the 1994 Institute video titled *Religious Apartheid*, a thirty-minute tape inspired by a Whitehead book of the same name. The best way I can describe this video is to say it is a bizarre half-hour rant featuring Whitehead in an antigovernment tirade. Even that doesn't do it justice. It has to be seen to be believed. The overall theme seems to be that government, perhaps compelled by the worst excesses of popular culture and political correctness, is going to take away our freedoms.

Unintentionally humorous in spots, the video opens with Whitehead strolling among urban rubble, with feral children lurking in the background. Why the feral children are there and why they are throwing rocks at the windows of an abandoned factory is never explained.

Another scene depicts a man being brainwashed by Nazis while a voice chants the words "love," "tolerance," "diversity," and "choice." Periodically a stern-looking Whitehead emerges from the shadows to explain how the federal government is laboring to crush parents' rights and religious freedom.

But my favorite portion of the video centered on a depiction of a typical American family getting ready for their day. As mom, dad, sister, and brother sit at the breakfast table, geeky-looking, clipboard-toting government bureaucrats invade. They pull off mom's apron and force her into a business suit, stick a briefcase in her hand and shove her out the door. Dad is similarly dispatched because he was going to work anyway. Now the evil bureaucrats can focus their attention on the kids. Suddenly a rock band appears in the kitchen. Sister dresses provocatively and begins slathering on bright red lipstick. Brother is shoved in front of a pinball machine (that's right, a pinball machine—not even a video game).

Americans United had had the *Religious Apartheid* video around the office for a number of years, but no one had bothered to watch it until Whitehead's fifteen minutes of fame started. Reporters started asking if they could borrow it, so I figured it was time to take a look. One night I took the video home and my wife and I whipped up some microwave popcorn. I had told my wife only that we were going to watch a "Religious Right video." We were only a few minutes into the tape when she turned to me and said, "This is a joke, right? Someone put this out to make fun of these groups, right?"

Alas, it was for real. Watching the thing, I got the impression that two sophomore film students at a second-rate institution had been given a video camera and some money and set loose to run amok. In fairness to Whitehead, I should point out that *Religious Apartheid* was directed by Frank Schaeffer, an evangelical Christian author (who later converted to Eastern Orthodoxy) and aspiring filmmaker. But since Whitehead narrates the video and appears on camera in several sequences, I think it's safe to assume that he had some input into the final product.

Whitehead is clearly uncomfortable with the video today. The only time he squirmed during our interview was when I asked about it. He told me that artistic control of the video was left in the hands of Schaeffer. Whitehead indicated he was not pleased with the final product, saying, "It's not so much the message, it's the way it was shot and some of the rhetoric. . . . We didn't have a lot of control over the director. I won't say more on that."

Nevertheless, Whitehead clearly had high hopes for *Religious Apartheid*. The video and book were sold as a package along with workbooks and marketed to churches for adult study groups. The Institute marketed the *Religious Apartheid* package aggressively through its own publications and other conservative Christian journals. I have a feeling there are a lot of those tapes left in the Institute's basement. During my visit to the Institute, one staffer chastised me for bringing up the video, asserting that the project was "a flop."

The Institute stopped selling the *Religious Apartheid* video in 1997. And, despite the organization's prior enthusiasm for the project, Whitehead seemed to want to forget that it had ever existed. Late in that year, Cable News Network (CNN), in the course of preparing a profile of Whitehead, asked the Institute for a copy of the video. The group declined to provide one.

But no worries, Americans United was there to save the day. We lent our copy to CNN, and clips appeared nationally on the all-news channel on January 16, 1998. Americans United also lent the tape to *60 Minutes* when the CBS newsmagazine profiled Whitehead on October 4, 1998.

My point here is not to ridicule Whitehead or the Institute for putting out a silly video. We all do things we later regret. People are capable of changing their minds. But in Whitehead's case, those conversions seem to happen awfully quickly. That they were happening at the same time Whitehead was getting a lot of media attention gave me cause for suspicion. Was Whitehead trying to cover something up? I thought it was a fair question.

Consider the issue of gay rights, for example. As far as I'm concerned, the constant gay bashing employed by Religious Right groups is one of their most loathsome and despicable practices. These attacks are clearly designed to demonize gay people and make followers of the Religious Right hate and/or fear them. Imagine how this affects gay people who have parents, siblings, cousins, aunts and uncles, or other family members caught up in Religious Right groups. Anyone who thinks that this type of activity promotes "family values" is so detached from the real world that they might as well be living on Mars. Dividing families and urging people to treat certain members of their own families like outcasts or objects of scorn on the mere basis of sexual orientation is the very antithesis of family values.

The Rutherford Institute has done its share of gay bashing in the past. In fact, homophobia formed the basis for a string of Rutherford letters in the early 1990s. One notable letter, mailed in July of 1993, carried the signature of Whitehead's wife, Carol, in which she explained, in fervid language, how upset John Whitehead was over the prospect of gay marriages being legalized in Hawaii. Supposedly, he couldn't even sleep at night.

Observed Mrs. Whitehead, "Unless we act, and I mean soon, homosexual marriages and homosexual 'families' will be placed on equal and possibly preferential footing with the traditional heterosexual marriage and the traditional family." The appeal was accompanied by a snapshot of a gay-rights parade captioned, "Here is an example of what the courts call a family. . . ."

Again, Whitehead insists that his opinions on gay rights have changed. He told the *Washington Post* he now regrets the antigay mailings, a stance he reiterated during my interview with him. "About 95 percent of my opinion on the whole gay thing started changing a while ago," he said to the *Post*. "I was working with some gay people on a video project and I talked to them and started reading about the subject, and I saw that not only was I wrong but a great majority of evangelicals are out to lunch on the subject. Christ would not have been that way. . . . Homophobia is wrong."[10]

Whitehead told me that the Institute once represented a group of antiabortion gays who wanted to march in a gay rights parade in Boston and said he will defend homosexuals in the future. "We will protect gay people, but getting them to call here is the thing," he said. "You have to give us time. We're taking on our first AIDS discrimination case right now." (That case dealt with a young man, HIV-positive but not gay, who was denied admission to a karate class.)

As proof that his newfound views are sincere, Whitehead cited the fact that his recent comments in the media about gays and Clinton brought the wrath of the right-wing down on him.

"I had this guy call me up from one of the big Christian Right groups and said I was attacking the brethren. . . . The thing was that some of my recent statements have not sold well to the brethren, whatever he was talking about," Whitehead said. "And I told him to shut up. I was in a bad mood that day, I shouldn't have said that, but I said, 'Just shut your mouth. I'm not talking with you,' and I hung up. . . . I'm getting as many attacks from the Right now as I ever got from the Left."

Perhaps Whitehead's views on Clinton and gays have evolved, but his thinking on the separation of church and state has remained more consistent over the years, albeit with fine-tuning. As I mentioned, Whitehead's first book, *The Separation Illusion*, puts forth a familiar Religious Right argument: Separation of church and state is a myth conjured up by the Supreme Court in modern times to impose a secularist order on society.

In the volume, Whitehead correctly traces the separationist philosophy to Thomas Jefferson, who coined the metaphor "wall of separation between church and state." But from there his analysis becomes unusual. In a chapter of the book titled "Primal Antichrist," Whitehead takes issue with Jefferson's religious skepticism and implies it led our third president astray on the proper relationship between religion and government.

"A man can pretend God is not there or he can separate himself from God by erecting an illusionary wall," writes Whitehead. "Either way man lies to himself. Jefferson, courting illusion, had erected a wall between himself and God. Subsequently, he attempted to erect such a wall between the church and state governments. He used as his authority for this illusion the Constitution. Careful study shows him wrong."

Elsewhere in the chapter Whitehead asserts that the United States was founded to be a "Christian nation" and that the Constitution was written to protect the right of states to uphold Christianity through law. He charges that the Supreme Court, in striking down government-sponsored prayer and Bible reading in public schools, has actually violated the First Amendment.

In the school prayer rulings, Whitehead asserts in the book, the High Court declared that all religions are equal in the eyes of the government. This is a rather noncontroversial axiom to most Americans, and indeed it would be difficult to imagine our country operating any other way. Whitehead found the idea offensive. "The Christian faith is not reducible to the level of every other religion," Whitehead wrote. "Christianity offers the only path to the one true God. To hold that the Christian religion is no better than Buddhism or Judaism is blasphemy. . . . The Court is in essence assailing the true God by democratizing the Christian religion. This is suicidal. . . ."[11]

In his 1982 book, *The Second American Revolution*, Whitehead echoed that theme. He blasted the Supreme Court for striking down religious qualifications for public office in the 1961 case *Torcaso* v. *Watkins*. In that ruling, Whitehead wrote, the High Court "rejected Judeo-Christian theism as the religion and foundation of the United States."

In my view, the Supreme Court made the only call it could, holding that religious tests for public office are unconstitutional because the United States has no official religion or anything like one. As recently as 1982, Whitehead disagreed.

It's rare today to find a Religious Right leader who will be as blunt as Whitehead was in those books. Pat Robertson still occasionally launches crude and uninformed broadsides against non-Christian religions (and he spoke favorably of religious tests for public office in his book *The New World Order*[12]), but most Religious Right leaders have stopped talking about the United States as a "Christian nation," having long ago tossed that term aside for what they see as the more inclusive, less threatening "Judeo-Christian nation." In their hearts, they may not really mean the "Judeo" part, but in public they know what phrases to mouth.

So, does Whitehead still stand by what he wrote in those books, twenty years later? Once again, Whitehead says his views have evolved. Today he says he agrees with the result in the school prayer cases, if not the High Court's reasoning, and he criticized an effort that was underway when we talked to add a school prayer amendment to the Constitution. Sponsored by Rep. Ernest Istook (R-Okla.) and religious conservatives, the so-called Religious Freedom Amendment would have permitted coercive prayer in public schools, required government to give financial support to religion, and permitted the display of sectarian symbols on government property. Whitehead called it "a mistake."

Whitehead these days seems to favor a church-state philosophy known as accommodationism. In a nutshell, the view holds that government can give financial aid and other types of assistance to religion as long as it does so on a nonpreferential basis. I reject this view, holding that it is nonhistorical and at odds with our traditions. If it is wrong for the government to officially establish one religion and give it preference, it only compounds the problem by allowing the government to establish fifty or sixty religions by giving them support.

During our talk, Whitehead seemed irritated that I kept bringing up *The Separation Illusion*. At one point he said to me, "You know, that book's not the Bible." Nevertheless, I thought it was important to clarify how Whitehead's views might have changed since 1977, since much in the book is so startling.

The book predicts the imminent demise of religious freedom in America—a sentiment echoed in two other early Whitehead books, *The Second American Revolution* and *The Stealing of America*[13]—but Whitehead told me he does not believe that will happen now. "Partly through Clinton's efforts, partly through our efforts, things have gotten better out there," he said. "They've improved; you won't get that from the other Christian groups because they have to raise money."

Another issue about which Whitehead says his views have evolved is censorship. In 1988, after Universal Studios released the film *The Last Temptation of Christ*, which many Christian fundamentalists condemned as blasphemous, Whitehead wrote in one of his newsletters that unspecified "legal action" might be necessary. He did not say what form this action might take, and for good reason: It would be a failure, as U.S. law no longer recognizes blasphemy as a crime. (Indeed, some fundamentalists did file suit against the film without Whitehead's help. The case went nowhere.)

Also, Whitehead once issued a fund-raising letter demanding that the National Gallery of Art in Washington, D.C., stop selling a book of photography by Jeff Koons that Whitehead deemed "hardcore pornography." But now he says he regrets the move and opposes censorship. (However, it was not that long ago—1993—that the anti-Koons letter went out.)

Whitehead's relationships with Religious Right leaders have also changed over the years. Prior to forming the Rutherford Institute, Whitehead did brief pro bono consulting work for Jerry Falwell when the Lynchburg TV preacher considered setting up his own legal group, and he defended Falwell's Liberty University in 1991 after Americans United successfully sued to stop the city of Lynchburg from giving the school tax-exempt development bonds (see chapter 3). The Rutherford Institute handled Liberty's final appeal to the U.S. Supreme Court, but the High Court refused to hear the case.

Falwell speaks highly of Whitehead. In his January 27, 1998, *Falwell Fax* bulletin, the Lynchburg televangelist asked supporters to "be in prayer for Rutherford Institute President John Whitehead. . . . Whitehead is a fine Christian man who has dedicated his life to securing the rights of Christians in this age of politically-correct persecution." Columns by Whitehead used to run in Falwell's newspaper, the *National Liberty Journal*, and in 1995 *Rutherford* magazine ran a laudatory cover story on Falwell. But Whitehead told me he had not spoken to Falwell in several years and has not sought his endorsement.

However, Whitehead remains a member of the Council for National Policy (CNP), a secretive group of far-right leaders who meet regularly to plot strategy. CNP meetings are not open to the public or the media. The group has no office and refuses to answer any inquiries. Numerous Religious Right leaders belong to the CNP, including TV preacher Pat Robertson, former Christian Coalition Executive Director Ralph Reed, Phyllis Schlafly of the Eagle Forum, the American Family Association's Donald Wildmon, Focus on the Family founder James Dobson, Gary Bauer of the Family Research Council, and Coral Ridge Ministries' D. James Kennedy.

Whitehead said he has not attended a CNP meeting since the early 1980s and dismisses the organization as nonthreatening. "I see it as mainly a speaking group," he said.

Is it possible that Whitehead's views have changed this much in just the past four years? Some things have certainly changed at the Rutherford Institute during that time. The group's fundraising letters, for example, are less florid, and the amount of gay bashing in them has dropped noticeably. Whitehead says that's because Institute fundraising appeals are now being produced in-house. The kinder, gentler letters, he said, bring in less money, but he plans to stick with them.

I've always believed you can learn a lot about a Religious Right group by readings its fund-raising letters (also called "direct mail"). One of my rules of thumb is, "Ye shall know them by their direct mail." If an organization claims to be interested in issues A, B, C, and D, yet 95 percent of its fund-raising letters deal with issue D, that tells you what the group's real focus is. If an organization swears it is not homophobic, but then raises money by sending out gay-bashing fund-raising letters, then the denial does not mean much. Actions still speak louder than words.

Direct mail can tell you what an organization's members really care about. Sometimes groups try to take on new issues, with varying degrees of success. If the group keeps returning to certain themes time and time again, it's a good sign those are the issues the members really care about.

In the post-Jones days, the Rutherford Institute's direct mail took on a sad, almost pathetic tone at times. After the case fared poorly in court and the media stopped traveling to Charlottesville to interview Whitehead, some Institute letters almost took the form of an apology, pointing out that the group had lost money in the venture and begging past supporters to return to the fold. Others warned of dire financial crises.

In some letters, Carol Whitehead complained about health problems John was having and his sleepless nights. Some of the letters have an extremely personal focus. One mailed in June of 1999 actually contains copies of the Whiteheads' wedding pictures from 1967.

"John is tired now, and so am I," writes Carol Whitehead, who also works at the Institute. "With these projects and the demands of the work of The Rutherford Institute, we have been burning the candle at both ends. We still have a lot of work to do, but hopefully a period of rest will fit in somewhere. John may be weary and in need of rest, but he is faithful to God's call and to his duties as a Christian leader, as head of The Rutherford Institute and as a husband and father."

Elsewhere in the letter, Carol Whitehead refers to "the tension and strain" that John's work causes in their marriage.

What struck me about this letter was that it never really pinpointed a problem donors were expected to fix. I would suggest a more direct approach. A few years ago, Whitehead sued a Pennsylvania school district for giving children state-mandated physicals, during which some girls were given superficial genital exams. A Rutherford fund-raising letter about the incident opened, "First let me say, I'm outraged! Young girls were forced by public school officials to strip down and endure genital examinations!" I miss those days when Whitehead got right to the point. In this June 1999 letter he just sounds weary, almost like he's ready to give up. Reading it, I had to wonder what the potential donor was supposed to do? Chip in to finance a vacation? Marital counseling? Perhaps some sleeping pills?

(I should point out that Americans United was once the target of a Rutherford Institute fund-raising letter. The letter was mailed in April of 1996, after we launched an initiative called Project Fair Play and announced it would report to the Internal Revenue Services churches and religious nonprofit groups that violated their tax-exempt status by intervening in partisan politics. Whitehead accused Americans United of wanting to "spy on American church-going voters" and included an "Open Letter of Outrage" to Americans United Executive Director Barry W. Lynn for supporters to sign demanding the project be stopped. We received a couple hundred letters at the our office, which we tossed in the dumpster.)

There have been other changes at the Institute in the post-Jones era. *Rutherford* magazine, once the group's flagship publication, was rechristened *Gadfly* and turned into a journal of popular culture, not politics. Whitehead hoped to turn *Gadfly* into a general-interest publication, something anyone could buy at a newsstand. To date, that project has met with limited success.

Whitehead's interest in popular culture sets him apart from other Religious Right leaders. Most of them seem to have nothing but disdain for the entertainment business and frequently assault Hollywood as the great defiler of children. Whitehead takes a more nuanced view. He is an avid movie buff whose office is covered with pop culture icons. His desk is literally covered with rubber space aliens, plastic models, small toys, and whatnot.

The January 1998 issue of *Gadfly* contained a cover story on "Over 100 Films That'll Change Your Life," and the February issue dealt with the Sex Pistols, a raucous British band that ushered in the punk rock movement of the late 1970s. In looking it over, one would be hard-pressed to identify *Gadfly* as a publication produced by a religious organization.

In 1999, Whitehead completed a seven-part film series titled *Grasping For Wind*, which is described as a "series on humanity's search for meaning." I'll admit I haven't watched it yet—the sting of the *Religious Apartheid* debacle is still fresh—but I'm intrigued, especially since Whitehead, who wrote and directed the film, has indicated a desire to market it to public schools. (To be fair, I should note that some folks like *Grasping for Wind* quite a lot. In 1999 it won a "SilverWorld Medal" at the New York Film Festival.)

Is Whitehead sincere? Is he a Religious Right leader who has changed his mind on many issues? The short answer is unsatisfying: I don't know. I do know that Whitehead has lately taken public stands that challenge Religious Right orthodoxy. This has won him few friends. In the Religious Right world, few sins are worse than apostasy.

I can also say this: If I had to be trapped in an elevator for three hours with the Religious Right figure of my choosing, I'd pick Whitehead. He is at least interesting to talk to and speaks with passion. With someone like Jerry Falwell, I've always had the impression that he has not reconsidered—let alone changed—an opinion since the Eisenhower administration. He merely regurgitates those set-in-concrete views, over and over and over again.

Whitehead also has a sense of humor, a quality often sadly lacking among Religious Right figures. When I visited his office, he allowed me to photograph him while he put his arm around a blow-up figure of the shape from Norwegian artist Edvard Munch's famous painting "The Scream." At the time, Whitehead was wearing a necktie featuring images from the cover of the Beatles' album *Sgt. Pepper's Lonely Hearts Club Band*.

Try as I might, I couldn't imagine Jerry Falwell doing that.

The Rutherford Institute
Leader: John W. Whitehead
Budget: $4.3 million
Membership: The Institute says it is not a membership organization but reports that it has about fifty thousand supporters.
Address: P.O. Box 7482, Charlottesville, VA 22906-7482
Website: http://www.rutherford.org

NOTES

1. John W. Whitehead, *The Separation Illusion: A Lawyer Examines the First Amendment*, 3rd ed. (Milford, Mich.: Mott Media, 1977) pp. 129-30.

2. Robert G. Clouse, Robert N. Hosack, and Richard V. Pierard, *The New Millennium Manual: A Once and Future Guide* (Grand Rapids, Mich.: Baker Books, 1999), pp. 124–30.

3. John W. Whitehead, "Questions About the President," *Rutherford* (June 1995).

4. Karen Augustine, "How Clinton is Transforming America," *Rutherford* (April 1994).

5. Ibid.

6. Megan Rosenfeld, "On the Case for Paula Jones," *Washington Post*, January 17, 1998.

7. John W. Whitehead, "Health Care Police: The New Fascism," *Rutherford* (April 1994).

8. Ibid.

9. Nisha N. Mohammed, "In Search of the Truth about Clinton," *Rutherford* (June 1995).

10. Rosenfeld, "On the Case for Paula Jones."

11. Whitehead, *The Separation Illusion*, pp. 85–94.

12. Pat Robertson, *The New World Order* (Dallas: Word Publishing, 1991), p. 219.

13. John W. Whitehead, *The Second American Revolution* (Elgin, Ill.: David C. Cook, 1982); *The Stealing of America* (Westchester, Ill.: Crossway Books, 1983).

Chapter 6

DARE TO BE A RELIGIOUS RIGHT HACK

Dr. James Dobson and the Politics of "Family Values"

My biggest mistake was in assuming that Focus on the Family is a building. It's not—it's a compound. North of Colorado Springs, not far from Interstate 25, is Explorer Drive. A helpful sign points the way: "Focus on the Family Welcome Center."

I soon learned that Focus on the Family is a bona fide tourist destination. I pulled a rental car into the parking lot one July day in 1999 and saw that the place was full. Cruising around to find a parking spot, I noticed that most of the vehicles (lots and lots of vans) did not have Colorado license plates. People had come from all over, drawn by Dr. James Dobson's Christian fundamentalist mecca in the shadow of Pike's Peak.

My guess is that if you polled Americans, you would find that Dobson's Focus on the Family is probably not as well known as the Christian Coalition or even Jerry Falwell's old Moral Majority. And if you asked the people who have heard of Focus on the Family what it does, they would say it is a family ministry, not a political operation. Yet Focus on the Family is an incredibly large and growing organization that is increasingly political and hews to the Religious Right line 100 percent.

I will grant that the organization is not as knee-deep in partisan politics as the Christian Coalition. Focus on the Family still poses as a family ministry and dispenses enough advice about strong marriages and disciplining children to provide some cover. The national Focus on the Family office does not produce voter guides, although some of Focus on the Family's state affiliates do. But the stands Focus takes on various contemporary issues could have been lifted directly from the Christian Coalition's activism manual, and Dobson is working overtime to become a major player in ultraconservative politics. There's a lot more going on in Colorado Springs than the mere promotion of "family values."

Dobson is a child psychologist, not a minister. He reaches millions daily through his a thirty-minute *Focus on the Family* radio broadcast that is heard on fifteen hundred U.S. and Canadian stations. He has a regular newspaper column, and his organization produces dozens of magazines, books, pamphlets, position papers, and other materials. Dobson's commentary is heard in ninety-five countries and translated into nine different languages. Every minute of every day, no matter what time it is, a station somewhere in the world is broadcasting the voice of James Dobson.

At Americans United we've been keeping an eye on Dobson since the 1980s, when he first began to emerge as a national figure. Fifteen years later, we still have trouble convincing some people that Dobson is a Religious Right leader. Many people know of Dobson because of his child-rearing books. The advice in these books is conservative—Dobson made a name for himself by endorsing spanking at time when many child care experts were advising against it—but the volumes themselves are not overtly political.

But over time, another side of Dobson has emerged. He may not care to acknowledge it, but Focus on the Family has become an increasingly political entity, and Dobson himself is up to his eyeballs in efforts to keep the Republican Party as far to the Right as possible. His rhetoric is becoming more extreme by the day. In other words, the mask has been ripped off. Anyone who still claims that Focus on the Family is not a Religious Right organization has simply not been paying attention.

For years I had heard about Dobson's operation in Colorado Springs. I wanted to see it for myself. In July of 1999 I got the chance when Americans United business took me to Denver. I arranged to go early, flew into Colorado Springs, and spent a morning at the Focus on the Family campus.

Focus on the Family consists of three buildings, with a fourth under construction. The Welcome Center opened in September of 1994, paid for entirely by Elsa and Edgar Prince of Michigan, the same benefactors who helped pay for the Family Research Council's fancy digs in Washington, D.C. (Remember, Focus on the Family and Family Research Center are legally separate but "spiritually one." In my book, that means Dobson runs them both.)

The Welcome Center is an impressive structure. And it features something most people really like: lots of free stuff. Copies of Focus on the Family's numerous magazines, newsletters, and other publications lay about in piles, yours for the taking. The walls are covered with photos of Dobson and the Focus on the Family staff. Downstairs is an ice-cream parlor and a play area for children (featuring a three-story-tall twisty slide). Costumed characters wander about to entertain the young ones. I won't say it's like an amusement park, but the draw for the children is obvious. Three-quarters of a million people have visited the center since it opened.

I joined about sixty others for the noon tour at the Administrative Building. (Focus runs tours daily, Monday through Saturday, on the hour from 9 a.m. until 4 p.m.) Two bubbly college students acted as our guides. They explained to us that they had come from out of state to spend their summers working for Focus; their dedication to the group's mission was obvious.

That mission, by the way, is very straightforward: "Focus on the Family's primary reason for existence is to cooperate with the Holy

Spirit in disseminating the Gospel of Jesus Christ to as many people as possible, and, specifically, to accomplish that objective by helping to preserve traditional values and the institution of the family."

On paper, Focus on the Family sounds like a strictly evangelical group determined to bring the "Good News" to the world. This is not an uncommon practice. Many Christians call it the Great Commission. But in Focus's case, apparently, part of their cooperation "with the Holy Spirit" involves advocating right-wing politics, because that's primarily what Dobson and Focus on the Family do these days. The sad thing is, many people don't even realize that when they first contact the group. (More on that later.)

But first, back to the tour. We were informed early on that "God has blessed this ministry tremendously." People may disagree about God's role in the matter, but there is no denying that the growth of Focus on the Family has been nothing short of remarkable. Dobson founded the group with a friend in 1977. Two years later it had ten staff members. It now has thirteen hundred employees and sits on a forty-seven-acre campus worth $4 million. That land, incidentally, was given to Focus on the Family by an outfit called the Polmar Foundation, a conservative group that doles out cash to right-wing causes, which enticed Focus on the Family to move from Southern California to Colorado Springs in 1991. Because the land was free and the buildings were paid for by benefactors, the ministry's current debt level is zero. Focus on the Family's annual budget is $114 million.

Material making up 12 to 15 percent of Focus on the Family's physical plant, the guides told us, was donated by well-wishers. Walking around, I was most struck by a cavernous room containing 120 people who do nothing but answer letters all day. Focus on the Family receives about ten thousand letters per day and has its own zip code. However, 90 percent of those letters are orders for materials or other mundane requests. The other 10 percent come from people who are seeking help or asking a specific question. Those letters end up in this room.

The vast majority of letters are addressed to Dobson. Of course he never sees them. Instead, correspondence specialists tap into a massive database containing Dobson's views on hundreds of issues. This material is culled from his many books, and is simply printed out for people who write in. In other words, when people receive a reply answering their question, it doesn't really come from Dr. Dobson; it comes from a giant computer containing all of Dr. Dobson's combined wisdom.

Lots of people write in with simple questions—"When is a good time to start toilet-training my toddler?" and the like. But sometimes people treat Focus as a type of crisis counseling center. The guides told us stories about people writing in or calling—the organization receives between thirty-five hundred and seven thousand calls per day—who were grappling with serious problems. Specially trained staff members deal with these calls and letters. They may send out Focus on the Family materials, refer people to fundamentalist Christian counselors (who are screened beforehand to make sure they are doctrinally pure before getting the Dobson seal of approval), or simply talk with people about their problems.

Focus produces so many publications that it is hard to keep them all straight. No matter what your situation in life, it seems, Focus on the Family has a magazine, tape, or other publication to deal with it. And that's where the problem begins.

Focus on the Family insists it is not a political organization. As one of the guides told us, "Focus on the Family is not a political organization, nor do we intend to be."

That statement is simply not true. In fact, Focus on the Family publications are loaded with politics, and Dobson himself has been a key player in trying to keep the Republican Party as far to the Right politically as possible.

Even during the forty-five-minute tour, it was hard not to see material with political content. It was lying around everywhere. In one room there was a stack of articles blasting the so-called gay agenda. Another article criticized legal abortion and feminism. I came home with a bagful of FOF magazines and materials. They are loaded with standard-issue Religious Right positions: attacks on public education; demands for vouchers and other types of private school aid; calls for religious instruction in public schools; creationism; gay bashing; assaults on legal abortion; general grumbling about "the liberals" in Washington; and complaints about higher education, popular culture, and the like. It all promotes a right-wing line, and it's political whether Dobson cares to acknowledge that or not.

To me, it's sad to think that some people call Focus at a genuine moment of crisis because they believe it's merely a family-oriented organization. They may get some help, but they also end up, eventually, getting sucked into right-wing politics. This is a simply unavoidable consequence of anyone who is exposed to Focus on the Family materials for any length of time. Let me state it again: Just about all Focus on the Family materials contain Religious Right political propaganda. Most of the time it isn't even subtle.

Equally amazing to me is that this organization, despite its clear bias and overwhelming Christian fundamentalist perspective, manages to get its materials into public schools. Focus on the Family produces a variety of videotapes and other materials that it markets aggressively toward public schools. Our guide explained that the tapes are often slightly edited for public school use—that is, the overt proselytism is watered down—but, she added, "we still manage to get the Christian message out." (Again, this group uses "Christian" like all other Religious Right groups: as a synonym for the fundamentalist interpretation of Christianity.)

Thus, Focus on the Family has managed to pull off the ultimate coup: The organization has interjected its Religious Right, fundamentalist propaganda into thousands of public schools, *and it has convinced the public schools to pay for the privilege*! How many public schools use Focus on the Family materials? I don't know, and I doubt anyone does outside of Focus on the Family, but our guide told us that "millions" of public school students have seen its tapes.

Some schools do learn to regret purchasing Focus on the Family materials. In 1995 members of the Fairfax County, Virginia, school board voted to stop using the Focus video "Sex, Lies . . . and the Truth," which promotes sexual abstinence for teenagers. Some minority parents had complained that minorities were treated negatively on the tape, and some medical professions said it was medically inaccurate.

Focus on the Family sells to public schools even while Dobson runs down public education and actively works to undercut it. Focus on the Family works for voucher plans through the Family Research Council in Washington and its state affiliates, even though such plans would have a devastating effect on public school funding.

Dobson is an enthusiastic supporter of school vouchers. In October of 1993, he devoted two segments of his daily radio program to promoting Proposition 174, a voucher initiative then on the California ballot. He also sent supporters a four-page letter endorsing vouchers, calling the issue "a matter of awesome significance, not only for that great state [California] but also for the nation." (California voters failed to take his advice, rejecting Prop. 174 by a 7 to 3 margin.)

Five years later Dobson struck again, this time issuing a letter of support for Proposition 226, a California ballot measure designed to curb the power of unions in the state. The measure's backers had hoped to place curbs on political activity by teachers' unions and then push vouchers through. Golden State voters rejected the measure, 53 percent to 47 percent.

Dobson has endorsed the well-worn view that "secular humanists" have taken over public education, and tells his followers that the schools are hostile to religion. The idea that some sinister force called "secular humanism" has taken near-total control of American society is a constant Religious Right obsession. I wonder how they can say it with a straight face, especially when one examines the religion-soaked political system of America. Yet in his 1990 book, *Children At Risk: The Battle for the Hearts and Minds of Our Kids*, coauthored with Gary Bauer, Dobson asserts, "I indicated earlier that the secular humanists hold sway in every American center of power and influence except two, the church and the family."[1] Even these last two institutions, Dobson says, may not be able to hold out much longer.

For those of you who don't speak Religious-Rightese, let me translate this passage for you: "Millions of Americans have rejected my narrow, ultraconservative, fundamentalist, exclusionary version of Christianity. This annoys me, so I call all of those other believers names and assert that they aren't really believers at all. So there."

Children At Risk, by the way, is a treasure trove of Religious Right calumny. If you have friends who continue to insist that Dobson is just a nice, grandfatherly guy who dispenses advice on how to raise kids, get them a copy of *Children At Risk*. That should end all doubt.

Dobson's fundamentalist worldview of literal interpretation of the Bible and strict adherence to narrow doctrinal policies leads him to see issues like abortion, gay rights, and religion in public schools in black-and-white terms, with no room for subtle nuances or special circumstances. Similarly, he sees an ongoing struggle for the soul of America with clearly delineated sides: God-fearing, moral "Christians" (i.e. fundamentalists) who agree with his interpretation of the Bible versus "secular humanists."

A Dobson letter mailed in February of 1998 asserted that "Secular Humanism, the sexual revolution and the New Age movement" have taken a heavy toll on America. Despite the fact that public opinion polls show that the United States is overwhelmingly religious and that nearly 90 percent of the population identifies itself as Christian, Dobson concludes that the country is now "post-Christian" and says "spiritual confusion" reigns. Like many Religious Right leaders, Dobson seems to believe that Christians who do not hew to his literal, fundamentalist interpretation of the Bible are not really Christians.

Because Dobson is convinced that only fundamentalist Christianity is valid, he naturally wants to see that version propagated in as many public institutions as possible, including the schools. He was in on the drive, which began in 1995, to replace the First Amendment's religious freedom guarantees with a so-called Religious Freedom Amendment that would have mandated religious worship in public schools. (The House of Representatives voted down the measure in June of 1998.) He works constantly to find new ways to violate the religious neutrality of public education. One Focus on the Family magazine, *Teachers in Focus*, is essentially dedicated to encouraging public school teachers to proselytize students and work fundamentalist Christian references into the curriculum. In December of 1993, Focus on the Family sent out misleading materials implying that public school teachers could preach about the birth of Jesus Christ in class at Christmastime under the guise of objective study about religion. The booklet in question, produced by an outfit called Gateways to Better Education, reminds teachers that Christmas is "about the baby Jesus as a gift from God" and recommends that they replace secular holiday carols with religious songs in the classroom.

In 1996, Focus on the Family produced a series of "folders" for teachers on topics that included America's "Christian heritage," creationism, and character education. The material was rife with inaccuracies and was wholly inappropriate for use in public schools. Some of the historical material, for example, was little more than Religious Right revisionism designed to show that separation of church and state was not intended by the founders. One section asserted that the early federal government was expected to "enforce civil laws according to orthodox Christian standards." There is nothing in the language of the Constitution that supports this view, and in fact the First Amendment, with its guarantee that "Congress shall make no law respecting an establishment of religion . . . ," mandates the exact opposite.

In 1998, *Teachers in Focus* took the extraordinary step of advising public school teachers to supplement school lesson plans if they fail to measure up to the teacher's fundamentalist religious views. An article in the October issue advised teachers to take their concerns to the principal but if that failed it recommended "modifying classroom activities, changing homework assignments, passing out supplementary readings, presenting alternate viewpoints or making other changes."[2] The author of the piece specifically criticized instruction about evolution and blasted public schools for failing to teach moral absolutes.

This last item is a common complaint among Religious Right activists, many of whom do not send their children to public schools and have not darkened the door of a public school since the 1950s. Perhaps if they visited one, they would see that the schools punish students for cheating, failing to turn in homework, doing sloppy work, fighting, skipping class, and so on. It sounds as if a few fairly rigid rules are indeed being enforced in public schools.

What else do Dobson and Focus on the Family believe? Not surprisingly, Dobson has little use for the separation of church and state. Over the years I have talked with people who have attended legal seminars or "Community Impact Seminars" sponsored by Focus on the Family or related entities. Speakers there tell attendees that separation of church and state was never intended by the founders, that it is a recent invention of the Supreme Court, and so on.

In 1993, I interviewed some Colorado Springs residents affiliated with Citizens Project, a local group that serves as a watchdog of the Religious Right in Colorado. One man who had attended a Focus on the Family seminar later wrote in a Citizens Project newsletter, "The objective . . . was clear. It was to show that America was and always has been a thoroughly Christian nation. The separation of church and state was revealed to be a very recent and completely unprecedented misapplication of a casual phrase [Thomas] Jefferson had once used in an obscure letter to a friend."[3]

The newsletter also reported that one conference speaker told the crowd, "As far as the founders were concerned, to try to separate Christianity from government is virtually impossible and would result in unthinkable damage to the nation and its people. Much of the damage we see around us must be attributed to this separation."[4]

Focus on the Family's misreading of history is nothing new for the Religious Right. See my 1993 book *Why the Religious Right Is Wrong About the Separation of Church & State* for a thorough debunking of the Religious Right's view of the development of the separation principle. The book includes a discussion of Jefferson's famous "wall of separation" letter to the Danbury Baptists and why it should be considered authoritative.

Dobson is also not really keen on the idea of tolerance or respecting other religions. In February of 1994, the group's most political journal, *Citizen*, attacked the Girl Scouts for promoting "humanism and radical feminism."[5]

The Girls Scouts are best known for selling cookies, but according to Dobson they were guilty of the ultimate crime: being nice to non-Christians. Delegates at the Girl Scout convention the previous year had voted overwhelmingly to make a reference to God in the organization's oath optional. The vote came because increasing numbers of girls were joining the group who were from non-Christian religions with non-Western concepts of God. The Girl Scouts wanted to make sure these girls knew they were welcome in the group.

Keep in mind, the oath was not dropped, the reference to God was merely made optional. Any girl who wanted to could still recite the old oath—"On my honor, I will try to serve God and my country, to help people at all times, and to live by the Girl Scout law."

On November 4, 1996, Dobson was even more explicit in condemning tolerance. He aired an address by a woman named Luci Swindoll who talked about her disappointment when she learned as a child that her father had been previously married and divorced. Her father told her that Christians make mistakes sometimes and urged her to be tolerant.

Dobson endorsed much of Swindoll's message but then added, "[I]n the context of today's culture . . . the word 'tolerance' has a double meaning in our society." Tolerance, said Dobson, is a "kind of watchword of those who reject the concepts of right and wrong. You know, there are no absolutes, there is no right and wrong, there is no eternal truth and we should be tolerant and accepting of every-thing—anything and everything. It's a kind of desensitization to evil of all varieties. Everything has become acceptable to those who are tolerant. And they brag—the Republican National Convention kept bragging about how tolerant they were, accepting of all points of view. But the Scripture teaches that we are to discriminate between right and wrong, good and evil. And that we are to be intolerant of evil. Romans 12:9 says, 'Learn to be sincere. *Hate* what is evil. Cling to what is good.'"

Continued Dobson, "Now, that's not tolerant. You know, that's intolerant of evil. Not intolerant of people, but of wickedness and evil. And you have to discriminate between the two. Tolerance is not the greatest good in all contexts as it's being taught in the world of political correctness today."[6]

I found these comments interesting and have quoted them at length here because I think they are crucial to understanding Dobson's beef with America: He does not like the fact that people are willing to put up with things that he, Dobson, finds offensive.

Homosexuality is a good example. Like many Religious Right leaders, Dobson seems to obsess over the fact that homosexual people exist. But deep inside, I think what's really eating him is that an increasing number of Americans are no longer bothered by this. In his 1987 book, *Parenting Isn't for Cowards*, Dobson pined for the days of his childhood when gays were considered "very weird and unusual people."[7] After the U.S. Supreme Court struck down an antigay Colorado measure in 1996, Dobson favorably cited remarks by conservative honcho Paul Weyrich, calling for impeaching the members who had voted against his view.

Dobson seems to have trouble coming to grips with the fact that American views about gay people are changing. While in Colorado Springs, I picked up a new Focus on the Family magazine called *plugged in*, which examines pop culture. A column in the magazine criticized TV networks for airing shows depicting gays in a positive light. "Put simply, people are getting used to homosexuality . . . ," reads the article. "Now the goal of portraying homosexuals on television isn't about ratings; it's about altering cultural conscience. Normalization. Mainstreaming. In the end, it's educating teens that being gay is okay."[8]

Dobson trades on his credentials as a psychologist to give authority to his views. However, it is worth noting that his views on homosexuality are not shared by the American Psychological Association, which no longer considers homosexuality a psychological disorder. Also, most of the professional associations working in psychology and psychiatry reject so-called reparative therapy, which asserts that homosexuals can be "cured" of their sexual orientation and can become heterosexual.

Focus on the Family and other Religious Right groups assume that television shows drive trends. In other words, their argument seems to be that TV has foisted gay characters on the American people in an effort to make society more accepting of homosexuality. The people in turn have been brainwashed and now, lemming-like, believe that gay is okay.

I'm not a social psychologist, but I think the situation calls for a more nuanced and sophisticated analysis. I would flip the equation and assert that television reflects social trends, it does not cause them. In fact, it often lags behind. Gay liberation has been under way since the 1970s, yet the first network TV show with an openly gay lead character was ABC's *Ellen*, which aired in 1997. (Furthermore, the show was not conceived as a "gay sitcom." When it first started airing, the character's sexuality was not mentioned. Ellen did not "come out" until the program had been on the air for at least a year.)

Television networks want to make money. If shows do not attract large enough audiences to interest advertisers, the shows get cancelled. (*Ellen* is a case in point. After the character came out, the plots grew stale, many people lost interest, and the show got axed. If ABC's goal were to brainwash Americans, they would have kept the show on the air. But their goal wasn't brainwashing people, it was making profits.) That's the bottom line. At some point, networks decided that Americans were not so threatened by homosexuality that gay characters had to be excluded. Thus, gay characters began to appear on some shows. Most Americans did not think this was a big deal. Religious Right groups obsess over it. The rest of us grew up a long time ago.

Dobson's ideal is an America that no longer exists—an America where groups that he finds personally distasteful stayed under wraps. The reality is that in modern America, groups that had been excluded are now demanding to be included. They don't want to live in closets anymore. Dobson may prefer it if they did, but times have changed.

I also believe that deep down, what really bothers Dobson and the Focus on the Family staff is not so much that gay people are winning legal and political victories right and left, because the truth is, they really are not. What bothers them is that attitudes have changed in the country. Polls show consistently that more and more Americans have adopted a live-and-let-live attitude toward gays. In short, the Religious Right is slowly but surely losing its battle to demonize gay people and drive them back into the closet. This is naturally unsettling for them. They can't accept the fact that regular Americans disagree with them, so they make bizarre claims—that people have been brainwashed by TV, led astray by secular humanists, and so on. They sure don't give the American people much credit.

Dobson also believes that certain programs of higher education can lead young people astray. He once warned parents not to let their daughters take women's studies programs in college. These classes, Dobson asserts, can persuade women to become lesbians.

As much as Dobson enjoys bashing gays, it is legal abortion that really puts him into a state of frenzy. To mark the twenty-fifth anniversary of *Roe* v. *Wade*, the 1973 Supreme Court ruling that legalized abortion, Focus on the Family issued a copy of its *Focus on the Family* magazine with a cover story titled, "25 years, 35 million dead." Inside, Dobson explained why abortion should almost never be legal, even in cases of rape or incest. The only exception Dobson would make is in the case of a grave threat to the mother's life, which he calls very rare.

Many people believe that requiring a woman who gets pregnant as a result of rape to carry the fetus to term is cruel. Dobson not only disagrees with this, but he argues that doing so would be best for all concerned, including the rapist, whom he has the temerity to refer to as the "father." According to Dobson, "Of special concern is the woman who is carrying a baby conceived during a rape. Her pain and agony are beyond expression. I am convinced, however, that such a mother, if she carries the baby to term and either keeps her baby or places it up for adoption, will never regret her decision. What is right and moral for the unborn child is ultimately best for the mother and father, too. I know this statement will be inflammatory to some, but it is what I sincerely believe."[9]

Dobson's right-wing attacks on gays, public education, legal abortion, women's rights, and other issues are but one example of his political agenda. A more telling example is found in his personal political involvement, which has been extensive. Dobson seems eager to turn himself into a Pat Robertson–type power broker in the Republican Party. But Dobson is not always a GOP team player. In fact, he has repeatedly criticized the party for not being right-wing enough—in other words, he "dares to discipline" the party.

The Republican Party today kowtows to the Religious Right constantly, but for Dobson that is not enough. He seems to want the party to reflect his personal religious views as public policy. This has led to a great amount of conflict between Dobson and party officials.

Dobson began his saber rattling in the spring of 1996, when he offered encouragement to right-wing firebrand Pat Buchanan, who was at that time toying with the idea of leaving the GOP and running for president on a third party. Dobson asserted that the party establishment had offended Buchanan and "pro-life" voters as well. "The insulting things that Republican leaders have said about Pat Buchanan have not only wounded him, but they also irritated millions of pro-life and pro-family voters," Dobson told the *Washington Times*. "That is the source of the 15-point gap between Dole and Clinton."[10]

But Dobson could still be a team player. On May 2, 1996, he took to the airwaves to interview "Christian nation" propagandist David Barton, a Texas man who runs WallBuilders, a group that distributes material attacking the separation of church and state. During the interview, Dobson urged fundamentalists to vote so that the "excellent, God-fearing men and women in Congress" would not lose their seats. "I wish," Dobson said, "that our listeners knew and fully understood the meaning of the fact that there are perhaps thousands of attorneys and lobbyists in and around Washington, D.C., who drive to work on those roads and freeways every day with one primary objective, which is to remove God from all vestiges of public life—and private [life] if they can do it—but to eliminate the Christian ethic. And they work on that throughout the day and they have the inside track."[11]

That summer Dobson endorsed Republican senatorial hopeful Sam Brownback of Kansas. Brownback sought the seat vacated by Sen. Robert Dole, who gave it up to concentrate on his presidential campaign. Moderate Republican Sheila Frahm had been appointed to the seat, but, thanks in part to Dobson's endorsement, Brownback defeated her in the primary, 55 percent to 42 percent. (Brownback went on to win the general election as well.) During the primary campaign, Brownback flooded Christian radio with Dobson's endorsement.

As the 1996 presidential election heated up, several GOP hopefuls trekked to Colorado Springs to meet with Dobson. (Dole met with him in Washington.) At one point, Dobson appeared ready to endorse Texas Sen. Phil Gramm. But Gramm angered Dobson during a Washington, D.C., meeting when he told Dobson he would not make his campaign a moral crusade, reportedly saying, "I am not running for preacher. I am running for president. I just don't feel comfortable going around telling other people how to live their lives."[12]

Ralph Reed, at that time the executive director of the Christian Coalition, was present. In his book *Active Faith*, Reed wrote that Dobson left the room with flushed cheeks and said, "I walked into that meeting fully expecting to support Phil Gramm for president. Now I don't think I would vote for him if he was the last man standing."[13]

A year later Dobson seemed to be growing disenchanted with the entire Republican Party. During the summer of 1997, he began criticizing the GOP in harsh terms in an effort to flex some muscle in the party and get more attention for his agenda. In July of 1997 he issued a *Family News From Dr. James Dobson* newsletter lambasting the GOP for failing to act on "family values" issues. "It appears that the electoral victory Republicans were granted in 1994 and again in 1996 accomplished little that matters to families," observed Dobson. "Instead of working to advance the causes on which they ran, many GOP leaders appear anxious to avoid controversy or tackle anything that will threaten their power base."[14]

The following February, Dobson appeared at a meeting of the Council for National Policy, a secretive cabal of ultraconservative leaders from the nation's top Religious Right groups, who meet regularly to plot strategy, where he pledged to abandon the GOP if it continues to "betray" religious conservatives. Dobson promised to "do everything I can to take as many people with me as possible."[15]

Dobson insisted he was speaking as an individual, not as the head of Focus on the Family (nice trick, splitting himself in two like that) but added that he would use his radio network as much as is legally possible to spread his message.

Dobson told the crowd of about three hundred he had not voted for Robert Dole in 1996 but had instead backed Howard Phillips, candidate of the fringe U.S. Taxpayers Party. Dobson described the action as a "protest vote." Two years earlier, Dobson had met with Phillips for ninety minutes at his Colorado Springs office.[16]

(Meetings of the Council for National Policy are not open to the press. The report on this one appeared in a newsletter published by the Institute for First Amendment Studies, a Religious Right watchdog group, which, understandably, did not name its source.)

Dobson kept the pressure on. In a March 1998 interview with the Associated Press, Dobson said the Republican Party could go the way of the Whigs, (a nineteenth-century party that collapsed due to internal divisions) if it did not shape up. "I would really like to see millions of people call or write Newt Gingrich, Dick Armey, Trent Lott, and others and put them on notice the ground is shifting underneath their feet," said Dobson, "that they are aware that they have been ignored . . . and if that lack of commitment to the things in which they believe continues, then they will abandon the Republican Party."[17]

Right-wing House members began to get a little nervous over Dobson's saber rattling. Gingrich sent Rep. Tom Coburn, an Oklahoma Republican who is close to Dobson, to ask Dobson to send the GOP leadership a list of his top legislative priorities. Dobson did so, then distributed a copy to every GOP House member. To up the ante, Dobson had Focus on the Family release his letter to Coburn and the list publicly through PR Newswire. Interestingly, the news release about the letter was on Focus on the Family letterhead and listed contacts at Focus on the Family to call for more information, even though Focus is supposedly nonpolitical and this effort was supposedly done by Dobson the private individual, not Dobson the Focus on the Family leader.

Dobson's wish list is interesting, as it sheds more light on his hard-line views. Eight priorities are listed. They are: defunding Planned Parenthood and other "pro-abortion" organizations; defunding federal "safe sex" programs and condom distribution programs; enacting a federal law guaranteeing parental consent for abortions and receipt of contraceptives by minors; banning human cloning and fetal tissue research; defunding the National Endowment for the Arts; enacting the so-called Religious Freedom Amendment; passing some type of school voucher legislation; and eliminating the so-called marriage penalty tax.

Dobson added that it is so obvious that he also wants to see a ban on all late-term abortions and blockage of any attempt to expand gay rights that he did not bother to list them.

Shortly after that things really got nasty for a while. Dobson traveled from Colorado Springs to Washington, D.C., to meet with top leaders of the Republican Party. Undoubtedly, a certain amount of tension hung in the air.

Both sides had hoped to smooth over recent differences, but things did not work out exactly as planned. During a closed-door meeting with Majority Leader Dick Armey (R-Texas) and Majority Whip Tom DeLay (R-Texas), Dobson found himself and Bauer under fire.

A source close to DeLay told the *Washington Post* that the Texas congressman, known for his blunt style, "let them have it." DeLay chastised Bauer and Dobson for running strident antiabortion television ads in a recent special-election House race in California, where Democrat Lois Capps defeated social conservative Tom Bordonaro. Polls showed that most voters in the district support legal abortion and the ads, DeLay asserted, were not helpful.

"Thanks but no thanks, if you guys are going to do things that are counterproductive," fumed DeLay.[18]

Dobson was livid. Before coming to Washington he had announced plans to continue his attack on the Republicans in interviews with the *Washington Post* and the *New York Times* if the party did not continue its policy of appeasement toward him. Religious Right members of Congress persuaded him to cancel the interviews, and they hoped to find a way to neutralize further broadsides. Instead, Dobson left angrier than ever.

In a letter he circulated immediately after the meeting to twenty-five ultraconservative GOP congressional allies, Dobson vented his anger about the meeting. DeLay, he wrote, "was argumentative, defensive and accusatory. Instead of grappling with Republican failures . . . he denied that a paralysis has occurred and trumpeted meager accomplishments. Then he attacked Gary Bauer for causing the loss of a seat in the Bordonaro race. It is also my understanding that after we left, DeLay was highly critical of us and said, 'They just don't get it.' " Dobson wrote that he wished he had gone through with his plan to attack the GOP in the *Post* and the *Times* and added, "There is still time to do that."[19]

Even while under intense fire, Dobson did not hesitate to play hardball. In an April 3, 1998, letter he circulated to supporters, Dobson said it is time for the Republicans to "fish or cut bait" and added, "They have to understand that we will abandon them if they continue to ignore the most important issues. The threat must be real for us to have integrity, and I am determined to deliver on the promises to campaign against them if nothing changes. But I'm praying that won't be necessary."[20]

The following month, top GOP leaders met with Dobson again and caved in. After a three-and-a-half-hour meeting at the Library of Congress, Gingrich and DeLay emerged to say they had agreed to push Dobson's agenda items and to establish a GOP "Values Action Team" that would report weekly to Dobson and other Religious Right leaders.

In return, Dobson declared a temporary truce. He made the rounds on television talk shows to outline his views. While his rhetoric was less strident toward the GOP, he continued to insist that party leaders had to deliver or face his wrath. Appearing on May 3 on NBC's *Meet the Press*, Dobson said his threat to bolt the GOP was not hollow. "I have said that," he said. "And it would be a disaster if that would be necessary. First of all, there are a lot of good, solid, pro-life, pro-family congressmen and senators in the Congress. And they would be hurt in the process. I know who would inherit the power. It would be the Democrats in the White House and the Congress, so that would be unfortunate. But you never take a hill unless you're willing to die on it. And we must die on this hill if necessary."[21]

There was more talk of dying on hills four days later when Dobson appeared on CNN's *Larry King Live*, where he told King, "I believe we're going to see some change. I've been encouraged this week. I met for an hour with Trent Lott this afternoon, and I believe there are good things coming. But if there is not, we have to be willing to die on that hill."[22]

Republican moderates were dismayed by the party's capitulation to Dobson. Rep. Chris Shays, a Connecticut moderate, told CNN, "To have us jump every time Mr. Dobson speaks means that we'll become a very small party pretty quickly."[23]

Business leaders were also angry. Many business leaders are Republicans and enjoy close ties to the GOP. However, they are chiefly concerned with fiscal issues and taxes and get worried when the party goes overboard on the social issues.

One anonymous representative from a Fortune 500 company told the *Washington Post* in June, "Everything went south in a big way after Newt and the rest of the leadership tried to make up with James Dobson and the other Religious Right guys. They gave away the store, and we were on the shelves."[24]

One year later, much had changed. Gingrich resigned after the Republicans suffered setbacks in the 1998 elections. As for Dobson's wish list, it has seen little activity. The misnamed Religious Freedom Amendment was voted on in the House on June 4, 1998, and fell sixty-one votes shy of the two-thirds vote required for passage. (It was introduced in the Senate but never got so much as a subcommittee hearing there.) The National Endowment for the Arts was not defunded, nor were sex education and condom distribution programs discontinued. Attempts to ban late-term abortion were vetoed by President Clinton. Other items saw no activity at all.

Dobson was not pleased. Prior to Gingrich's resignation, Dobson accused him and congressional Republican leaders of caving on the "pro-family" issues. He demanded that Gingrich and Lott resign.

As of this writing, Dobson confederate Gary Bauer is still seeking the GOP nomination for president. However, Texas Gov. George W. Bush appears to be the man to beat. Bush opposes legal abortion, but there has been speculation that he would pick a pro-choice running mate in an attempt to balance the ticket. If that happened, Dobson told CNBC's Chris Matthews on November 10, 1998, "I will do everything I can to beat him."

Dobson and Bauer continue to talk about bolting to a third party. In July of 1999, New Hampshire Sen. Robert Smith publicly resigned from the GOP, in part because he said the party had gone soft on social issues. Bauer endorsed Smith's move and speculated that more Republicans would leave the party if it did not start taking a harder line on social issues. (Just three months later, however, Smith returned to the GOP.)

In late July of 1999, Dobson lashed out against the Republicans again. In a Focus on the Family *Citizen Issues Alert* fax bulletin, he blasted the GOP for not moving fast enough to eliminate the so-called marriage penalty tax, a glitch in the federal tax code that requires some married couples to pay higher taxes than they would if they remained single. (Religious Right leaders assert that the "marriage penalty tax" encourages cohabitation.) Dobson complained that a year ago GOP leaders had promised him they would eliminate the "marriage penalty" but so far had done nothing.

The GOP tax-cut plan, Dobson said in the newsletter, amounts to a "betrayal of pro-family conservatives" by the Republican Party.

On his daily broadcast for July 16, Dobson exhorted listeners to bombard House GOP leaders with calls and demand that the tax glitch be totally eliminated in one fell swoop instead of incrementally, as party leaders proposed. The fax bulletin reported that thousands of people had called top GOP leaders in Congress.[25]

It's also worth noting that Dobson has begun issuing endorsements of certain conservative candidates. When extreme antiabortion activist Randall Terry (of Operation Rescue) sought to win the GOP nomination for a congressional seat in New York in 1998, Dobson issued a letter endorsing him. The endorsement letter, issued on Dobson's personal letterhead, read in part, "I rarely do political endorsements, but I'm making an exception now to personally endorse Randall Terry because I believe in this man. He's been a great friend of the family who is now running for election to the U.S. House of Representatives. I wish we had a dozen more like him in Congress."

Dobson has since endorsed other right-wing candidates, including ten candidates for the U.S. House in California.

For a man who heads a "nonpolitical" organization, Dobson sure seems to have a lot of interest in conservative politics. It's also worth noting that not everyone is fooled by his claims to be apolitical. In February of 1996, the evangelical Moody Broadcasting Network refused to air a Dobson interview with Bauer. Moody standards say that broadcasts must be nonpartisan and "acknowledge respectfully the existence of differing viewpoints on political matters within the body of Christ." This Focus on the Family broadcast, Moody officials said, failed that standard.

The Dobson foray into Washington and its aftermath are telling for a number of reasons. It underscores the increasingly contentious relationship between Religious Right conservatives and the Republican Party and the GOP leadership's uncertainty over how to deal with them. But perhaps more importantly, it demonstrates the growing influence and power of Dobson. Dobson is rapidly becoming the radio version of Pat Robertson. He may be even more dangerous because, unlike Robertson, Dobson has greater self-discipline. Robertson is prone to make off-the-cuff remarks and say strange things on national television time and again. He shoots himself in the foot on many occasions. Dobson's views are just as extreme, but he presents them in a nonthreatening, "family-friendly" package. Thus, Robertson has high negatives in the polls. Dobson is still thought of as avuncular and grandfatherly. (Or, more likely, people don't know who he is.)

Dobson and Bauer represent a different breed of Religious Right strategist. Unlike former Christian Coalition director Ralph Reed, who eagerly sought "insider" status in the Republican Party and relished his role in the halls of power, Dobson and Bauer have little desire to join the party establishment if that means giving even an inch on the far-right, hypermoralistic agenda they champion. They want action and they want it now.

How does Dobson get away with passing himself off as a mere kindly family counselor while brokering backroom deals with GOP leaders and parroting the Religious Right's line on politics? It's a good question.

In the spring of 1998, I interviewed Gil Alexander-Moegerle, who helped Dobson found Focus on the Family in March of 1977 but has since broken with him, to get his thoughts on this question. Alexander-Moegerle told me he remains astonished at Dobson's ability to downplay his obvious political agenda.

"It's an amazing phenomenon," Alexander-Moegerle told me. "I think one answer is that there has always been a most unfortunate feature about Dobson: He does his politics in a deceptive way. It's a straight-on strategy, a hit-and-run, punch-and-duck, and then he essentially lies when he has to about the formidable political agenda he has and how a large portion of what Focus does is political. His spin is simply, 'We're not political.' "

Author of the book *James Dobson's War on America*, Alexander-Moegerle worked at Focus on the Family cohosting radio broadcasts with Dobson in the late 1970s when the ministry first started to become political. He remembers that Dobson got his first taste of power when he asked listeners to call the White House and demand that he be invited to an upcoming conference on the family. Sixty thousand listeners did, and Dobson got his invitation.

Later, says Alexander-Moegerle, Dobson learned the art of using his listeners to create meltdown in congressional offices to block legislation. The first few times this happened, says Alexander-Moegerle, Dobson "was giddy like a schoolkid with excitement over how much influence he could wield."

Alexander-Moegerle says Dobson has compared Focus on the Family's activists to "guerilla forces camped in the woods around Capitol Hill." His listeners would hit congressional offices with "mortar shells," and the representatives would rush outside to figure out where the fire was coming from. Dobson reportedly remarked, "I love that they can't find me."

Alexander-Moegerle agrees with me that these days Dobson's work is rife with right-wing political content. In fact, he believes that Dobson's immediate goal is to create a "Christian Republican Party."

Alexander-Moegerle notes that a good chunk of Dobson's daily radio broadcast is political in nature, as is the monthly *Focus on the Family* magazine. A separate broadcast, *Family News in Focus*, often promotes right-wing politics. In addition, Focus on the Family publishes *Citizen*, which is totally devoted to politics, and every week issues a fax briefing, again with near 100 percent political content.

Additionally, Dobson's monthly letters to supporters are increasingly little more than far-right political rants. Every January, for instance, Dobson mails a letter to supporters reviewing the past year. The 1998 letter was a good example because it hit all of the Religious Right's favorite targets.

In the letter, Dobson celebrates private school "choice" legislation in the states, writing, "School choice is an idea whose time has come, and parents who agree should be working to achieve it." He goes on to bemoan the fact that at that time state courts in Wisconsin and Ohio had declared voucher laws unconstitutional, noting, "Again, the phantom 'separation of church and state' clause was cited as the justification."

Elsewhere in the letter, Dobson calls for the display of the Ten Commandments and other sectarian symbols in courthouses and other government buildings, demands curbs on abortion, blasts a federal judge in Alabama who ruled that public schools must stop promoting religion, and assails efforts to in several states to extend legal protections to gays.

Dobson asserts that God will judge America for tolerating legal abortion and sexual improprieties. "The overriding question for believers now concerns how a God of justice can bless and preserve a nation in which murder is its centerpiece—and sexual immorality its pastime," he writes. "History teaches that the Holy One of Israel can not—and He *will* not—withhold judgment from those who flaunt [sic] the moral law of the universe. I don't know how or when His wrath will befall those who wallow in evil, but Scripture assures us that it will come."

Dobson's aggressive style and willingness to criticize the Republican Party leadership is already shaking up the Religious Right. What remains to be seen is how Focus on the Family and the Christian Coalition will coexist.

After Ralph Reed stepped down as executive director of the Christian Coalition, Robertson hired two men to replace him—Don Hodel, formerly Secretary of the Interior under President Ronald Reagan, and Randy Tate, a one-term congressman from Washington State. Hodel has longstanding ties to Focus on the Family. He serves on the group's board of directors and once worked as an unpaid "executive vice president" for the organization. Hodel's presence at the Christian Coalition led some observers to speculate about a coming nexus between the Coalition and Focus on the Family.

But it was not meant to be. Hodel was soon fired. (For more on this, see chapter 2.) Hodel probably could not have bridged the gap between the two groups anyway. The fact is, Religious Right groups will always maintain a certain amount of intergroup rivalry. The pool of potential donors for such organizations is limited, and the groups are well aware that they often end up chasing the same dollar.

Furthermore, a great deal of personal animosity reportedly exists between Dobson and Robertson. It stems in part from an incident early in Dobson's broadcasting career when he appeared on Robertson's *700 Club.* Dobson felt he was snubbed by Robertson and was upset when the Virginia TV preacher referred to him on the air as "James Dotson."

In addition, significant theological differences separate the two men. Dobson was raised in the Church of the Nazarene, a strict fundamentalist group. Robertson was raised as a Baptist but now practices a Pentecostal theology marked by speaking in tongues and direct "words of knowledge" from God, practices deemed heretical by many fundamentalists.★

It often seems that everything Dobson touches is tainted with right-wing politics. For several years his wife Shirley has served as chair of the National Day of Prayer Task Force, a private group that promotes observances of the National Day of Prayer, the first Thursday in May. Every year the task force issues a kit loaded with "Christian nation" paraphernalia and attacks on the separation of church and state. The materials quote Supreme Court decisions out

---

★Pentecostalism, an emotional form of worship marked by its adherents' belief that they can receive messages directly from God, is growing in popularity in the United States and has appeared in many Christian denominations, including even the Roman Catholic Church. Many Christian fundamentalists, however, remain highly skeptical of the validity of Pentecostal practices and doubt that speaking in tongues, faith healing, and "words of knowledge" really come from God. Although Pentecostal practices are described in the New Testament, many fundamentalists maintain they were gifts given by God to Jesus' small band of original followers and are not available for people to experience today.

of context and contain fabricated quotes allegedly uttered by the Founding Fathers in an effort to buttress the view that America was founded to be a "Christian nation." In years past, the task force had recommended activities in public schools that would be patently unconstitutional.

The first time this happened, Americans United wrote to Mrs. Dobson and urged her to clean up the materials. She wrote back saying she appreciated the feedback. Yet the kits that have been issued subsequently are no better and arguably worse. The 1999 kit, for example, practiced religious exclusion and pointed out that the National Day of Prayer is a "body of Christ" event and said event organizers had no obligation to permit "Mormons, Muslims, etc." to take part. Anyone could attend the events, the kit said, but the only people with access to the microphone should be "those we know have a personal relationship with Christ."[26] Leave it to Dobson and his wife to take a bland exercise in civil religion like the National Day of Prayer and attempt to turn it into a revival service.

And, if you plan to tangle with Dobson, get ready for a real fight. The man has a bunker mentality. In 1995 he defended the use of military metaphors to fight the so-called culture war. Dobson wrote a column in *Christianity Today* responding to criticism from John D. Woodbridge, an Illinois university professor who had charged that the Religious Right's constant use of battlefield imagery is "problematic for several reasons," chiefly in that it put evangelicals in a bad light.

Dobson fired back with both barrels. "Do we as Christians need to be liked so badly that we chose to remain silent in response to the killing of babies, the spreading of homosexual propaganda to our children, the distribution of condoms and immoral advice to our teenagers, and the undermining of marriage as an institution?" he wrote. "Would Jesus have ignored these wicked activities? Would the One who severely threatened those who would harm a child have ignored the bloody hands of today's abortionists? No, I am convinced that he would be the first to condemn sin in high places, and I doubt if he would have minced words in making the point."

Dobson chastised those Christians who choose to sit out the "culture wars" and concluded, "Sometimes in our zeal we may fail to show the love of Christ, which is central to everything we believe. You are justified in criticizing us when that occurs. But while you're there on the sidelines, I ask that you not make our task any more difficult than it already is. . . . The world of the Christian activist can be a very lonely place. War is always tough on those who are called to fight it."[27]

I'd like to conclude with a few thoughts that came to me as I toured the Focus on the Family compound. To start with, the place has the feel of a cult of personality. The guides spoke of Dobson in reverential tones as they pointed out mundane features. ("There's the chair where Dr. Dobson sits when he tapes radio broadcasts!") Guides went on at length about what a great man of integrity Dobson is, how he takes no salary from the organization and lives on book royalties. (For more on Dobson's egoism, I recommend Alexander-Moegerle's book.)

At one point, we were shown a large world map with points of light indicating cities where Focus on the Family shows are broadcast. I was surprised to see several in China, a country not known for its openness to Christian evangelists. The guide explained that the more overt religious references are removed, just as they are in the tapes marketed to public schools. But still, the guide assured us, the Christian message gets through. (One other thing struck me about this map: Greenland has so far fended off Focus on the Family.)

In the end, I came to conclude, Dobson is guilty of an old-fashioned bait-and-switch. People are lured into Focus with the promise of finding family harmony or perhaps healing after a personal tragedy. That's the bait, and attractive it is indeed. But alongside an answer for their uncertainty or a balm for their pain these folks in need get the switch—a huge dollop of right-wing politics and an intolerant version of Christianity. When do people get these messages? When they are at their most vulnerable.

As we walked the corridors of Focus on the Family, our guides told us stories, undoubtedly meant to be heartwarming, about people who called the organization in the middle of crises and got the help they needed. One story was about a woman whose husband had died and left her with a small child. Depressed and unsure of what to do, she called Focus on the Family on a friend's recommendation. The organization sent her free materials and a box of books and videos for her son. The boy was almost immediately drawn in and, we were told, soon accepted Jesus on his own. He then confronted his mother and told her she "needed to accept Jesus now." The happy ending was that she did. Mother and son had supposedly traveled to Focus earlier in the year to tell their story.

Maybe Focus did help the woman. But I suppose the group did nothing that a competent grief counselor could not have done as well. And I have to wonder how the woman's life was improved by all of the other baggage Focus on the Family straddled her with. Will hating and fearing gay people make her a better mother? Will voting for the most reactionary right-wingers in an election help her raise her son alone? How does the embrace of an intolerant, exclusionary brand of Christianity make it easier to cope with life's often turbulent ride?

If Religious Right leaders were capable of feeling shame, then Dobson would be sorry for what he has done, for taking people when they are at their most vulnerable and drafting them as foot soldiers in his Religious Right campaign to remake America in his own image. As it is, he simply leans into the microphone and unleashes more invective daily.

And Focus continues to grow. When I was there, the fourth building was still under construction. We were told it will house, among other things, an international division dedicated to continuing the spread of Focus on the Family's message worldwide. Someday, maybe they'll even conquer Greenland.

In the end, what does Dobson want? I'll let Gil Alexander-Moegerle answer that question. After Dobson "Christianizes" the Republican Party, that is, makes it submissive to fundamentalist dogma, he'd like to do the same to the rest of the county, Alexander-Moegerle told me. "I believe it is accurate and justified and reasonable to say that Jim wants theocracy," Alexander-Moegerle said. "I believe it's really true. I'm not just trying to scare people about Dobson. His perfect president would be someone with a law book in one hand and a Bible in the other, someone who defers to the fundamentalist interpretation of the Bible. Jim really believes that until that happens, America is on its last legs and is gasping its last breaths. Jim is desperate and fearful. And he really believes that only a theocracy can save us."

Focus on the Family
Leader: Dr. James C. Dobson
Budget: $114 million
Membership: Daily audience of radio program reportedly tops five million.
Address: P.O. Box 35500, Colorado Springs, CO 80935-3550
Website: http://www.family.org

NOTES

1. James Dobson and Gary L. Bauer, *Children At Risk: The Battle for the Hearts and Minds of Our Kids* (Dallas: Word Publishing, 1990), p. 37.

2. Francis J. Beckwith, "Is Public Education Really Neutral?" *Teachers In Focus* (October 1998).

3. Rob Boston, "Out of Focus," *Church & State* (March 1993).

4. Ibid.

5. Scott DeNicola, "Girl Scouts Lose Their Way," *Citizen* (February 21, 1994).

6. "Beware Of Tolerance, Says James Dobson," *Church & State* (December 1996).

7. Quoted in Gil Alexander-Moegerle, *James Dobson's War On America* (Amherst, N.Y.: Prometheus Books, 1997), p. 193.

8. Steven Isaac, "The Rippling Effects of TV's Gay Culture," *plugged in* (May 1999).

9. James Dobson, "Dr. Dobson's Solid Answers," *Focus on the Family with Dr. James Dobson* (January 1998).

10. E. Michael Myers, "Group's Offer Puts Buchanan on a Hot Seat," *Washington Times*, March 28, 1996.

11. "If 'Christian Vote' Stays Home in '96, Congressional Allies Could Lose, Says Dobson," *Church & State* (June 1996).

12. Ralph Reed, *Active Faith* (New York: Free Press, 1996), p. 240.

13. Ibid.

14. James Dobson, *Family News From Focus on the Family*, (July 1997).

15. Ben Winton, "Dobson Declares War on GOP," Institute for First Amendment Studies Internet bulletin (February 1998).

16. Rob Boston, "Family Feud," *Church & State* (May 1998).

17. "Dobson's Warning," *Washington Times*, March 10, 1998.

18. Thomas B. Edsall and Ceci Connolly, "A Gaping GOP Rift," *Washington Post*, March 27, 1998.

19. Boston, "Family Feud."

20. Ibid.

21. Joseph L. Conn, "Taking the Hill," *Church & State* (June 1998).

22. Ibid.

23. Ibid.

24. Thomas B. Edsall, "GOP Angers Big Business On Key Issues," *Washington Post*, June 11, 1998.

25. "Promises, Promises: Marriage Tax-Relief Plan Betrayal, Dobson Says," *Citizen Issues Alert* (fax bulletin), July 21, 1999.

26. "Prayer Day Task Force Excludes Non-Christians," *Church & State* (June 1999).

27. James Dobson, "Why I Use 'Fighting Words,' " *Christianity Today* (June 19, 1995).

Chapter 7

IT CAME FROM DARKEST COLORADO (AND MICHIGAN)

A Visit to the Family Research Council

The Family Research Council (FRC) occupies a brand-new, six-story office building on the edge of Washington, D.C.'s Chinatown. Staffers are not shy about telling you where they got it. The facility, erected in 1996, was essentially a gift from two wealthy Michigan families: Richard and Helen DeVos of Grand Rapids (Richard DeVos is founder of the Amway multilevel marketing company) and Elsa Prince and her late husband Edgar of Holland, Michigan. No other donor funds were spent on the building, a sign inside reads.

I arrived at FRC headquarters for a personal tour on an overcast July day in 1999. My guide was running late, so I browsed the FRC museum and store on the ground floor. The "museum" consists of two glass cases, on this day filled with information about the life of the Rev. John Witherspoon, a clergyman who signed the Declaration of Independence. The store is mainly a collection of shirts and assorted items bearing the FRC logo. (My favorite was the FRC guest towel.) Pictures of FRC head Gary Bauer hobnobbing with noted political leaders adorned the wall. The guide later told me that due to a quirk in D.C.'s zoning laws, the FRC had to agree to have a store and museum on the premises before getting permission to build in the neighborhood, which is undergoing redevelopment.

Bauer was on a leave of absence when I arrived. He was out seeking the Republican nomination for president. He remained mired in the single digits in the polls at that time, and, quite frankly, many people were wondering what he was even doing in the race—although I'm sure that many, many more had no idea he was even in it.

It took a certain amount of chutzpah for Bauer to seek the presidency. The man has never held elective office. He served briefly as an undersecretary of education during the Reagan administration and later as a domestic policy advisor to the president. That is the sum total of his public service. Yet I imagined, as I examined the FRC golf balls and posters promoting abstinence for teenagers, that Bauer was out there somewhere, probably Iowa, standing on a box speaking to a crowd—probably not a large one—under the hot sun. I suspected he would be back at the FRC helm before too long, perhaps having imitated Pat Robertson and having used his quixotic campaign as a vehicle to gain exposure and win new followers.

Bauer founded the FRC in 1983 after his service in the Reagan administration. The group struggled along in near obscurity with a handful of employees until 1988, when it was adopted, so to speak, by radio counselor James Dobson, founder of Focus on the Family. Then it began to take off.

Dobson was at that time based in California, but he had been looking for an outlet for his conservative political views in the nation's capital. Taking over Bauer's fledgling operation made a lot more sense than trying to build something entirely new from the ground up.

Religious Right leaders had helped elect Reagan, but they were disappointed with what they got for all of their labors. As the Reagan years drew to a close, many were wary of Vice President

George Bush. Some backed rival candidates, like TV preacher Pat Robertson and former New York representative Jack Kemp.

After Bush's election, Bauer made an attempt to put some pressure on him. In one of his early speeches, Bauer told a crowd at the Heritage Foundation in May of 1989 that he expected President George Bush to give social issues equal attention with economic concerns. "It's time to stop assigning the social issues and the family issues to the back of the public policy bus," Bauer said. He identified two of the most important social issues as a ban on abortion and passage of some type of private school aid scheme. Bauer asserted that the United States is in the middle of a "civil war" over social issues and added, "The social issues are the binding agents of the conservative movement."[1]

The FRC served as an arm of Focus on the Family for four years. In October of 1992, Dobson severed the official relationship between the two groups. It was an amicable split. Reportedly, Dobson was concerned that the FRC's political work might jeopardize his group tax-exempt status.

Although legally separate, the groups still work closely together. Both the FRC and Focus are 501(c)(3) tax-exempt organizations. They are, as Dobson himself has said, "legally separate but spiritually one." (Dobson serves on the FRC board of directors.)

The FRC-Focus partnership dramatically boosted Bauer's public profile. In 1990, scholar Matthew C. Moen, a University of Maine political science professor and author of several books on the movement, singled Bauer out as one of a new breed of Religious Right leaders. This new breed, Moen said, was more politically sophisticated than Jerry Falwell and his Moral Majority and, being more familiar with the workings of government, had the potential to be much more effective politically.

Under the Dobson-Bauer nexus, the FRC has seen an explosion of growth. In the early 1990s, the group had twenty employees. The day I toured the facility, the FRC was up to one hundred staffers and still growing. (My guide even urged me to check out the organization's website in case I was interested in employment opportunities myself.) In fact, my guide said wistfully, the lovely new building was already starting to feel overcrowded. (An additional thirty people work out of an order fulfillment center in Holland, Michigan.)

There's not much to the tour. The ground floor consists of a guard station, the museum/store, and a conference room. The fourth floor is off-limits entirely. ("It's just administrative offices," my guide mumbled.) The sixth floor is used mainly as a work space for college students who come to the FRC under a fellowship program to get thoroughly immersed in the organization's point of view. Other floors house the FRC's worker bees—graphic artists, writers and editors, public policy analysts, lawyers, and lobbyists. It's the usual assortment for any public policy organization.

The growth of the staff is impressive. Equally impressive has been the growth of the FRC's budget. In 1990, the year Americans United first started keeping serious tabs on the FRC, the group's budget was $1.5 million. In 1999 it was projected to be $15 million. The FRC raises that budget from a mix of individual donors and right-wing foundations. In fiscal year 1998, 24 percent of the FRC's money came from foundations. Sixty-three percent came from individual donors. Seven percent came from businesses, and churches gave 2 percent. The remainder came from "other sources."[2]

When the Christian Coalition began experiencing internal difficulties in the late 1990s, some commentators speculated that if Robertson's organization entered a period of decline, the Family Research Council would step up to the plate and assume the task of being the nation's leading Religious Right organization.

That could happen, but it's also important to note that there are significant stylistic differences between the Christian Coalition and the Family Research Council. The two groups are not simply interchangeable. While they pursue the same goals, they have different strategies for achieving success.

The Christian Coalition sought to merge with the Republican

Party and force the GOP to bow to whims of religious conservatives. Its ploy of distributing voter guides in churches was designed to politicize as many houses of worship as possible and convert them into cogs in a giant GOP political machine. To that end, the Christian Coalition always strived to build a grassroots presence.

The FRC is more of a Washington-based entity. Its parent organization, Focus on the Family, maintains chapters in some state capitals that serve as a focus for grassroots organizing. That leaves the FRC free to focus on the U.S. Congress. As far as the Republican Party goes, the FRC is also much less of a team player than the Christian Coalition. Dobson, in fact, announced publicly that he did not vote for GOP presidential candidate Robert Dole in 1996. Instead, he backed Howard Phillips of the fringe U.S. Taxpayers Party. Robertson may occasionally harp about the GOP mistreating religious conservatives, but he would never publicly threaten to bolt the party, as Dobson and Bauer have already done. Bauer, in fact, went so far as to tell a conservative newspaper in 1994 that religious conservatives should form a third party if the GOP softened its stance on abortion. (In an attempt to mollify him, GOP officials appointed Bauer to a Republican policy group called the Policy Council on Strengthening the Family.)

The way it is configured today, the FRC would not be prepared to mimic all of the activities of the Christian Coalition. It lacks the necessary grassroots presence. However, the organization may be positioning itself to build that presence, and Bauer's long shot presidential campaign may be part of that effort.

No matter what happens to the Christian Coalition, it's clear that Bauer is seeking a higher profile both for himself and his organization. There is an obvious case of institutional rivalry between the two groups, and until now the Christian Coalition has tended to enjoy the upper hand.

I recall attending an FRC media event at the National Press Club in Washington, D.C., the morning after the November 1998 elections. the FRC's event, which was billed as an analysis of the results (in which the Religious Right fared poorly) began at 9:30. The Christian Coalition was sponsoring a similar press event down the hall at 10. Turnout for the FRC's event was mediocre at best, and just before 10, many of the reporters who were there got up, walked out of the room and strolled down to the Coalition's standing-room-only event. (It didn't help that the FRC had asked Kellyann Fitzpatrick, a Republican pollster who masquerades as a political commentator, to analyze the election results. Fitzpatrick said nothing of interest and said it quite poorly.)

The FRC is making a play to be a big-league Religious Right organization. Its budget comes close to the Christian Coalition's. Its leader is trying to increase his public profile. The group is backed by the formidable financial resources and star power of James Dobson in Colorado Springs. Anyone concerned about the Religious Right needs to be informed about this organization.

So what does the FRC want? Having watched the FRC's growth over the years, having examined many of its publications, and having listened to Bauer and other group leaders expound on the issues, I'm prepared to say that there is nothing in the FRC agenda that doesn't ape what every other Religious Right organization is saying. Its agenda is tired, uncreative, and mind-numbingly familiar—criminalize abortion, defeat gay rights, reject feminism and public education, encourage censorship and Christian fundamentalism in the public schools, and support school vouchers.

But it's still worthwhile to take a closer look. Let's begin with the FRC mission statement. It reads, "Family Research Council's primary reason for existence is to reaffirm and promote nationally and particularly in Washington, D.C., the traditional family unit and the Judeo-Christian principles upon which it is built."

To achieve this end, the FRC promises to undertake four tasks. I have taken the liberty of interpreting some of the lofty rhetoric for readers:

- "Promote and defend the family in the media." (This means the FRC will maintain a staff of public relations professionals who will spend time getting the organization's name in newspapers and magazines, seeking appearances on national television, and sending ideas for shows to right-wing talk radio hosts.)
- "Develop and advocate legislative and public policy initiatives which strengthen and fortify the family and promote traditional values." (The FRC spends most of its time assailing legal abortion and gay people and trying to censor the World Wide Web and public libraries. How any of this "strengthens families" is unclear.)
- "Establish and maintain an accurate source of statistical and research information which reaffirms the importance of the family in our civilization." (In English: "We plan to churn out lots of propaganda, claiming that it is reliable research.")
- "Inform and educate citizens on how they can promote Biblical principles in our culture. (Translation: "That's 'biblical' as we define it, of course.")

One of the things that irks me most about Religious Right groups is their use of the word "family." So the FRC exists to "promote and defend" the family? I did not ask it to promote and defend my family. I don't want it speaking for my family. I have a feeling that my definition of what constitutes a family is a good bit different than the FRC's.

Elsewhere the group talks about its support for the "traditional family." I suppose this means mom, dad, and the kids. I want to see these families supported. But I also know that there are lots of other families out there that need support—single-parent families, gay parents, grandparents raising grandchildren, children in foster care, and extended families that include aunts, uncles, and cousins. The FRC extols the "traditional family unit." Of course it is best for children to have a set of loving parents at home. But the reality of today is that, given our country's divorce rate and high incidence of out-of-wedlock births, many children are not living in that type of environment. It would make more sense to support *all* families, rather than make arbitrary distinction of which qualify as "traditional" (and are thus deserving of more support) and which do not.

Families are not isolated social units. They can and indeed must receive support from larger institutions. One of those institutions may be a house of worship. Many families draw strength, inspiration, and even material aid from faith communities. Another source of support for families, in an ideal world, would be public education. What does the FRC have to say about public education?

Nothing good. Like every other Religious Right group active these days, the FRC is reflexively anti–public education. Its attacks on this institution are crude, uninformed, and mean-spirited. They do a disservice to the people who work hard in our public schools for the betterment of children—people who, in many cases, are doing something concrete to shore up America's families, not just sitting in a plush office building in Washington issuing press releases or spouting rhetoric on CNN.

The FRC's main problem with public education is that it fails to indoctrinate children in the group's preferred version of Christianity. This is a common complaint among the Religious Right. (And by the way, forget all of this talk about the FRC promoting "Judeo-Christian values." The values they want to force onto the public school system have very little "Judeo" in them, and the Christianity is of a particular stripe as well—it's fundamentalist. Surprise!)

FRC either does not understand or does not care to acknowledge the changes that have taken place in American society since 1950. The fact that there are religious minorities in public schools does not faze the group.

Not surprisingly, the FRC advocates vouchers for private and religious schools or home-schooling. But, recognizing that 90 percent of American children still attend public schools, the group calls for adding a hefty dose of that old-time religion to the curriculum.

Explaining his advocacy of a school prayer amendment to the *Washington Post* in late 1994, Bauer remarked, "The liberals are screaming about religious differences, but there was not one ounce of that sensitivity when it came to some things like sex education. For years, our children have had to go to sex education classes that are deeply offensive to our values. And when we've suggested that our kids shouldn't be humiliated by having to bring a note to class saying, 'Bobby should be excused,' the educational establishment and civil libertarians haven't been very sympathetic to us. This [school prayer] would level the playing field, so if they're going to be cavalier to us on our values, I don't see how they can say the whole class must remain silent because an atheist in the class may be insulted."[3]

In a nutshell: Some fundamentalist Christian students have been embarrassed because their parents insisted they be removed from sex education classes. Therefore, the remedy for that is to embarrass and humiliate other people's kids by making them take part in Christian worship in public schools. That will teach them. Try as I might, I cannot imagine a situation in which I would teach my children this type of "get even" ethics—and I certainly would not call it "pro-family" or "Christian." Nor would I use my children as pawns like this. Why not? Because it isn't "pro-family." It's disgusting.

In 1997, the FRC attacked a federal judge in Alabama for ordering a public school in rural DeKalb County to stop sponsoring prayer and other forms of Christian worship during school hours. The record of abuses in the case was extensive, and, in his ruling, U.S. District Judge Ira DeMent went out of his way to say that only coercive, school-sponsored religious worship was unconstitutional. Individual students, DeMent pointed out, have the right to pray at any time during the school day, and students can pray with their friends or read Bibles during free time. This part of the ruling broke no new ground and essentially restated what had been the law for thirty-five years.

Nevertheless, the FRC went on the warpath. In a fax bulletin issued by Dobson's Focus on the Family, Bauer accused DeMent of issuing a "draconian" ruling and headlined his observations, "Dictatorship in Alabama?" Bauer and the FRC continued ridiculing DeMent and distorting his opinion for months afterward. The FRC's actions were reckless and clearly intended to inflame a situation already rife with bad information and emotional outbursts.

DeMent was faced with a difficult case. Some of the practices at the DeKalb schools had not been the subject of extensive previous litigation, such as permitting students to say prayers before sporting events. Some federal courts have upheld practices like this, while others have struck them down. A federal appeals court later upheld DeMent's ruling barring school-sponsored religious activity but lifted his ban on certain types of ostensibly "student-initiated" prayer. Having read both opinions, I believe DeMent's was correct. The appeals court, I believe, engaged in rampant right-wing judicial activism, as there is no precedent giving approval to some of the activities they declared constitutional.

My point is, DeMent found himself in difficult legal territory. He made the best call he could. His opinion is reasonable and well written. But all he got for efforts was ridicule from the FRC.

The FRC never lets the facts get in the way of a good smear against public schools. In early 1998 Bauer granted an interview to Associated Baptist Press on the issue of religion in schools. During the interview, Bauer said a federal appeals court had dismissed a case brought by a kindergarten student who had been expelled for praying over his lunch. According to Bauer's account, the Supreme Court had also refused to hear the case. In reality, there was no such case. Pressed to give specifics about it, Bauer could not do so. An FRC staffer later told the Associated Baptist Press reporter that Bauer had combined elements from several cases.

In the summer of 1998, Bauer came to the defense of Mildred Rosario, a public school teacher in the Bronx who was fired after she engaged in religious activities with her fifth-grade class. Rosario had prayed with students and "anointed" them by laying on hands. One student, a Jehovah's Witness, found her Pentecostal practices frightening and complained to her family. School officials asked Rosario to agree not to engage in the practices again. She refused and was let go.

Religious Right groups brought Rosario to Capitol Hill and used her as the star attraction in a sideshow designed to prove that the Constitution should be amended to allow mandatory school prayer. At one of these events, Bauer lauded Rosario as "an ideal teacher" and said America "needs countless more like her."

As it turned out, Rosario was on the verge of being fired before the ruckus started. Officials with the city school system charged her with unsatisfactory ratings and said she had been cited for poor teaching methods and absenteeism.[4]

Observed a spokeswoman for the New York City Board of Education, "[It is] an irony that there is a cause célèbre on the Religious Right to maintain a teacher who would have been dismissed for unsatisfactory performance."[5]

Imagine the uproar that would occur across the land if thousands of public school teachers suddenly began following the example of Bauer's "ideal teacher" Rosario. Rosario's Pentecostal beliefs are undoubtedly sincere, but that does not make them any less controversial. In fact, many fundamentalist Christians reject practices such as speaking in tongues, laying on of hands, and the exuberant forms of worship that mark Pentecostalism. How would a Southern Baptist react if a teacher led his child in these practices?

How would Protestant students feel if a Roman Catholic teacher told them Martin Luther was a crank and that the only path to salvation is through the Church of Rome? What if a liberal Protestant told the kids that all of this talk about being "born-again" was really just nonsense and asserted that Jesus was actually little more than a first-century peacemaker who just wanted everybody to get along? Personally, I don't see any of this going down too well. For a few hundred years, hundreds of thousands of people were killed over these very questions.

I've limited my discussion to Christian groups here for a reason. Groups like the FRC use the term "Christian" in a reckless manner. They seem to imply that there is a universal collection of Christian teachings with which most Americans agree. There isn't. If that were the case, we would not have hundreds of distinct Christian denominations operating in the country today. Christian denominations disagree on how the Bible is to be interpreted; on the relationship of Jesus to God; on whether salvation is obtained through good acts, faith alone, or a combination of both; on whether worship and communion with those of other beliefs is acceptable; on the question of salvation outside the faith; and many other doctrinal issues. These are not minor differences that can cavalierly be papered over. They mean something to people.

I haven't even touched on the political issues. Is abortion murder? Some Christian groups say emphatically yes. Others say no. Still others say it depends. Is homosexuality a sin? You'll find Christian groups all over the map on that one. Christian groups can't even agree on how to order the Ten Commandments!

Some Christians don't even recognize other Christian groups as Christian. I recall sharing a television appearance once with an extreme right-winger. We were arguing over religion in public schools. He wanted "Christianity" taught in the schools. I asked him if he would be willing to accept the version of Christianity taught by the Seventh-day Adventists, the Christian Scientists, and the Mormons. "No," he replied, "those groups aren't Christian." My reply was simple: "I rest my case."

Now add in the non-Christian groups—the Jews, the Buddhists, the Muslims, the Hindus, the atheists, the agnostics, the secular humanists, the Wiccans, the Zoroastrians, the Pagans, the Sikhs, the New Agers, the Jainists, and on and on.

Is it the FRC's belief that only teachers who seek to indoctrinate students in *certain forms* of religion—namely, right-wing, fundamentalist Christianity—are to count as "ideal" teachers? I suspect it is, and if that's so, then what they are seeking is not freedom, it is special treatment and government favoritism toward Protestant fundamentalism. That's what they want, and they ought to just come out and say so. It will feel good to get it off their chests.

(Oddly enough, for all of his holier-than-thou attitude, Bauer, like a lot of other Religious Right leaders, can't resist the lure of Sun Myung Moon's millions. Moon, head of the Unification Church, claims to be the messiah sent to complete the failed mission of Jesus Christ. In 1996, I stopped by a meeting of Moon's Family Federation for World Peace at the National Building Museum in Washington, D.C., and was surprised to see Gary Bauer on the program. He later defended himself by saying he often speaks to groups whose theology he does not agree with, such as Jews and atheists. I had to wonder how many atheist organizations Bauer had addressed recently.)

At about the same time he was advocating fundamentalist Christianity in the public schools, Bauer and the FRC were hard at work on another plan to interject religion into public schools and the government at large. The FRC drafted a "Ten Commandments Defense Act," a bill stripping the federal courts of their ability to declare government-sponsored displays of the Ten Commandments unconstitutional.

The FRC had one of its congressional allies, in this case Rep. Robert Aderholt (R-Ala.), sponsor the measure. It went nowhere that year, but in 1999 a modified version of it was passed by the House of Representatives when attached as a rider to a juvenile justice bill. The rider attempted to force the federal courts to declare such displays constitutional.

Over the years, right-wing firebrands in the House and Senate have promoted various "court-stripping" measures. Sen. Jesse Helms (R-N.C.) used to promote them as a way of getting around the High Court's ban on government-sponsored school prayer. Other members of Congress promoted proposals telling the federal courts they could no longer rule on issues relating to abortion.

Of course there is one drawback to these schemes: They are blatantly unconstitutional. Congress does not have the power to limit the federal courts and take certain issues out of their jurisdiction. This is elementary civics, but here the problem: The three branches of government, legislative, executive, and judicial, are *independent.* That's deliberate. The framers made it that way. The three branches perform a system of checks and balances over one another. (Remember this from fifth grade?) This is called the separation of powers. Just as the courts can't force Congress to pass legislation, Congress can't force the courts to hand down only rulings it likes or take certain issues out of the jurisdiction of the courts completely. The power of the courts to declare acts of Congress unconstitutional was settled more than two hundred years ago. Legislation like the Ten Commandments Defense Act is the product of a mind that is either very foolish or very venal. Take your pick.

I suspect that backdoor court-stripping measures like the Ten Commandments Defense Act have more to do with impressing gullible FRC members than advancing a legitimate public policy idea. In the FRC's case it is all part of a larger plan of court bashing that has been going on for several years now. The FRC's court bashing is one of the most tiresome features of the group's agenda. It insists that a liberal judiciary has imposed liberal views on America. How and why this happened after twelve years of conservative appointments to the federal courts by Presidents Reagan and Bush is a mystery.

Ira DeMent, the federal judge the FRC attacked so savagely in the Alabama school prayer controversy, is a case in point. DeMent was appointed by Bush and is considered a conservative. A Methodist, DeMent reportedly keeps a Bible on his desk at work. His ruling is actually in keeping with conservative principles, as it cites the legal precedent and strikes down practices that have long ago been declared unconstitutional. That's what federal judges are supposed to do. Handing down a ruling that ignores all existing precedent and charts a totally new course might have pleased right-wingers in this case, but it would have been a radical step, not a conservative one.

Bauer and the FRC have attacked the federal judiciary with reckless abandon over the years. In grade school, I was taught to respect the government and its legitimacy. I was also taught about the role of dissent in a democratic society and the appropriate channels for protesting a court ruling one perceives as misguided (like filing an appeal). The FRC's uninformed attacks on the federal courts make me long for the days when conservatives supported the government. All they seem to do these days is question its very right to exist and flirt with recommending that people defy court or government actions they don't like. Didn't they criticize leftists for doing the same thing in the 1960s?

Consider this: After Judge DeMent handed down his ruling, the FRC and other Religious Right groups called for his impeachment, declared the federal courts illegitimate, and spread wild stories about the scope of his ruling in a string of hysterical fund-raising letters designed to inflame passions and mislead people. When the appeals court reversed portions of DeMent's ruling, Americans United was displeased, but our organization did not call for impeaching the judges or suggest that their ruling should be ignored. Instead, we pulled our lawyers together and discussed our legal options. Who took the more responsible course?

Bauer so dislikes the federal courts that a few years ago the FRC began sponsoring an annual banquet where "Court Jester Awards" are handed out to judges who have dared to issue rulings that Bauer does not like. The right-wing media gives the event some play, but sensible people ignore it, realizing that the only fools connected with the ceremony are the people who conceive, plan, and attend it.

Public schools and the U.S. courts take a lot of flak from the FRC. In 1994 the FRC attempted to add public libraries to its list of targets as well. Joining forces with Focus on the Family, the FRC held a press conference in Washington the same week as the American Library Association's annual "Banned Book Week" to insist that books are not actually banned in America. (This must come as a surprise to all of the teachers who have had to wage battles for the right to teach John Steinbeck's *Of Mice and Men* and J. D. Salinger's *The Catcher in the Rye* over the years.)

For a while the FRC and Focus attempted to found a national anti–public library group, Family Friendly Libraries, which advocated blocking young people's access to certain "controversial" books or putting some titles on restricted access. I once had occasion to interview the group's head, a Springfield, Virginia, woman named Karen Jo Gounaud, who had a bad habit of lapsing into gay bashing during media interviews. The group seems less active today, but still, the issue is worth keeping an eye on. The FRC and other Religious Right groups have successfully blackened the reputation of public education. They would like to do the same to public libraries.

The FRC pretends to be concerned about young people. But its constant attacks on public education and libraries actually do a great disservice to teenagers. Similarly, the group in 1996 did all young people another great disservice when it helped block a federal job-training bill in Congress that would have offered help to youngsters who enter the workforce after graduating from high school.

At least half of high school graduates do not go on to college. Of those who do enter college, about 25 percent drop out before graduating. This means that a lot of young people must enter the workforce every year with a high school diploma. Some of these young people are interested in vocational careers. The federal bill was designed to streamline services to help them. The FRC opposed it on the grounds that kids were going to be categorized academically by public schools, denied the opportunity to go to college, and forced to enter certain professions against their will. Nothing in the bill said anything like that. Yet an FRC spokeswoman told the *New York Times*, "It's not clear that this is going to be an optional vocational track."

Robert Reich, then the Secretary of Labor, called the objections raised to the bill by the FRC and the Eagle Forum "incomprehensible." U.S. Rep. Howard P. McKeon, a conservative Republican, added, "[It] boggles the mind, but it's out there."[6]

The job-training bill enjoyed bipartisan support and had passed both the House and Senate by large margins, but thanks to pressure from the FRC and the Eagle Forum, it was gutted by the conference committee. The bill that emerged was so watered-down that most Democrats and Republicans who had backed it withdrew their support, and President Clinton promised to veto it.

"This is like a dead mouse in the middle of the ballroom floor that everybody is ignoring and nobody wants to retrieve," said Rep. Pat Williams (D-Montana). "It is shocking that the governors, the president, the vice president, the leaders of the House and Senate and various business groups can unite behind something and it can be scuttled on the rocks of the far-right."[7]

Helping young people fresh out of high school get training so they can land medium- or high-wage jobs instead of languishing in the world of the minimum wage would seem to be "pro-family." It's possible the FRC knows something the rest of us don't, but my guess is its leaders are just paranoid, or they automatically oppose most federal spending programs.

Similarly, in 1996 the FRC helped kill another measure aimed at helping young people that would seem to fit the definition of "pro-family." The proposal would have encouraged members of the National Guard to work in local communities combatting substance abuse and delinquency among teenagers. The theory behind the program was that in peacetime a minuscule amount of resources could be allocated to these programs without harming military readiness. A spokeswoman for the National Guard noted that similar programs had worked in the past. "The one-on-one work that Guardsmen do with youth has cut the rate of delinquency, the bad things that happen to kids these days," she said.[8]

The FRC would have none of it and joined other right-wing groups in successfully prodding Congress to require the National Guard to find funding for the program from new sources, as opposed to relying on the larger defense budget.

Public schools and libraries are juicy targets for the FRC, but an equally appealing bull's-eye for the group's wrath is gay people. The FRC has a staff member named Robert Knight, whose title is "director of cultural studies." It might as well be "director of gay bashing" as that is primarily how Knight spends his time.

Elsewhere in this book I recounted how, during a session at TV preacher D. James Kennedy's 1999 "Reclaiming America" conference, Knight denied being a gay basher but then moments later went on to make remarks about how most lesbians are overweight. Knight spends most of his time making the same arguments over and over again: homosexuals account for far less than 10 percent of the population; homosexuality is a chosen lifestyle, not something a person is born with; and homosexuals can choose to stop being homosexual through "reparative therapy." The FRC regularly spews out heavily footnoted, pseudoscholarly reports leveling various charges against gay people or claiming to have uncovered evidence that homosexuality is not genetically based.

In 1995, Knight issued an FRC briefing paper highlighting a National Institutes of Health study that he claimed "rekindled the debate over whether homosexuality has a genetic component." The study in question dealt with fruit flies. Researchers altered the body chemistry of male fruit flies and found that they formed mating chains with one another. Although many media outlets reported this study as evidence of a genetic component to homosexuality, Knight begged to differ, writing in his paper that "normal" male fruit flies "resisted sexual advances by the altered males for up to two hours and then succumbed to the same-sex activity [indicating] strongly that homosexual behavior is environmentally induced."[9]

I will resist the temptation to make obvious jokes. To me, any attempt to extrapolate human behavior from a fruit-fly study is clearly going to be fraught with difficulties. I will point out, however, that in Knight's case there is another angle to be considered: the FRC denies the validity of the theory of evolution and rejects a connection between humans and lower forms of life, since humans, according to creationists, are the product of special creation. This makes Knight's position on the fruit-fly study all the more ridiculous. Chimpanzees share 98 percent of human DNA, yet according to the evolution deniers, they aren't really related to humans. According to their logic, a fruit-fly study should tell us nothing about human behavior.

Another one of the FRC's favorite tactics is a type of bait-and-switch maneuver during which statements made by extreme and fringe gay groups are projected onto the larger homosexual community. The organization makes frequent references to the North American Man-Boy Love Association (NAMBLA), a fringe group that advocates sex between adults and children. Knight loves to quote Kevin Bishop, a NAMBLA member, who allegedly once said, "Scratch the average homosexual and you will find a pedophile."[10]

This attempt to link homosexuality to child molesting reflects a certain type of desperation on Knight's part. Public tolerance of homosexuals has steadily increased since the 1970s. In the wake of the gay liberation movement, many Americans began to have contact with gay people who were suddenly out of the closet. Many Americans realized that gay people were their coworkers, neighbors, friends, and in some cases even their children.

To make matters worse from the Religious Right's perspective, many segments of the business community have been eager to tap into the lucrative gay market. Even Coors brewing, a Colorado beer company owned by ultraconservatives, has gay-friendly work policies and advertises in gay publications.

Polls show that the majority of Americans no longer believe that gays should face discrimination or that companies should be able to fire them for no other reason than the issue of sexual orientation. Gay characters appear in television shows and feature films. The Southern Baptists' recent call for a boycott of Disney for its alleged promotion of homosexuality was widely ridiculed and did not hurt the company's bottom line. In short, most Americans now realize that gay people exist, and they don't seem to mind that fact. It's only the Religious Right that can't grow up and get over it.

The Religious Right is losing this battle. They know it. Most Americans are no longer in a mood to hate and fear gay people. The FRC tries to reverse that mindset by linking homosexuality to loathsome practices like child molestation. It doesn't work. The overwhelming majority of homosexuals are not child molesters, just as the vast majority of heterosexuals are not child molesters. Some child molesters victimize children of the same sex, others victimize children of the opposite sex. The offender's crime is not in his or her sexual preference, the crime is in viewing children as acceptable outlets for sex.

Thanks largely to the efforts of the FRC, efforts to add gays to the list of groups protected under federal "hate crimes" legislation has been stalled repeatedly. Federal law currently limits "hate crime" protections to those who suffer injury or death on the basis of race, religion, or national origin. In October of 1998, Matthew Shepard, a young gay man in Wyoming, was pistol-whipped and left tied to a post in freezing weather by two thugs. In the wake of his death, there were calls to add sexual orientation to the hate crimes list.

The FRC and other Religious Right groups have spent countless hours and funds lobbying against the measure. How have these right-wing groups, which normally trumpet their "tough on crime" stance, justified this activity? According to their somewhat creative logic, giving gay people protection under the hate crimes statute would essentially outlaw the "pro-family" message.

The legislation, said FRC analyst Steven A. Schwalm, would "criminalize pro-family beliefs. This basically sends a message that you can't disagree with the political message of homosexual activists."[11] Another FRC staffer said the group opposes the measure because "Basically, it's a thought crime—it's getting into someone's head."[12]

I find it hard to believe that these "pro-family" leaders cannot see the difference between writing an article critical of homosexuality and beating a gay person to death with a baseball bat. The former is a protected activity under the First Amendment; the latter is a crime. One may be criticized for the first, but one can't be put in prison for it. One can and will for the second.

If what the FRC is asserting about the hate crimes bill were true, then it would stand to reason that anyone who has criticized people on the basis of race, religion, or national origin would be in prison now, since existing hate crimes laws protect these groups. Obviously this is not the case. Even extreme hate groups enjoy First Amendment protections. The Ku Klux Klan, for example, still exists. It can publish articles attacking any racial or ethnic group, and does so. The KKK can even march in public and hold rallies. It's the group's First Amendment right. Other extremist groups regularly publish wild conspiracy theories about Jewish control of world governments, international banking, and the media with no sanctions.

The Supreme Court has never ruled that publishing an article critical of an ethnic group or airing critical comments about them on radio or TV is a hate crime. In fact, the Supreme Court and lower federal courts have stated quite clearly that even critical or unpopular speech is entitled to full First Amendment protection. (One school of thought holds that the First Amendment protects this type of speech especially. After all, who is going to try to stop you if you get up and give a speech about how great motherhood, apple pie, and baseball are?)

Hate crimes statutes are intended to protect people from violent, physical acts. FRC staffers know this, yet they continue to make baseless claims about "thought crimes." Perhaps that's because without this cover, their sole reason for opposing extending hate crime protections to gay people would be, "Homosexuals don't deserve this protection because we don't like them."

When the FRC isn't gay bashing, it is harping about legal abortion. It opposes abortions for virtually *any* reason and lately has taken to criticizing "morning-after" pills (alternatively, "emergency contraception") that are often given to rape victims. The pills work by blocking the implantation of a fertilized egg.

On July 30, 1999, the FRC issued a press release blasting a new form of "morning-after" pill that supposedly has less severe side effects than other similar pills. According to FRC spokeswoman Janet Parshall, the new pill "disrespects human life and does not warrant approval of the FDA." The press release quotes Parshall as saying: "In the debate over the ethics of family planning, it's critical that both sides define their terms. The pro-life community strongly believes pregnancy begins at conception, when the sperm penetrates the egg. Any harmful interference with the development of a fertilized egg is immoral and therefore should not be supported."

The FRC talks constantly about "late-term" abortions and describes, in graphic detail, how fetuses are removed during these procedures. The group frames the argument in this way and keeps raising this specific issue because it knows that many Americans have qualms about the legality and appropriateness of abortion beyond a certain point. But every so often the truth slips out: The FRC opposes abortion from the moment of conception for any reason (even in the case of rape) and believes, apparently, that a fertilized egg is the legal equivalent of a fully grown adult.

Gary Bauer and the FRC have worked hard to keep the Republican Party antigay and antichoice on abortion. In late 1995, Bauer joined a bevy of Religious Right heavy hitters in Washington at a press conference to blast Gen. Colin Powell, who was at that time being touted as a possible GOP presidential candidate. Powell never did more than test the waters in a very superficial way, but that was enough to bring the wrath of the FRC down on him. Powell, Bauer and others said, had committed the cardinal sin of being moderate on social issues.

At the FRC's headquarters, visitors can watch a tribute to America's veterans via CD-ROM. By touching the screen, viewers can activate audio clips of veterans giving their recollections about World War II, the Korean War, and the Vietnam War. This isn't the only instance of Bauer seeking to capitalize on the heroism and sacrifice of veterans, even though he himself has never served in uniform. Given this, there was great irony watching Bauer run down Powell, a genuine hero of the Gulf War. Powell, said Bauer in interviews, is little more than "Bill Clinton with [military] ribbons."[13] At least Powell earned those ribbons, which is more than can be said for Bauer.

Bauer will not hesitate to rip a Democrat or a moderate Republican war hero to shreds, but he is not in the habit of criticizing conservative Republicans as long as they parrot his line on social issues. Earlier that year, Bauer had essentially given Texas Sen. Phil Gramm absolution after the media reported that Gramm had invested $7,500 in a soft-core porn movie in 1974.[14] Bauer said it was no big deal because it had happened so long ago. At the same time, Bauer was bashing Clinton right and left because he didn't serve in Vietnam in 1970. (Imagine, for a moment, what Bauer's reaction would have been had the senator involved been Ted Kennedy instead of Gramm.)

In November of 1996, Bauer decided to jump into partisan politics in a big way. He formed a political action committee (PAC) called the Campaign for Working Families. (It is now the nation's sixth-largest PAC.) Note again the clever use of language. If I didn't know better, I would assume from the name that this PAC had something to do with issues that concern working families, such as access to affordable health care or increasing the availability of quality child care.

Nothing doing. The Campaign for Working Families obsesses almost exclusively over abortion and gays. I'm on several right-wing mailing lists and for a while received regular solicitations from the Campaign for Working Families. Most of the letters attacked legal abortion. The rest attacked gays. Bauer has yet to explain how making all abortions illegal and stripping homosexuals of their rights helps "working families."

Actually, the name of the PAC is probably another component of Bauer's phony attempt to claim to be a man of the people. Bauer was born in northern Kentucky in a blue-collar home, a fact he frequently plays up in the media. He occasionally tries to pass himself off as a champion of the working class. A quick look at the FRC's agenda dispels that myth. In 1998 the FRC issued a "Ten Year Progress Report" listing its chief accomplishments for 1998. These include seeking various restrictions on abortion, banning federal funding for federal education testing, working to abolish the capital gains tax, trying to shut off funding for the National Endowment for the Arts, seeking to censor the World Wide Web, opposing gay marriage in Hawaii and Alaska, and lobbying Congress to reject calls for a heavier federal presence in child care.

Working families have legitimate concerns: affording good health care, finding quality child care, helping build good neighborhood public schools, making a living wage, creating safe neighborhoods with moderately priced housing, and saving money for the higher education of children. These issues aren't even on the FRC's radar screen.

Bauer's PAC claims spectacular results. In election years, it pours some money into the races of GOP shoo-ins. This is a sure-fire recipe for success and enables the PAC to claim great victories afterward. But in close races, the PAC is less effective. In a January 1998 special election in California, the Bauer PAC heavily funded social issues conservative Tom Bordonaro in his primary race against GOP moderate Brooks Firestone. Bordonaro and Firestone were vying to go up against Lois Capps, widow of Rep. Walter Capps, who had died the previous year.

Money from the Campaign for Working Families helped Bordonaro edge out Firestone in the primary, but in the general election many Republicans found Bordonaro too right-wing and defected to Capps. She was elected 53 percent to 45 percent.[15]

In 1998, Bauer's PAC pumped $3 million into 225 federal and state races around the country. Many of the candidates were defeated, as the Religious Right faced one of its worst years ever at the ballot box.[16]

The day after the election, Bauer struggled to explain away the disaster. Republicans, he told reporters at the National Press Club, had fared poorly because they had run away from the Religious Right's message. Voters perceived them as bland and opted for Democrats. In other words, since conservative candidates fared poorly, the obvious thing to do is run candidates who are even more conservative.

Rep. Chris Shays of Connecticut, a leading GOP moderate, had perhaps a more realistic assessment of the situation. Shays told the *New York Times*, "As soon as my [congressional] leadership started to jump when the Christian Coalition and Gary Bauer and others said jump, we lost a lot of voters."[17]

Nevertheless, Bauer strikes me as one of those types who would rather stand on principle and go down to defeat than compromise and win. He must be Ralph Reed's worst nightmare. In 1998, Bauer went on the attack after Reed suggested that all any religious conservative wants is "a place at the table" in the Republican Party.

Bauer wants a lot more, probably ownership of the table outright—and the right to determine who else gets a seat there.

"Nobody's going to put on your tombstone, 'He had a place at the table,' " said Bauer. "The thing you want on your tombstone is, 'He liberated the slaves' or 'He stopped the slaughter of the innocents.' That's what men and women of faith in both parties ought to be involved in."[18]

As my tour at Family Research Council ended that July day, an incident occurred that to me served as a sort of clumsy metaphor for what this "pro-family" group is really all about. I had left the house that morning under clear skies, but now it was cloudy and starting to rain. My guide felt bad for having kept me waiting and promised to make it up to me with a gift: a Family Research Council umbrella.

Pulling a long blue-and-white umbrella embossed with the FRC logo from a storage closet, she explained to me that the group couldn't sell them because they were made in China. The FRC is a frequent critic of President Clinton's policy toward China and has called for tough economic sanctions against that country for its repressive policy toward Christians. The year before, the group had been embarrassed when critics pointed out that the FRC, which had urged a boycott of Chinese goods, was distributing mugs made in China.

"There's just one thing I need to do," said my guide as she lifted up the umbrella. With a quick motion she pulled out a pair of scissors and snipped the "Made in China" tag off of the umbrella. Smiling brightly, she handed the umbrella to me, thanked me for coming, and wished me a good afternoon.

Outside I walked to the subway with the umbrella tucked under my arm. It was only a slow rain, and I decided I'd rather just get wet.

Family Research Council
Leader: Gary Bauer
Budget: $15 million
Membership: The FRC says it is not a membership organization but reports that about five hundred thousand people receive its materials.
Address: 801 G St., N.W., Washington, D.C. 20001
Website: http://www.frc.org

NOTES

1. "Conservatives Should Push Social Issues, Activist Says," *Church & State* (June 1989).

2. "A Decade of Progress," Family Research Council Ten-Year Progress Report, November 1998.

3. Laurie Goodstein, "Conservatives Refining School Prayer Strategy," *Washington Post*, November 22, 1994.

4. Timothy J. Burger, "Whip Flays Apple Over Booted Teach," *New York Daily News*, June 26, 1998.

5. Ibid.

6. Adam Clymer, "Job-Training Bill Is Being Attacked By Conservatives," *New York Times*, March 31, 1996.

7. Judith Havemann, "Job Training Bill Conference Degenerates," *Washington Post*, July 18, 1996.

8. Rowan Scarborough, "Republicans Take Social Work out of Pentagon's Funding Bill," *Washington Times*, February 5, 1996.

9. Robert H. Knight, "New NIH Study Indicates Homosexuality Is Learned," *Family Research Council Insight* (n.d.).

10. Knight cites a source for this in one report: *The Electronic Mail & Guardian*, the on-line version of a newspaper published in South Africa, June 30, 1997.

11. James Brooke, "Gay Man Dies From Attack, Fanning Outrage and Debate," *New York Times*, October 13, 1998.

12. Sean Scully, "Democrats See Student's Death Helping Revive Hate-Crimes Bill," *Washington Times*, October 13, 1998.

13. "Fight Over Colin Powell Splits Religious Right," *Church & State* (December 1995).

14. "Buchanan Calls for New Religious Crusade," *Church & State* (July–August 1995).

15. Rob Boston, "Family Feud," *Church & State* (May 1998).

16. Joseph L. Conn, "Election '98 After Shock," *Church & State* (December 1998).

17. Alison Mitchell, "So Just Whose Party Is It? A GOP House Divided," *New York Times*, November 12, 1998.

18. Linda Feldman, "Religious Right's New Mandarin," *Christian Science Monitor*, March 18, 1998.

Chapter 8

THE BOTTOM-FEEDERS

Wall Bashers, Born-Again Atheists, Stoners in the Name of Christ, and More

Every movement has its stars and its second-stringers, its home run hitters and its back-benchers. So it is with the Religious Right. In reality, there are only a handful of prominent Religious Right groups in the country. I'd include in this list the Christian Coalition, Focus on the Family, and the Family Research Council.

Other groups certainly exist but have much lower profiles. Some organizations achieve national prominence and then fade away. Phyllis Schlafly's Eagle Forum enjoyed a high media profile during the struggle over the Equal Rights Amendment. When the amendment failed, everyone forgot about the Eagle Forum, although the organization still exists. A few years ago I called the group in Alton, Illinois, to request membership information. Schlafly herself answered the phone and told me that she was temporarily out of membership brochures. I got the strong impression she was standing in her kitchen at the time. This is not a good development for any organization that seeks a national presence. (But don't think the Eagle Forum is totally dead. I'm told the group remains influential in Utah, where, in 1998, it led a drive to block adding fluoride to the water. Sure, they tell us it will prevent tooth decay, but everyone knows it's a communist plot.)

Antifeminist crusader's Beverly LaHaye's Concerned Women for America was all the rage during the Reagan years. The Washington-based group opposed communism, homosexuality, "secular humanism," abortion, and so on. Concerned Women still cranks out loads of fund-raising mail, but its influence in Washington seems to have declined sharply since the Berlin Wall fell.

Donald Wildmon and the American Family Association had quite a run in the early 1980s. Wildmon, based in Tupelo, Mississippi, is still urging people to boycott "indecent" television shows and actually puts out a newsletter that tallies up all of the raunchy talk and "antireligious" material on network programs and gives plot summaries. Yet risqué shows seem to be proliferating, and now an entire network, Fox, exists that seems devoted to scantily clad women, UFOs, and police cars chasing bad guys. Is anyone listening to Wildmon anymore?

Other second-tier Religious Right groups struggle to break into the big leagues. This seems to be the case with D. James Kennedy's Florida-based Center for Reclaiming America. Kennedy would love to play with the big boys. Perhaps he will someday, but for now, he's strictly in the farm league.

Yet the Religious Right's "lesser lights" plug on. Some organizations, I really do believe, are nothing more than letterhead operations that exist primarily to mail out fund-raising letters. These letters, if they have even a scintilla of information in them, can qualify as "educational" mailings. Thus, sending out even more fund-raising letters becomes the organization's main purpose. It's good work if you can get it—and can sleep at night while doing it.

Over the years I've had various and sundry encounters with Religious Right second-stringers. I'll look at some of them in this chapter.

DAVID BARTON'S WALLBUILDERS

The first time I saw a book by David Barton, I was convinced it was a joke. The book was titled *America: To Pray or Not to Pray*. It was self-published—by WallBuilders Press, which Barton founded and owns—and looked like it had been slapped together in someone's garage. The main argument of the book was that ever since the Supreme Court struck down mandatory prayer in public schools in 1962, America has gone to hell. The book contains a series of charts designed to prove this assertion. Barton will display a chart of, say, the rate of venereal disease in America and indicate that it has increased since 1962.

I have, since the fifth grade, known what is wrong with this argument. It's a common fallacy of logic called the *post hoc ergo propter hoc* fallacy. The phrase is Latin for, "after this, therefore on account of this." I read about this fallacy in a magazine for children when I was ten years old (although the magazine did not use this fancy Latin phrase). The article was about common mistakes people make when framing arguments. The example the magazine used was someone saying, "Ever since men went to the moon, the world has been getting hotter." This may be true, but it's a non sequitur. The second statement does not follow from the first. They make no sense together.

Just because two things occur in sequence does not mean that one caused the other. It *may* be the case that one caused the other, but one has to find some proof of it. If a man drinks six martinis then smashes his car into a tree while driving home, it is safe to assume that he was probably drunk while driving. But we can test that hypothesis by giving him a blood-alcohol or field sobriety test. Plus, in this example, it helps that the link between intoxication and reckless driving was proven many years ago.

Barton can make the assertion about the High Court's school prayer cases spawning negative social trends, but he can't prove it.

That's why his argument collapses like a house of cards under even casual scrutiny.

Occasionally I speak before organizations that promote science education or critical thinking. I have blown up several of Barton's graphs, and I take them along to show the crowd. They never fail to elicit gales of laughter. Though Barton's research is shoddy, and, in the final analysis, downright silly, that has not in any way stopped him from becoming a hero to the Religious Right. Through his Texas-based, for-profit group WallBuilders, Barton disseminates his books and other types of "Christian nation" propaganda. (WallBuilders takes its name from a Bible passage, Neh. 2:17, which reads, "Ye see the distress that we are in, how Jerusalem lieth in waste, and the gates thereof are burned with fire: come, let us build up the wall of Jerusalem that we be no more a reproach." Barton apparently sees himself akin to the Old Testament prophet, chosen by God to rebuild the nation's moral foundations.) I have heard Barton speak many times at the Christian Coalition's "Road to Victory."

Barton poses as a historian on the basis of his second self-published book, *The Myth of Separation* (now titled *Original Intent*), a double-barreled assault on the separation of church and state. In 1998, he was asked by a right-wing member of the State Academic Standards Commission to critique California's proposed history standards. One of the things he tried to do was delete all positive references to the separation of church and state.

In its original 1989 version, *The Myth of Separation* was a classic example of slipshod research, the type of thing common among Religious Right groups. In the book, Barton attempts to prove that separation of church and state is a myth that was never intended by the framers. Instead, he asserts, they sought to officially establish the United States as a Christian nation.

The back cover of *The Myth of Separation* contained a long list of quotations allegedly uttered by Founding Fathers lauding Christian principles in government or otherwise advocating church-state union. Nearly all of them turned out to be bogus, as Barton himself admitted in 1996. No wonder *The Myth of Separation* was revised and given a new title.[1]

My personal favorite of the bogus quotations was this one, supposedly stated by James Madison: "We have staked the whole future of American civilization not upon the power of government, far from it. We have staked the future of all of our political institutions upon the capacity of each and all of us to govern ourselves according to the Ten Commandments of God."

I don't claim to be an expert on James Madison, but I know a few things about him. To me, he is one of America's great unsung heroes. I always thought it unlikely that Madison actually said this. Madison was a strong advocate of separation of church and state, stronger even than Thomas Jefferson in my view. Plus, as an adult, Madison, to be frank, had a rather indifferent attitude toward religion. I was suspicious of this quote from day one. My suspicions were heightened because I noted that I often saw different versions of this quote in print. Sometimes words or phrases were omitted or changed. But still, I could not definitely debunk the quote, so I told the people who asked me about it that I merely suspected that it was false.

Finally, in 1993, Prof. Robert S. Alley of the University of Richmond (and a member of Americans United's Board of Trustees) asked the curators of the Madison Papers at the University of Virginia to see if they could verify this quote. The curators reported back in the negative. Furthermore, they added that the quote seemed to conflict with Madison's well-known views on the separation of church and state.

Can I prove definitively that Madison never said it? No. I also can't prove that Madison didn't once do the cancan on top of a flagpole to celebrate Independence Day. In the absence of any evidence indicating that he did that, I'm going to assume that he did not. It seems the wise and prudent thing to do.[2]

Nevertheless, this bogus Madison quote about the Ten Commandments keeps circulating. As recently as July 3, 1999, I was forced to write to the *Washington Post* and debunk it again. An earlier letter writer had cited it in defending the House of Representatives for passing a bill urging public schools and government offices to post the Ten Commandments. In my letter, I pointed out that there is no proof that Madison ever said it. Thus, those who advocate government-sponsored display of the Ten Commandments will have to look elsewhere for allies. They can't claim Madison.

Barton's bogus history has put down deep roots in the Religious Right. One of Barton's more outrageous claims is that Thomas Jefferson intended for his famous "wall of separation between church and state" to protect only the church from encroachment by the state, not the other way around. Jefferson's wall, Barton asserted, was "one directional" and he always intended for there to be "Christian principles" in government.

I can't tell you how many times I've had fundamentalists throw this at me on talk radio. It's easily debunked because it's such folderol. As I pointed out in my first book, *Why the Religious Right Is Wrong About the Separation of Church and State,* Jefferson's views on the evils of mixing church and state are well known and easily verified. He definitely saw his "wall" as good for both church and state. Jefferson knew what the combination of church and state had done to Europe. He had no desire to bring that conflict to the United States. He saw church-state separation as the way to ensure that it never happened.

Barton supplements his income traveling around the country giving speeches on why the United States was founded to be a Christian nation and offering up his little cut-and-paste revisionist history. He gets angry when I point out in the media that on two occasions he has given speeches before white supremacist organizations. I am not saying, and never have said, that Barton has any sympathy with racist hate groups. Indeed, I do not believe he does.

However, he did on two occasions speak to such organizations. That is a fact. I believed he showed bad judgment.[3]

When peddling his bogus history, Barton's favorite technique is to cite instances of church-state union from the colonial or post–Revolutionary War periods and insist that these somehow mean that separation of church and state is a bad idea. He seems unable to grasp the fact that the country has changed since 1740 and that certain practices that may have seemed to make sense then would not be acceptable now.

In the eighteenth century, when the nation was overwhelmingly Protestant, it was not uncommon for government to discriminate against Roman Catholics, Jews, and members of other faith groups or for the government to assume the religious trappings of the majority. That seemed the "natural" way of doing things, just as for a long time owning slaves and denying women the right to vote seemed to be the proper way to order society. Today we know better and should never hesitate to label those old practices just plain wrong, even though they are historic and in some sense even "traditional."

Here's one example: In 1994 Barton lectured to the Christian Coalition and showed a slide of Delaware's 1776 state constitution. It required officeholders to profess faith in the Trinity and a belief that the Old and New Testaments were divinely inspired. These types of "religious tests" for public office were common in many of the colonies. (Remember, most of the colonies had state-established churches.)

I am always amazed when I hear anyone in this day and age speak approvingly of religious qualifications for public office. What exactly are they saying—that only fundamentalist Christians should have full citizenship rights? Would they exclude Jews, mainline Protestants, Muslims, and those skeptical of religion from public office? If that's a "Christian nation," I think most Americans will say no thanks. Barton insists his views are mainstream. Requiring people to believe certain things about religion before they can hold public office may be mainstream in Afghanistan, but it isn't here.

The following year Barton resurfaced at the Coalition's "Road to Victory." This time he played past and loose with the facts about the drafting of the Constitution. Barton asserted that Gouverneur Morris, a colonial leader from Pennsylvania, "wrote the Constitution." This is simply not accurate. Morris served on a committee that drafted the Constitution. He was later asked to make the document stylistically uniform—in other words, give it a good edit.

For some reason, Barton was absent from several "Road to Victory" gatherings in the late 1990s, though he was back in 1999. But he still makes the rounds in other Religious Right circles. On May 2, 1996, he appeared on James Dobson's Focus on the Family radio program, where he spread more misinformation about Thomas Jefferson's famous 1802 letter to the Danbury Baptists of Connecticut, which contains the well-known "wall of separation between church and state" metaphor. During that interview, Barton told Dobson, "In Jefferson's full letter, he said separation of church and state means the government will not run the church, but we will still use Christian principles with government."[4]

Let me state this, once again, as clearly as I can: Jefferson's letter to the Danbury Baptists says *no such thing*. It simply is not in there. Barton must know the truth by now, yet he continues to spread false stories. It is breathtaking to me that Barton continues to say these things, when anyone could look up the letter and see that his claims are plainly made up out of whole cloth. Perhaps he knows that his target audience will never bother to do this. As for what this says about Barton's credibility, draw your own conclusions.

It is simply incredible for anyone to believe that Jefferson would have advocated fundamentalist Christian principles in government. This is the man, after all, who took a pair of scissors to the Bible, cutting out all of the references to Jesus' divinity, the miracles, and other stories that Jefferson considered too fantastic to be true. Jefferson admired Jesus' moral teachings, but he strongly doubted that Christ was the Son of God. Jefferson has nothing in common with today's Religious Right, and if he were alive and running for office today, I can only imagine the character assassination they would use against him. After all, their predecessors did it to him in the late eighteenth century.

As I was writing this book, Barton sent me—and a few thousand others, I would guess—a short video clip promoting his new "Spiritual Heritage of America's Capitol" project. Barton asked for funds to make a video showing the religious heritage of the Capitol Building and other Washington institutions. During the clip, Barton said his video will prove that "religion and morality were part of our public life" during the founding period. The problem with this statement is that it's not Barton's argument. No one in his right mind would dispute that religion and morality were part of public life during the founding. (And guess what, they still are today.) That's not what the debate is about. The debate is over whether the country was founded to be some type of Christian fundamentalist theocracy or a secular state that guarantees religious freedom for all.

Barton, who has issued several videos promoting his views, said this new one will be a "first-class professional production" featuring dramatizations and even animation. But the dramatizations on the preview clip looked as cheesy as any other Barton production. (Note to the producers: Find a way to keep those powdered wigs from slipping off the actors' heads!) Although I did not contribute to the video's estimated $150,000 price tag, I am eagerly awaiting its release.

To sum up: I do not believe David Barton is qualified to critique history or social studies standards in any state. He is not a historian, he is a propagandist. Barton is the type of person whom the Religious Right, if it had any sense, would have long ago sent out to pasture. Instead, they have made him a hero. Only in the Religious Right can one pass off slipshod research and win kudos for it. Barton wouldn't last five minutes in a real academic setting.

THE CATHOLIC LEAGUE FOR RELIGIOUS AND CIVIL RIGHTS

The Catholic League for Religious and Civil Rights is a New York City-based organization run by William A. Donohue that exists primarily to scream bloody murder any time anyone dares to criticize the political goals of the Roman Catholic Church.

It's an effective strategy. By equating criticism of the church's political efforts with criticism of the Catholic religion generally, Donohue has managed to intimidate many people. But not everyone cowers before him.

I've had a few run-ins with Donohue over the years on television (not nearly as many as Americans United Executive Director Barry W. Lynn). His standard operating procedure is to yell a lot and interrupt frequently. I simply yelled back. I don't suppose this made for fascinating television, but often it's what passes for a dialogue on the issues these days.

Prior to his elevation at the Catholic League, Donohue made his living cranking out books attacking the American Civil Liberties Union. The League, originally founded by the late Rev. Virgil Blum, advocates government funding of parochial schools, opposes abortion and gay rights, works to counter alleged "anti-Catholic" bias in the media, and the like. The group has been around for a while, and in many ways it is a historical curiosity. The League seems to cling to a rapidly fading view of ultraconservative Catholicism, common in the country prior to the moderating reforms of Vatican II, which ran from 1962–1965. One doesn't quite know whether to think the League is quaint or scary.

Needless to say, the vast majority of American Catholics disagree with the stands taken by the League, and although the group claims to have an outrageously high membership, the real figures are probably negligible, especially when one considers that there are at least fifty million Roman Catholics in the country. The group was nearly moribund in the early 1990s and was brought back to life only through the efforts of John Cardinal O'Connor of New York.

The Catholic League seems to see anti-Catholicism or, more generally, hostility toward religion, lurking behind every tree. A few years ago at Christmastime I remember debating a League staffer on Fox News Channel about a controversial painting a department store in New York had displayed in the window.

The painting depicted Santa Claus being crucified on a cross. The League went ballistic. On the air, I tried to explain to the League representative that maybe the artist was actually on his side. It seemed to me that the painting was making the statement that, by substituting Santa for Jesus at Christmas, we have misplaced our priorities and lost sight of what the holiday is supposed to be all about.

The League rep just didn't get it. He insisted that the painting would frighten small children, but a moment later suggested that if the artist were trying to make a statement about the overcommercialization of Christmas, perhaps he should have painted Santa being lynched. (I'm sure that would have made the kids feel better.)

By shouting and huffing and puffing, the League is occasionally able to win concessions from television networks, advertisers, and such. In 1999, the group complained about a reference to the Catholic Church in Fox TV's animated *The Simpsons*. The segment in question was an ad parody that depicted scantily clad women provocatively washing a car while wearing crosses around their necks. The tag line was, "The Catholic Church—we've made some changes!" When the episode was run again, the word "religion" was substituted for "the Catholic Church."

In 1997 the League bombarded ABC with protests after the network began airing *Nothing Sacred*, a weekly drama about an unconventional, liberal priest in an inner-city parish. Donohue took the credit when the show was cancelled, but in reality it was axed because it failed to find an audience and was plagued by low ratings. (Having seen one episode, I understand why.)

Other League protests have been less successful. In 1998, the group complained after a theater in New York City agreed to stage a production of a play called *Corpus Christi*, which allegedly depicted Jesus as a gay man. The Catholic League and other groups protested, but the play opened. It had a short run and was not a hit with the critics.

The League is unique among Religious Right groups because of its Catholic origins. Most Religious Right groups are Protestant in character. The Christian Coalition, for example, has only a small Catholic membership. When Ralph Reed was at the Coalition, he talked a lot about finding ways to bring Catholics on board. For a while the Coalition even had a Catholic affiliate, the Catholic Alliance. (It is now a separate organization.) Donohue would seem a natural ally for Robertson, but their relationship has been strained by the Coalition's occasional lapses into anti–Catholicism.

In 1996, Americans United criticized Ralph Reed for endorsing an off-the-wall prophecy book written by John Wheeler Jr., former editor of the Christian Coalition's *Christian American* newspaper. The book, *Earth's Two-Minute Warning*, really was strange. It warned that the Catholic Church could merge with mainline Protestant groups and become the "Great Whore" of the biblical book of Revelation. Furthermore, Wheeler wrote, the Vatican could become "satanically empowered" and "one day run amok."[5]

Americans United pointed out Reed's endorsement to Donohue, who issued a statement criticizing Reed. But Reed called Donohue and smoothed his feathers by saying he had provided the endorsement as a favor and had not read the whole book. Donohue then retracted the statement and issued one attacking Americans United instead.

I knew it would only be a matter of time before Robertson said something odd about Catholics again, so I bided my time and waited for the volatile televangelist to stab Donohue in the back yet again. Sure enough, Robertson went on a tear about six months later and criticized Catholic teachings on divorce during a *700 Club* episode and even dared to ridicule the pope. Donohue promptly fired off a letter of complaint.

The fact is, Robertson has a track record of ridiculing or misinterpreting Catholic theology. I discuss this in my book on Robertson, *The Most Dangerous Man in America?* Given Robertson's propensity to shoot from the hip and criticize other faiths, if Donohue wants to get cozy with the Christian Coalition, he'd better develop thicker skin—or simply remember that old saw about what happens when you lie down with dogs.

TRADITIONAL VALUES COALITION

The Traditional Values Coalition is a small Religious Right outfit run by the Rev. Louis P. Sheldon, a California minister who splits his time between that state and Washington, D.C. When Sheldon is not in the nation's capital, his daughter Andrea oversees lobbying. (Lou Sheldon was ordained in the Presbyterian Church in America, an ultraconservative strain of Presbyterianism.)

Sheldon was raised Jewish but converted to Christianity at age sixteen. He was ordained in 1960 and pastored churches in North Dakota before relocating to California in 1969. In the mid-1970s he worked briefly for Pat Robertson, commuting weekly between Virginia Beach and Anaheim, California.

In 1981, Sheldon founded the American Liberties Institute, later renamed the California Coalition for Traditional Values. When Sheldon decided to make the group a national organization, he changed its name to the Traditional Values Coalition (TVC). The group claims to be a coalition of conservative churches and says it represents some forty-three thousand congregations. It advocates all of the usual Religious Right positions: antiabortion, pro–fundamentalist Christianity in government, antigay policies, Christian fundamentalism in the public schools, and pro–private school vouchers.[6]

In the crowded world of Religious Right organizations, Sheldon has tried to carve out a niche for himself through constant gay bashing. Sheldon was riding this donkey long before other Religious Right organizations climbed aboard, but it hasn't made him a household name. Now the issue is being taken from him and exploited more skillfully by larger organizations, which see it as a cash cow. It can be a dog-eat-dog world in the Religious Right.

Nevertheless, Sheldon has some influence on Capitol Hill. In 1995 he persuaded conservative House members to hold hearings on the alleged homosexual infiltration of public education. The House Education Subcommittee on Oversight and Investigations held two days of vague and meandering hearings in December, during which no specific evidence or charges were presented. The move backfired, however, when some conservatives perceived the effort as an attempt at federal control of education. Former Education Secretary William Bennett testified, but, in a rare bout with lucidity, said local schools should be free to design and implement their own curricula. After the committee heard from a few disgruntled parents unhappy with tolerance programs in their local schools, the hearings ended.

Rep. Steve Gunderson, a gay Republican from Wisconsin, told a gay newspaper in Washington, D.C., "I don't think anyone can walk away from those hearings and say any case was made that homosexuality is being promoted in the nation's schools."[7]

A month before the hearing Sheldon came under fire after he was asked to deliver the opening invocation before Congress. Sheldon had been invited to give the prayer by a California Republican. When a group of Democrats got wind of it, they complained to then–House Speaker Newt Gingrich saying that Sheldon, a registered lobbyist, should not have had access to the House floor. (They also complained that his views are bigoted.) Gingrich dismissed the complaints, and his press secretary called Sheldon's appearance "perfectly appropriate."[8]

Sheldon immediately mailed a fund-raising letter to his supporters, charging that the "liberal, anti-family Democrats are attacking me for praying before an opening session of Congress."

I've had a few run-ins with Sheldon and his daughter in Washington over the years. I once debated Lou Sheldon on a now-defunct cable channel. Both Sheldons are pleasant enough on a personal basis, but they do hold far-right views. In 1985, for example, Lou Sheldon proposed that people suffering from AIDS be voluntarily isolated in "cities of refuge" similar to leper colonies.[9]

In 1993, Lou Sheldon spoke at an Americans United conference. He debated Skipp Porteous, a former fundamentalist minister turned church-state separation activist. To his credit, Sheldon did not try to soften his views before a hostile crowd and said, "I believe in a separated church and state; I do not believe in the separation of church and state. . . . It is very important for us to note that the phrase 'separation of church and state' was, in our modern time, to my knowledge, first really brought forth in a significant way by the Supreme Court in 1947."[10]

Despite his close ties to the GOP, Sheldon's TVC claims a tax-exempt status. In 1994, it received $47,000 from the state Republican Party for "voter education" activities. (Sheldon serves on the California Republican Central Committee.) He has in the past been something of a player in Golden State politics, where the state's Republican Party is dominated by the Religious Right. The recent Democratic ascendancy in the state has undoubtedly reduced his influence and may lead Sheldon to focus more time, attention, and money on Washington.

Sheldon's influence in California suffered another blow in August of 1999, when the TVC became embroiled in controversy after the *Orange County Register* reported that casino gambling interests had secretly paid Lou Sheldon's son, Steve, $156,000 since 1993 to persuade religious groups to oppose "card clubs" in California. The paper reported than an additional $20,000 of casino money went directly to Lou Sheldon's organization—$10,000 from a race-track in 1994 and $10,000 in 1998 from a group set up by Nevada casinos to fight a ballot proposal that would have allowed Indian tribes to sponsor gambling.[11]

Nevada-based casinos were eager to stop any expansion of legalized gambling in California, since the competition might decrease their business. They hoped to galvanize religious opposition to the expansion of gambling and enlisted Steve Sheldon, who serves as a legal consultant to the TVC, apparently hoping to influence Lou Sheldon as well. Steve Sheldon took on the assignment, but, the newspaper reported, many of the ministers he approached were not aware that he was on the casinos' payroll.[12]

"I never had a direct conversation with Lou," said Charles G. Westlund Jr., a consultant to the gambling industry. "However, it was clear what you were hiring Steve Sheldon to do. And then Lou Sheldon would turn up at the [antigambling] rallies. I hired Steve Sheldon and the Traditional Values Coalition to stir up anxiety in those communities."[13]

A California man who once worked for the Commerce Casino was more blunt. "God for hire, that's what I call it," said Hal Mintz, who worked with Steve Sheldon in 1995. "Everyone said, 'Steve's not too important, but his dad is.' . . . You wouldn't buy Steve unless you could buy Lou [too]. Everybody knows that."[14]

A minister in Pico Rivera said Steve Sheldon called him in 1995, mentioned his father, and asked the minister to join an effort to oppose card clubs in the community. The minister, the Rev. Richard Ochoa, told the *Register* that Steve Sheldon never mentioned his funding from the casino industry and if he had "I would have ousted him on the spot."[15]

Lou Sheldon's defense was creative. Asked about a $10,000 contribution he had accepted from Hollywood Park Racetrack in 1994, Sheldon replied, "Politics makes strange bedfellows. The devil had that money long enough. It was about time we got our hands on it."[16]

He added, "We want to stop the expansion of gambling. . . . If we can cut a deal with Hollywood Park [like] we did a number of years ago, that's fine with us. If they can meet our standard, we will accept a donation from them to help us fulfill our mission."[17]

But one religious leader who works full-time opposing the spread of legalized gambling disagreed with Sheldon's rationale. "This is a product that brings addiction, bankruptcy, crime, and corruption," said the Rev. Tom Grey, head of the National Coalition Against Legalized Gambling. "If you take the industry's money to fight it, you corrupt the message."[18]

One of the TVC's most recent activities was to launch a witch hunt—literally. On July 7, 1999, the organization mailed a fundraising letter, signed by Andrea Sheldon, claiming that a witch is casting evil spells over the Congress. In it, Sheldon talked about observing the Senate deliberate over a bill designed to combat juvenile crime and wrote that during the first few days of debate, "I could not believe the spirit of confusion that seemed to control the Senate. I do not remember a time when I sensed such confusion." She went on to say: "One morning I was waiting to speak with a Senator when I noticed a woman, who I had seen for years and always felt an emanating bad spirit. She had been walking around the room and then sat down and gave the appearance of praying. When I approached to speak to her, her face became contorted and she raised her hand to strike me. Shortly after that encounter I was told she is a witch who comes to the Senate every day and congers [sic] up evil spirits. She has a counterpart who joins her every Tuesday. It became clear to me then why there was such a spirit of confusion."[19]

I don't doubt that there was a lot of confusion in the Senate that day—both in Andrea Sheldon's head and among many of the Senators who are willing to do her bidding. I seriously doubt, however, that witches had anything to do with it.

CHRISTIAN ACTION NETWORK

There are some Religious Right organizations that little time should be spent worrying about. The Christian Action Network (CAN) is one of these organizations. The reason is that CAN doesn't appear to actually do very much of anything except mail out hysterical fund-raising letters.

The Christian Action Network is based in Forest, Virginia, and headed by Martin Mawyer, a former Moral Majority official. Just about all of its fund-raising letters deal with one of two issues: exposing the latest "nefarious scheme" cooked up by the gay community or trying to end government funding of the National Endowment for the Arts. Occasionally Mawyer does try to branch out. Several recent letters warned about the coming "one-world government."

Most of my knowledge of CAN comes from its fund-raising mail. To give you a flavor of what these letters are like, consider one Mawyer mailed in January 1998, after the title character on ABC's *Ellen* sitcom "came out" as a lesbian: "The title character in the ABC-TV sitcom 'Ellen' came out of the closet . . . AND DUMPED HER FILTHY LESBIAN LIFESTYLE RIGHT IN THE CENTER OF YOUR LIVING ROOM!! IT'S THE FIRST TIME IN THE HISTORY OF NETWORK TV THAT THE LEAD CHARACTER IS A SODOMITE!" Mawyer goes on to write, "Do you think TV ever portrays homosexuals as they really are? Having sex with hundreds of other perverts in 'one-night stands' . . . spreading their filthy sex diseases to millions of people . . . molesting innocent children . . . flaunting their grotesque lifestyle . . . committing murder and sex crimes more than any other group of people. . . ."

But my all-time favorite CAN letter did not deal directly with either gays, the NEA, or global government. Instead, Mawyer sought to raise funds because he and Executive Director Bob Hinkle had been in a bad auto accident on the way back from Washington while driving on "Interstate 29" in Virginia. (They meant U.S. Route 29; there is no such road as Interstate 29 in Virginia.) Thanks, we are led to believe, to the guiding hand of God, both men emerged with just scratches—although Hinkle, who was apparently not wearing a seatbelt, flew threw the windshield. But the CAN van took a real beating, and they would need to buy a new one. The really pathetic thing about this letter was that it was mailed in September of 1998—two years after Mawyer said the accident occurred!

In August of 1999, Mawyer tried that old right-wing fund-raising mail stalwart of sending out a letter over his wife's signature. I see this type of letter so often from Religious Right groups that I've coined a name for it: the "My Poor Husband" letter.

The "My Poor Husband" letter usually begins with a claim that, for some reason or another, donations to group X have dropped off sharply. Group X may not be able to keep its doors open and continue its valiant struggle against gays, public education, one-world government, the ACLU, anti-Christian fanatics, and so on. All of this has naturally affected the head of the organization, who bears a heavy burden as he labors to single-handedly save Western civilization from these forces of darkness.

Bonnie Mawyer seemed to know the script. After warning of the possible imminent demise of the Christian Action Network, she wrote, "Gifts to help the work of CAN are critically down this long, hot summer. I have never seen Martin so burdened. He checks the mail first thing every morning to see how many friends have written."

It's rare to see someone on the Religious Right be so frank about greed. I'll bet Martin looks every day to see how many "friends" have written. And if those friends don't send him big checks, they probably won't remain his friends for long.

For some reason, Bonnie Mawyer (or whoever prepared this letter for her) thought it would be a good idea to enclose some snapshots with it. One showed Martin Mawyer, dressed as Uncle Sam, demonstrating against "one-world government" at the United Nations in New York City. He was accompanied by six CAN activists. Four were dressed as Native Americans—or, more accurately, what someone at CAN believes a Native American looks like. (Yes, it was offensive.) One employee was dressed as the Grim Reaper. The last man was decked out like a Nazi.

Unfortunately, no context was given for the photograph. We were not told why Mawyer and his employees felt it necessary to don these outlandish outfits to battle UN globalism. As a result, the first thought that popped into my head was that things can't be all that bad at CAN. After all, Mawyer has enough money to buy or rent costumes and make a fool of himself and his employees during a junket to New York City.

Americans United tries to keep an eye on as many Religious Right groups as possible, and we pay special attention to their activities in Washington. CAN doesn't seem to have any significant activities in Washington—and few others elsewhere, for that matter. The group did manage to get itself sued by the Federal Election Commission in 1992 for running newspaper and TV ads attacking then-candidate Bill Clinton for supporting gay rights. CAN won the case when a federal court ruled that the ads were a permissible form of issue advocacy, not intervention in a partisan campaign.

In short, CAN seems to be a good example of how a Religious Right activist can lead a comfortable life without doing much work, provided he has the right ingredients—in this case a large mailing list of gullible people, access to the U.S. mail system, and absolutely no shame.

CITIZENS FOR EXCELLENCE IN EDUCATION

In 1988 I interviewed Dr. Robert Simonds, founder of Citizens for Excellence in Education (CEE), for the publication *Church & State* about his ambitious plans to take over the public school system for fundamentalist Christianity. Simonds's plan was simple: Find people who think like he does and get them elected to school boards to change local policies. End or water down the teaching of evolution. Toss out books considered "immoral." Work fundamentalism into the curriculum whenever possible.

Simonds founded CEE in 1983 as an arm of his National Association of Christian Educators. In an early fund-raising letter, he outlined his goals: "The enclosed information will tell you of our Lord's plans to bring public education back under the control of the Christian community. There are 15,700 school districts in America. When we get an active Christian parents' committee in operation in all districts, we can take complete control of all local school boards. This would allow us to determine all local policy; select good textbooks; good curriculum programs; superintendents and principals. Our time has come!"[20]

A September 1985 letter spoke of plans for "Christian parents and Christian teachers and students" to take "DOMINION over our schools and our nation."

The focus on local school boards made sense. In many parts of the country, voter turnout for local elections is modest at best. By mobilizing a bloc of Christian fundamentalist voters, CEE could manage to have a disproportionate effect on election outcomes.

When I talked to Simonds, I remember thinking that his movement would either be a spectacular success or a total flop. I doubted anything in the middle was possible. Now, eleven years later, I'm going to cast my ballot for "total flop."

But for a while, at least, it looked like "spectacular success" was possible. CEE claimed an impressive number of activists and chapters in the early days. Although his figures would vary from interview to interview, Simonds told me the group had representatives in all fifty states and fifteen hundred local chapters. Indeed, in the early days of the group we at Americans United used to get calls regularly from people asking, "What is this group called CEE?" CEE people seemed to be out there.

But something went wrong. By 1990, Simonds was claiming to have 550 chapters nationwide. At that time, his group, based in Costa Mesa, California, was marketing a "Public School Awareness Kit" for $195 that included audiotapes and brochures instructing fundamentalist Christians in how to get elected to school boards. Seven years after its founding, the group still seemed to be getting started.

In 1992, Simonds claimed to have 925 chapters nationwide and took credit for electing thirty-one hundred conservative Christians to local school boards. (Also that year, he branded separation of church and state "a Socialist myth.")[21] Since Simonds refused to provide a list of these board members to the media, there was no way to verify his claims. I suspect they were wildly inflated.

The year 1992 seems to have marked a turning point for CEE. Some of the group's supporters did manage to get elected to school boards. Many of them popped up on boards in Southern California after a spate of low-turnout elections. The candidates had run low-profile campaigns during which they stressed issues like taxes and fiscal responsibility, not religion in public schools. The tactic led the media to dub these office seekers "stealth candidates."

But few boards had an actual CEE majority. One that did, in Vista, California, gained national attention after newly elected board members tried to ban antidrug and self-esteem programs. One parent connected with the group requested that the nursery rhyme "Jack and Jill" be removed from the school, saying it was metaphor for a descent into Hell. Eventually the board went too far and tried to replace the teaching of evolution with creationism in science classes. The community was becoming a laughingstock. Concerned parents organized a recall election and removed the CEE pawns from the board.[22]

Throughout the 1990s, CEE spent much time attacking "outcome-based education"—an educational process that requires students to show mastery over a certain topic, usually through some type of demonstration or written test, before moving on to advance study—and working to stifle education reform in many states. There was less talk about getting "Christians" elected to school boards. The group suffered another setback when a voucher initiative Simonds had endorsed was rejected overwhelmingly by California voters in 1993.

In 1996, Simonds angered many of his supporters when he endorsed an effort spearheaded by several public education groups to find "common ground" with religious conservatives on contentious religion-in-public-schools issues. In one article, Simonds went so far as to write, "I now promote a peace process that seeks common ground. The idea is to focus on the principles that the aggrieved parties hold in common—in this case, to provide the best education possible for the nation's children."[23]

I ran into Simonds at a U.S. Education Department ceremony in February of 1996 announcing the release of the "common ground" document and was struck by how different his rhetoric was. It almost made sense. Had Simonds turned over a new leaf?

Alas, no. Even during the "common ground" effort, Simonds continued to attack public education in fund-raising letters, although he did tone his rhetoric down a bit. By February of 1998 he came full circle. He ratcheted up the rhetoric again, attacked the "common ground" effort, and endorsed Rescue 2010, a Religious Right plan calling on Christian fundamentalists to remove their children from public schools by the year 2010.

In a bitter letter, dated February 1998, full of denunciations and anti–public school rhetoric, Simonds said of the "common ground" effort, "School officials have used this for a stalling tactic, rather than an open dialogue for solutions. That's understandable, but just more of the same deceit tactics."

Elsewhere in the letter Simonds wrote, "Deception in our

schools is the rule, not sincerity; arrogance, not cooperation. Therefore, after 15 years of sincere efforts to gain parental rights, a 'safe passage' curriculum for our dear innocent children, the Lord has counseled me, and an impressive array of those associated in ministry have confirmed God leading, that Christians must exit the public schools as soon as it is feasible and possible. The price in human loss, social depravity and the spiritual slaughter of our young Christian children is no longer acceptable (and certainly never was!)."

I could have saved the "common ground" folks a lot time by filling them in on Simonds early on. The man is strange. His fundraising letters are rambling tirades full of capital letters and baseless charges. (They remind me of the "crank mail" Americans United often receives from irate fundamentalists. Usually the entire page is covered with typewritten copy, and there are handwritten notes on the margins—sometimes drawings. They always end with calls for us to "repent now!") To me, Simonds always seemed to be one of the least likely prospects for successful dialogue. Meaningful discussions require that all participants be reasonable. Simonds fails that test.

In April of 1999 Simonds issued another bizarre fund-raising letter, this one claiming that many of his supporters had deserted him over his endorsement of Rescue 2010.

"CEE is almost totally shackled because of the 50% drop in giving since we added rescuing our children from public schools to our agenda," he wrote. "If you think, beloved, we can do this alone—*it is over!*"

It has been a long, strange trip for Citizens for Excellence in Education. Is it over? One can only hope.

CHRISTIAN RECONSTRUCTIONISTS

Christian Reconstructionists believe that the legal code laid out in the Old Testament should be binding on Americans today. In a sense, I guess you could say they are the Religious Right taken to the extreme—pun intended.

It's tempting to believe that the Christian Reconstructionists were invented by a fiction writer to be colorful characters in some rollicking comic novel, but nope. They're real; they mean it.

Christian Reconstructionists would execute people for the following crimes: murder, striking or cursing a parent, kidnapping, adultery, incest, bestiality, homosexuality, "unchastity," rape of a betrothed virgin, witchcraft, offering human sacrifice, incorrigible delinquency, blasphemy, propagation of false doctrines, sacrificing to false gods, and refusing to abide by court decisions that uphold "Godly law." Some insist the Bible mandates death by stoning.[24]

When I read this list, the first thing I thought was, "Whoa! There aren't going to be a lot of people left when these folks take over." I'll admit, they aren't likely to get many people on the human sacrifice thing, but that "unchastity" business is going to bring a lot of folks down. Executing people for "propagation of false doctrines" could make the streets run red as well.

Back in 1988, I interviewed Rousas John Rushdoony, considered the dean of Reconstructionism and founder of something called the Chalcedon Institute in Vallecito, California. I was one of the first writers to take a serious look at this movement. Rushdoony was very polite, and he struck me as obviously well-read. He seemed completely sincere. He told me he strives to abide by every law in the Old Testament and even keeps the strict dietary regulations of Leviticus and Exodus. The biblical rules in question forbid the consumption of pork, shellfish, catfish, liver, and other foods as well as any food or drink that has sat uncovered in the same room as a dead person.[25] (Leviticus also warns against wearing clothing of mixed fibers, so I assumed that cotton/polyester shirts were out for Rushdoony, unless, technically, polyester does not count as a fiber. There are always loopholes.)

One of the problems with Reconstructionism is that its adherents tend to be a bit sure of themselves and their interpretation of the Bible. They brook no dissent. Thus, Rushdoony has reportedly not spoken to his own son-in-law, Reconstructionist writer Gary North, in nearly twenty years because they had a falling-out over some obscure doctrinal point.[26]

North is the author of dozens of books. Most of them are really thick and deal with arcane topics or the "biblical" view of finance. I have a bunch of them in my office and I defy anyone to actually read any of them all the way through.

North is fond of predicting the imminent collapse of American society. He used to live in Tyler, Texas, but the last I heard of him he was holed up in an isolated compound in rural Arkansas, convinced that the Y2K problem was going to bring America down. According to North, cities would quickly devolve into *Mad Max*–type war zones as panicky humans turned on one another to survive. If you are holding this book, and it is the year 2000 or later, it will be proof that Y2K doomsayers badly overestimated the extent of the problem—and that North is, once again, dead wrong.

Rushdoony, North, and the other Reconstructionists do tend to obsess over arcane points of law. Rushdoony's two-volume magnum opus, *The Institutes of Biblical Law*, attempts to spell out all that would be permitted and all that would not in a Reconstructionist society. But there are a few problems trying to graft ancient biblical codes onto modern society. *The Institutes*, for example, contains a lengthy passage dealing with what is to be done if an ox gores a man or another ox. I can't speak for everyone, but I do know that it has been a long time since there has been an ox-goring in my suburban neighborhood. I'm more concerned about what should be done if my neighbor's sport utility vehicle gores my economy car.

Rushdoony's *Institutes* also states that gossip should be illegal, asserts that unisex fashions are a rebellion against God, and mandates that a man refrain from having sex with his wife for forty days after the birth of a male child and eighty days for a female child.[27] (How on earth are they going to enforce this stuff?)

Their ideas may sound daft, but the Reconstructionists should not be dismissed. Their writings have influenced many Religious Right leaders. Pat Robertson has stated that he disagrees with Reconstructionist teachings, but Reconstructionists have been hired at Robertson's Regent University, and he sometimes seems to flirt with their rhetoric and at least once quoted North favorably on the *700 Club*.[28] Many Religious Right activists have discarded the more unpalatable aims of the Reconstructionists but have embraced their underlying theory, chiefly the idea that the Bible is more than just a religious text, it's also a blueprint for running a government.

James Dobson of Focus on the Family plays footsy with the Reconstructionists all the time. Dobson backed Howard Phillips of the U.S. Taxpayers Party (USTP) for president in 1996. The USTP is essentially the Reconstructionists' political arm. In the summer of 1995, Dobson met with Phillips for ninety minutes at Focus on the Family headquarters in Colorado Springs. "Jim Dobson was, I would say, very supportive of the work of the U.S. Taxpayers Party," Joseph Slovenec, executive director of the party, told reporters in Washington on August 8, 1995. "Now, are they going to jump over? I can't answer that question. Will they add some help to us? I believe they will."[29]

The USTP platform reads like the outline of a bad right-wing conspiracy theory novel. For instance, it denounces a United Nations–led plot to impose a "New World Order" on America. This is a frequent obsession of the far-far-right.

Also appearing at the August 8 press conference was radical antiabortion protestor Randall Terry. I attended the event, which the party held in front of the National Republican Center on Capitol Hill as a way to rebuke the backsliding GOP. There were precious few reporters there, so I took the opportunity to ask Slovenec if Phillips would be the party's presidential candidate again. Slovenec sneered and said that would not happen. The following year, Phillips, who founded the party in 1990, accepted its nomination.

Dobson's Focus on the Family also sells a Christian Reconstructionist book titled *A New World in View*.[30] The book is coauthored by Gary DeMar, who runs the Reconstructionist group American Vision in Smyrna, Georgia. Focus on the Family markets the book as a "teacher's aid," lauding it as "a glimpse at God's participation in history from the Classical Age (when Greeks and Romans battled the Christian worldview) through the early sixteenth century (the age of exploration)." DeMar has stated that the Bible mandates the death penalty for homosexuals and "abortionists."[31] (USTP officials also once met with TV preacher D. James Kennedy in Washington, and Kennedy once spoke at a conference sponsored by DeMar.)[32]

This business of executing nearly everyone in sight is the Reconstructionists' Achilles' heal. But they just don't seem to care. In January of 1999, Rushdoony's *Chalcedon Report* magazine carried an article by a Pennsylvania pastor, the Rev. William Einwechter, defending the practice of stoning disobedient teenagers. Einwechter cited Deut. 21:18–21, which says that parents should take a stubborn and rebellious son before city elders to be stoned to death if the youngster will not change his ways. Einwechter said the punishment is to be limited to older children—above "middle teens"— and is to be employed only after other methods of discipline have failed. Stoning, he argued, is not to be used for minor offenses such as talking back but rather when "a grown son (and by extension to a daughter as well) who, for whatever reason, has rebelled against the authority of his parents and will not profit from any of their discipline nor obey their voice in any thing."

According to Einwechter, the stoning of a naughty teen is actually a merciful act, as it preserves the moral order and "prevents the destruction of the family, society, and others. . . ." It also "strikes fear in the heart of other would-be rebels and restrains them from taking a similar ruinous course."[33]

Will America ever be free of these extremists? There is hope. In the mid-1990s a number of Reconstructionists became enamored of the central African nation of Zambia, lauding the alleged "Christian" regime of President Frederick Chiluba. Chiluba has declared the country officially Christian. Under his rule, abortion is illegal, censorship is common, and fundamentalist strains of Christianity are taught in public schools.

Chiluba's critics say he is a typical tinhorn dictator who oppresses the political opposition and declares emergency powers at the drop of a hat. But the Reconstructionists are keeping the faith, and some have speculated that once Zambia is totally "reconstructed" as a model society, it could be used as a base for missionary efforts to the United States. (I should point out that Pat Robertson is also chummy with Chiluba. On April 25, 1995, Robertson hosted Chiluba on the *700 Club*, lauded him as the type of president America should have, and called Zambia "a standard for not only Africa but the rest of the world.")

If the Christian Reconstructionists would just think this thing through, I believe they would agree with me that they should all relocate to Zambia immediately. It makes a lot more sense than trying to purify wicked, debased, immoral, ungodly America. (Aren't we long overdue to be destroyed à la Sodom and Gomorrah anyway?) The Reconstructionists have been plugging away for decades now, and we haven't had one decent stoning. Blasphemers and the unchaste walk the streets with impunity. Incorrigible children run amok in our houses. Oxen gore and go unpunished. There comes a time when, instead of throwing stones, one should throw in a towel. To the Reconstructionists I say: Onward, Christian soldiers! Zambia awaits.

WILLIAM MURRAY

There are well-known, well-funded, and active Religious Right organizations in America. Then there are a host of lesser-known, second-tier groups. Then there are third-tier groups. Keep going and you hit the real dregs. Go even lower than that and you hit William Murray.

Murray is the son of the famous (and missing) atheist Madalyn Murray O'Hair, who brought one of the cases that removed government-sponsored Christian worship from public schools. Murray rejected his mother's atheism and is now a born-again Christian (Murray calls himself an "evangelist") and right-wing political activist.

Murray has lurked for years on the fringes of the Religious Right, somehow managing to eke out a living. During the congressional debate over the Religious Right's so-called Religious Freedom Amendment in 1998, he occasionally appeared at Capitol Hill press conferences. But his efforts to become a national figure have been stymied. In 1995, Murray wrote a book about his life, *Let Us Pray*, which was picked up by a major publishing house.[34] It flopped. He sometimes speaks in churches, telling the crowd that his mother filed her lawsuit against school prayer on orders from Soviet Russia.

Religious Right activists love these types of conversion stories, and I'm surprised that Murray isn't more of a star in their world. Part of the problem may be that he frequently behaves oddly. I debated him once on the Fox News Channel. Whenever I started speaking, he tried to shout me down. At one point, I dared to gesticulate, and Murray, who was sitting next to me, grabbed my arm in an (unsuccessful) effort to keep me from making my point.

Murray runs something called the God Is Not Government political action committee, which he formed during the tenure of Newt Gingrich as House speaker (GING-PAC, get it?), probably hoping that easily addled far right-wingers would assume it was a Gingrich project and throw money at it.

He also tried to run a pro–school prayer group out of Texas for a while, but in 1996 he relocated to Stafford County, Virginia. (One has to wonder why this perfectly nice state has been cursed with so many Religious Right leaders—first Jerry Falwell, then Pat Robertson, John Whitehead, Martin Mawyer, and now Murray.) In one especially pathetic fund-raising letter dated November 1995, Murray begged for financial support so he could flee Texas because "satanists" or perhaps followers of witchcraft (the letter is confusingly unclear on this point) had been harassing him. "MY LAWN HAS BEEN POISONED. MY TREES HAVE BEEN KILLED. ACID WAS POURED IN MY AIR CONDITIONER," read the opening lines of the letter. It was even accompanied by pictures of the afflicted lawn and air conditioner, but unfortunately, they were of such poor quality that they didn't prove anything.

I've seen some rather wretched Religious Right fund-raising mail in my day, but I have to say if I were to award a prize for the worst, this one would probably get it. The Christian Action Network's "send-us-money-for-a-van-we-wrecked-two-years-ago-while-speeding" appeal gives Murray's letter a decent run for it, but in the end I have to say the Murray piece has the edge due to the sheer stupidity of the thing when looked at in its entirety.

In case I have been too subtle, I'll say that I was not impressed with this particular fund-raising letter. I'm supposed to give money to a guy to help him hightail it out of town because the forces of darkness are playing a little rough? Show some backbone, o ye of little faith! One would have expected this great man of God to stand up to these godless hooligans and rebuke them—unless of course the whole thing was just a cheap stunt to raise money from suckers, in which case . . . oh, never mind.

NOTES

1. Rob Boston, "Consumer Alert!" *Church & State* (July–August 1996).

2. Barton originally cited two other "Christian nation" authors as his source for this quote. He now concedes that it cannot be verified. The works cited were Russ Walton, *Biblical Principles of Importance in Godly Christians* (Marlborough, N.M.: Plymouth Rock Foundation, 1984), and Stephen K. McDowall and Mark A. Beliles, *Principles for the Reformation of the Nations* (Charlottesville, Va.: Providence Press, 1988).

3. David Cantor, *The Religious Right: The Assault On Tolerance & Pluralism In America*, 2d ed. (New York: Anti-Defamation League, 1994), pp. 55–56.

4. "If 'Christian Vote' Stays Home In '96, Congressional Allies Could Lose, Says Dobson," *Church & State* (June 1996).

5. John Wheeler Jr., *Earth's Two-Minute Warning* (North Canton, Ohio: The Leader Company, 1996), pp. 58–60.

6. Marla Jo Fisher, "Values Leader, Son Accepted Casinos' Cash," *Orange County Register*, August 1, 1999.

7. Lou Chibbaro Jr., "Congressional Hearings Take Surprise Turn," *Washington Blade*, December 8, 1995.

8. "GOP Invokes Free Speech for Minister's Invocation," *Washington Post*, November 3, 1995.

9. Fisher, "Values Leader, Son Accepted Casinos' Cash."

10. Rob Boston, "Church, State and the Religious Right," *Church & State* (November 1993).

11. Fisher, "Values Leader, Son Accepted Casinos' Cash."

12. Ibid.

13. Ibid.

14. Ibid.

15. Ibid.

16. Ibid.

17. Ibid.

18. Ibid.

19. Traditional Values Coalition fund-raising letter, July 7, 1999.

20. Rob Boston, "CEE: 'Taking Dominion Over Our School and Nation,'" *Church & State* (June 1988).

21. "CEE Escalates War On Public Education, Wall of Separation," *Church & State* (September 1992).

22. Robert L. Simonds, "Common Ground with the Religious

Right," *Education Digest* (January 1997). Condensed from *School Adminis-trator* (November 1996).

23. Sonia L. Nazario, "Crusader Vows to Put God Back Into Schools Using Local Elections," *Wall Street Journal*, July 15, 1992.

24. Rousas John Rushdoony, *The Institutes of Biblical Law* (n.p.: The Craig Press, 1973).

25. Ibid.

26. Rob Boston, "Thy Kingdom Come," *Church & State* (September 1998).

27. Rushdoony, *The Institutes of Biblical Law*, p. 428.

28. Boston, "Thy Kingdom Come."

29. "Dobson Meets with Third-Party Extremist in Colorado Springs," *Church & State* (September 1995).

30. Gary DeMar and Fred Douglas Young, *A New World in View* (Powder Springs, Ga.: American Vision).

31. Frederick Clarkson, *Eternal Hostility: The Struggle Between Theocracy and Democracy* (Monroe, Maine: Common Courage Press), p. 82.

32. "TV Preacher Kennedy Endorses Bible Classes in Public Schools," *Church & State* (October 1995).

33. William Einwechter, "Stoning Disobedient Children," *Chalcedon Report* (January 1999).

34. William Murray and Ken Ross, *Let Us Pray: A Plea for Prayer in Our Schools* (New York: William Morrow & Co., 1995).

Chapter 9

WHAT'S TO BE DONE?

Responding to the Religious Right

When I speak to groups around the country, I tell it like it is: The Religious Right is a well-funded, well-organized extremist movement that thinks it knows better than you how to run the country (and by extension, your own life) by virtue of what it believes to be its superior religious system.

Reasonable people try to resolve differences in an amicable way. They do not shy away from dialogue and they bring a willingness to compromise to the table. This is a good instinct that many Americans share. Most of the time it bears good fruit—but only if all sides in a dispute harbor the same attitude.

But this spirit of cooperation and dialogue can be difficult to use with Religious Right groups. I have, time and time again, heard the way Religious Right leaders and activists talk about their perceived enemies at the types of meetings I have described in this book. At these gatherings, there is no talk of finding "common ground" or compromise. Instead, Religious Right leaders talk of "reclaiming America" or "taking back our culture" and use violent warfare imagery to describe how they will vanquish their foes, crush all opposition, and triumph over their "godless" enemies. Rather than try to reach a compromise with such people, we would do better to work to convince the majority of Americans who are currently sitting out the "culture wars" to resist Religious Right overtures.

How is that to be done? I'd like to conclude this book by outlining several strategies.

Political involvement is key. Whether you like it or not, the effort to defeat the Religious Right will be won or lost on the political battlefield. Many Americans are fed up with politics these days, an understandable sentiment considering how polluted the system is with money and dirty deals. But if people of goodwill drop out, that creates a power vacuum. The Religious Right thrives in a vacuum.

The battle is political, but it is not partisan. This is an important distinction. More and more, as I travel the country, I encounter disaffected Republicans who are angry about what the Religious Right has done to their party. I tell them to take it back. But don't look to my organization to do it. We are not in the business of partisan politics. Some other organization must be formed to undertake the drawn-out battle for the soul of the GOP. Is it worth winning? I believe most moderate or fiscal Republicans would say it absolutely is.

Several times in the past few years, moderate Republicans have announced the formation of national organizations to oppose the Religious Right's growing influence in the party. These groups are announced with much fanfare and then vanish. Why is this? I suspect it's because the moderates get cold feet or are pressured by party leaders to compromise for the good of the party. These leaders don't want to see the GOP ripped apart. This is understandable. But the moderates must realize that every time they agree to disengage, they are handing another victory to the Religious Right. If they continue to do nothing or pursue policies of appeasement, then their party will sooner or later be the exclusive property of people like Pat Robertson, Jerry Falwell, Gary Bauer, and James Dobson.

Register people to vote. Regardless of party affiliation, everyone who is concerned about the influence of the Religious Right on politics should be registered to vote. Religious Right groups have achieved success politically not because a majority of people agree with them, but because many people are not registered to vote or because registered voters don't go to the polls. Voter turnout for national elections is hovering around 50 percent these days. With so many people out of the game, it is easy to see how a fringe group can have a disproportionate influence on the outcome.

Religious Right groups frequently undertake voter-registration drives. There is nothing illegal or unethical about this. It is good political strategy. The groups tell their members to identify people sympathetic to their causes and register them. This is a tactic they borrowed from the Left, as are many of the pages in the Religious Right's political play book. The Religious Right didn't invent this stuff; they don't own it. Opposition groups can use it as well.

Work to increase voter turnout. Registering people to vote is not enough. Some people must be reminded to vote on primary and general election day. The Christian Coalition organizes a telephone tree every election day. I know this because I receive calls from them each and every time there is an election. In some cases, Religious Right groups will offer to transport people to the polls or organize carpools. Our side needs to do the same. Remember especially to call the older folks who may have problems with mobility or be intimidated if the weather is foul. Many of them would appreciate a ride to the polls.

Again, there is nothing unethical about any of this. Buying votes or pressuring people to vote one way or another would be illegal, but merely taking people to the polls is not. It's time-tested, effective political organizing. The bottom line: *Registering sympathetic voters is not enough. To boost turnout on election day, remind people to vote and offer transportation to the polls.*

Pay special attention to local politics. Turnout for local races can be very low in some parts of the country. If you're not careful, you could end up with Religious Right candidates on the school board or city/county council. Pay attention to the local races. Organize or attend voter forums where all of the candidates field questions from the audience. Ask pointed, specific questions about church-state issues. School board candidates should be prepared to explain their views on vouchers, creationism, and religion in the classroom. If a candidate for school board has children of school age, find out if they are attending the public schools. (In some communities, private school parents have captured school board seats in an effort to divert tax dollars to private education or set up voucher plans.)

Urge the local media to run in-depth profiles of all candidates for local office. Consider asking local papers to run their own voter's guides—guides that are balanced and that cover a range of issues, as opposed to Religious Right voter guides, which are stacked in favor of some candidates.

Work cooperatively with like-minded groups. Many different interest groups are concerned about the Religious Right. To the largest extent possible, these organizations should work together, share information and pool resources. Just about any group that opposes the Religious Right should be looked at as an ally. Good places to look for support include the reproductive rights community, gay rights groups, pro–public school organizations, mainline religious groups, women's rights groups, civil liberties organizations, and so on.

Respond to the Religious Right in public forums. Religious Right leaders complain incessantly about the "liberal media," yet they do not hesitate to use general circulation newspapers, magazines, talk radio, and other media outlets to spread their viewpoint. This is their right, but that does not mean their views should go unchallenged. Anyone concerned about the Religious Right should be prepared to respond to their charges through letters to the editor, op-ed columns, radio and TV commentaries, and so on.

Some people get intimidated about writing for publication. I urge folks to remember that their voice deserves to be heard, and they don't have to be professional writers to be published in the local newspaper. If you need help framing an argument, or if you need assistance responding to specific charges raised by Religious Right activists, the staff of Americans United for Separation of Church and State stands ready to help with advice and research assistance.

I do not believe that most Americans are naturally inclined to agree with the Religious Right. I do believe they can start to lean that way if they see only one side of the argument. That's why I have always been a strong advocate of a rapid response to Religious Right misrepresentations. Religious Right arguments are often simplistic (mandatory prayer in school equals less violence in society, for example), but they can still hold powerful appeal to people who have not taken the time to think through an issue. A response giving the other side helps clarify matters for all of those people on the fence.

Defend the separation of church and state. Do not assume that everyone thinks the separation of church and state is a great thing, like apple pie and motherhood. The separation principle has been taking a beating from Religious Right groups for years now. It needs defenders.

I often make the point that separation of church and state is one of those things that should not require defense because its benefits are all around us. In other words, separation of church and state works. We know that. Every time you walk into the house of worship of your choice, that's separation of church and state in action. If you decide to venture into the "religious free marketplace" and find a new faith or give them all up entirely, that's separation of church and state in action. When you run for public office without fear that you will have to sign a religious oath or meet a government-mandated religious test, that's separation of church and state in action. When you send your children off to public school without fear that school officials will pressure them to adopt new religious beliefs, that's separation of church and state in action.

Now consider life without separation of church and state: mandatory church taxes, religious requirements for public office, minority religions having their rights violated, public schools that preach as well as teach, and members of the "right" faiths getting preferential treatment from the state.

It's no contest. Separation wins hands down. But that doesn't mean the concept is universally appreciated. Church-state separation has withstood the test of time, but it still needs defenders today. Be one of them.

Remind people that the Religious Right does not speak for all Christians. Several times in this book I have indicated my displeasure with how the Religious Right uses the term "Christian." They talk constantly about "getting more Christians" in government, when the overwhelming majority of people in government now already belong to Christian denominations.

The Religious Right defines "Christians" as people who interpret the Bible literally, who believe it is inerrant and infallible, and who hold ultraconservative political views, especially on social issues. Under this narrow definition, millions of American Christians would not qualify as "Christian" to the Religious Right. It is helpful to remind people of this. It shows how intolerant the Religious Right can be.

A few years ago I appeared on a television show on a now-defunct cable channel to debate the issue of teaching creationism in public schools with a representative from the American Family Association (AFA). During the debate, I mentioned that most Christians in America see no conflict between evolution and faith and that lots of believers see evolution as God's plan. The AFA representative responded, "Those people aren't real Christians!"

Talk about shooting yourself in the foot. Americans are a spiritual people, but they don't like to be judged or told they don't measure up religiously because they don't accept every facet of someone else's theology.

The Religious Right throws the word "Christian" around a lot because to most people that word has positive connotations. We need to constantly remind members of nonfundamentalist Christian denominations—including not just the denominations considered to be "mainline" Protestants but Mormons, Roman Catholics, Seventh-day Adventists, Christian Scientists, and others—"When the Religious Right says 'Christian,' they don't mean you."

Challenge the Religious Right's "pro-family" rhetoric. When responding to the Religious Right in public forums, it is important to challenge its rhetoric and use of terms. Religious Right groups frequently use the terms "pro-family" and "family values" as if they invented the concept of the family. It is important to remind people that when the Religious Right uses the term "family," they are talking about very specific types of families. Under their definition, millions of American families would come up short.

Also, phrases like "family values" and "pro-family" are loaded terms. What the Religious Right calls "family values" I call ultraconservative, right-wing politics. The idea that one must adhere to a certain brand of exclusionary Christianity coupled with far-right politics in order to qualify as "pro-family" is offensive to many Americans. We need to constantly remind Americans that the Religious Right uses "family talk" as a subterfuge for its oppressive agenda.

In my view, virtually nothing in the Religious Right's agenda is really "pro-family." In the introduction to this book, I talked briefly about how what I want for my children compels me to work against the Religious Right. Let me expound on that some more here.

I want my children to be well educated and appreciative of the sciences. The Religious Right wants them to learn creation stories masquerading as fact.

I want my children to grow up thankful for the rich religious pluralism and theological diversity of America. The Religious Right wants to tell them there is only one true version of religion—fundamentalist Christianity.

I want my children to grow up unafraid to question dogma, to explore the world around them without fear, and to think and reason for themselves. The Religious Right hoists up the Bible and says, "Stop looking. It's all in our interpretation of this book."

I want my children to have the freedom to read and learn about many different subjects, to explore different professional options, and to exploit their talents to the maximum. The Religious Right calls for censorship of our libraries and wants to put some topics off-limits.

I want my children to attend public schools that welcome children of all religious faiths, schools that do not squelch truly voluntary religious expression yet do not sponsor any sectarian practices. The Religious Right wants our public schools to be parochial schools for fundamentalism.

I want my children to be full citizens in the eyes of the government, no matter what they believe or do not believe about God. The Religious Right wants to saturate our government with fundamentalism and make Christians of its stripe preferred members of the body politic. Everyone else would be second-class citizens.

Lastly, I want my children to have the right to raise their children in a world safe from religious intolerance and religious coercion. And I am convinced, absolutely, that the only way to achieve this is to maintain a high and impregnable wall between church and state. The Religious Right wants to blast that wall to smithereens.

Yet having said all of this, and having sharply delineated my views from the Religious Right's, I want to freely concede that I believe followers of the Religious Right can be pro-family. To me, that term has nothing to do with what lever you pull in the voting booth or how many abortion clinics or gay bars you have marched in front of during a given month. Rather, the test of being pro-family is simply this: Having brought a life into the world, are you willing to do the hard work to nurture and raise it?

Being "pro-family" is not determined by where you stand on school prayer, vouchers, or the right to choose abortion. It is determined by where you're standing at 3 A.M. when your child is sick or wakens frightened from a bad dream and calls out for you. If you are with your child, providing aid, comfort, and love, then that's all I need to know. That passes the pro-family smell test.

The Religious Right is fond of military metaphors. Its publications and speeches are full of talk about battles, spiritual warfare, waging war to save America, and the like. I've never liked such talk myself. Wars involve destruction, death, and vanquishing your enemy. Is that really the Religious Right's vision for America? It sure looks like it to me most days. I am tired of people who dare to disagree with the Religious Right on political concerns being called names, having their reputations and motives attacked, and being demonized. Supporters of separation of church and state should refrain from such triumphalistic rhetoric, but they should remain deeply engaged in the day-to-day struggle to maintain American freedoms. I advocate a firm response to the Religious Right, but in doing so, we must be careful not to lapse into the same inflammatory language that our opponents often use.

Pat Robertson once said, "America is a prize worth having." He was right. America, as conceived and brought about by our founders and refined by two centuries of growth, learning, and achievement, is a prize worth having—an America that values its religious diversity; an America that gives all of its citizens, religious and nonreligious, equal rights in the eyes of the state; an America that protects the freedom to read and learn and question; an America that still serves as a beacon for those suffering religious oppression abroad.

But the Religious Right's America, little better than a fundamentalist theocracy, isn't worth having. Despite what they would have you believe, Religious Right groups are not about "reclaiming America." To "reclaim" it, they would have had to have once owned it. They never did. Their goal is not a return to something old but the creation of something new—America as a fundamentalist Christian state where the goals and opinions of men like Pat Robertson, Jerry Falwell, D. James Kennedy, and James Dobson are written into our legal code. It's an America where narrow-minded fundamentalist Christians run our schools, our libraries, our reproductive freedoms, and ultimately our lives.

That's not an America worth having; it's an America worth keeping where it belongs—in the realm of fantasy in the late-night, fictionalized machinations of the Twilight Zone. May it always and only lurk there.

SOURCES FOR FURTHER RESEARCH

Readers who want to learn more about the Religious Right or the separation of church and state can access a variety of useful resources at a public library, local bookstore, or on the World Wide Web. Here are some resources I have found especially helpful:

WEBSITES

Americans United for Separation of Church and State Homepage: http://www.au.org. Contains regular updates on breaking church-state news, analysis of important court decisions, a state-by-state rundown of church-state legislation, information about what church-state bills Congress is considering, and more. You can also read issues of Americans United's monthly *Church & State* magazine on-line.

The Constitutional Principle: Separation of Church and State Homepage: http://members.tripod.com/~candst/ index.html. This is a good site to go to for information debunking the Religious Right's phony history and its claims that America was founded to be a "Christian nation." This site is especially useful for refuting the spurious history put forth by Religious Right propagandist David Barton.

Institute for Church–State Studies at Baylor University: http://www.baylor.edu/~Church_State/Welcome.html. Somewhat academic in tone, this site is a good place for researchers to visit.

Mainstream Opinion: http://www.mainstreamop.org. This site is maintained by the Rev. Jim Watkins, a United Church of Christ minister in Kirtland, Ohio. It contains opinion columns that refute the Religious Right.

I also recommend that activists who want to monitor the Religious Right regularly visit the websites of groups like the Christian Coalition, Focus on the Family, Family Research Council, and so on for up-to-date information on what these groups are doing.

BOOKS

My first book, *Why the Religious Right Is Wrong About the Separation of Church & State*, debunks the Religious Right's view of American history and the development of church-state separation. It is written for laypersons.

My second book, *The Most Dangerous Man in America? Pat Robertson and the Rise of the Christian Coalition*, is an expose of the theocratic worldview of TV preacher Pat Robertson and contains a generous sampling of extremist quotes taken from Robertson's own mouth.

Other useful books include:

The Godless Constitution: The Case Against Religious Correctness, by R. Laurence Moore and Isaac Kramnick, traces the evolution of church-state separation in America and explains why Americans have a "godless" Constitution instead of a "Christian commonwealth."

With God on Our Side: The Rise of the Religious Right in America, by William Martin, is a well-written, objective history of the Religious Right in America. It provides much perceptive and interesting information on how this movement rose to power.

Blinded By Might: Can the Religious Right Save America? by Cal Thomas and Ed Dobson. Thomas, a former official at the Moral Majority, and Dobson, a conservative pastor, argue that the Religious Right has erred by placing too much emphasis on politics. Although the book contains much far-right content, such as harsh attacks on the public school system, it provides good arguments that counter Christian Coalition claims about the value of political activity in churches.

The Manufactured Crisis: Myths, Fraud and the Attack on America's Public Schools, by David C. Berliner and Bruce J. Biddle, amasses a wealth of statistical data to refute Religious Right claims that public education is on the verge of collapse. It is a valuable antidote to Religious Right calumny.

Setting the Record Straight: Responses to Misconceptions About Public Education in the United States, by Gerald Bracey. Similar to the Berliner and Biddle book, this tome uses statistical data to debunk right-wing assaults on public education.

James Dobson's War on America, by Gil Alexander-Moegerle, is an eye-opening look at James Dobson's supposedly "nonpartisan" group, Focus on the Family.

Eternal Hostility: The Struggle Between Theocracy and Democracy, by Frederick Clarkson, a journalist who has tracked the Religious Right for years exposes the movement's goal of transforming America from a democracy to a theocracy.

Without a Prayer: Religious Expression in Public Schools, by Robert S. Alley, profiles several families who have had the courage to stand up to coercive programs of religious worship in public schools. It provides a powerful response to those who ask, "What's wrong with a little prayer in schools?"

Church and State in America, by Edwin Gaustad, is an excellent layperson's guide to the issue of church-state separation. Written in clear, concise language, this is one of the best "Church and State 101" volumes ever written.

The Constitution and Religion: Leading Supreme Court Cases on Church and State, edited by Robert S. Alley. This is the book for anyone who has ever wondered what the Supreme Court has really said about issues like school prayer, tax aid to religious schools, the display of sectarian symbols on government property, and other church-state issues. This accessible, affordable book contains the text of the high court's major church-state cases, along with some commentary. A must for scholars and laypersons alike.

AMERICANS UNITED CHAPTERS

Alabama
Mobile Bay Area Chapter
e-mail: vbeckerle@aol.com

Arkansas
Arkansas State Chapter
1114 Indiana Street
Pine Bluff, AR 71601

California
Los Angeles Area Chapter
P.O. Box 34-1651
Los Angeles, CA 90034
e-mail: ETABASH@aol.com

Sacramento Chapter
e-mail: smogull@juno.com

San Diego Chapter
e-mail: pilgrimucc@aol.com

San Fernando Valley Chapter
P.O. Box 8061
Northridge, CA 91327-8061
e-mail: Murgoldman@aol.com
http://www.ausfv.org/index.html

San Francisco Bay Area Chapter
P.O. Box 424455
San Francisco, CA 94142
(415) 436-0658
e-mail: mkassman@tsoft.com

Colorado
Denver Chapter
P.O. Box 481943
Denver, CO 80248-1943
(303) 273-2838
e-mail: audenver@aol.com

Connecticut
Connecticut Chapter
P.O. Box 210
Watertown, CT 06795
e-mail: JaneHad@aol.com
http://www.auct.org/

Florida
Northeast Florida Chapter
P.O. Box 23486
Jacksonville, FL 32241-3486
e-mail: bwjax@sprintmail.com

Northwest Florida Chapter
P.O. Box 13631
Pensacola, FL 32591-3631
e-mail: ekernstock@juno.com

Tampa Bay Area Chapter
P.O. Box 66694
St. Pete Beach, FL 33736-6694
e-mail: jcpugh@juno.com

Georgia
Georgia Chapter
P.O. Box 13905
Atlanta, GA 30324-0905
(404) 607-0660
e-mail: auga@auga.org
http://www.auga.org/

Hawaii
Hawaii Chapter
P.O. Box 1352
Kurtistown, HI 96760
email: Anson.Chong@pobox.com
http://www.freeyellow.com/members8/au-hawaii/index.html

Idaho
Idaho Americans United
e-mail: TGilbert@nea.org

Illinois
Chicagoland Chapter
P.O. Box 4331
Naperville, IL 60567-4331
e-mail: auchicago@aol.com

Kansas
Wichita Area Chapter
P.O. Box 3089
Wichita, KS 67201-3089

Kentucky
Bluegrass Chapter
e-mail: phimille@acs.eku.edu

Maryland
Maryland Chapter
e-mail: penelope@erols.com

Massachusetts
Massachusetts Americans United
340 Main Street
Room 717
Worcester, MA 01608
e-mail: WCACLUM@Earthlink.net

Missouri
St. Louis Chapter
4374 McPherson Ave.
St. Louis, MO 63108

New York
Buffalo Area Chapter
e-mail: jlip@acsu.buffalo.edu

Rochester Chapter
3553 West Ridge Road
Rochester, NY 14626-3452
e-mail: rochesterau@juno.com
http://www.ggw.org/au

North Carolina
East Carolina Chapter
P.O. Box 1749
Kinston, NC 28503
e-mail: ici1239@mail.icomnet.com

North Carolina Chapter
P.O. Box 40397
Raleigh, NC 27629-0397
e-mail: buddyrayo@aol.com

Ohio
North Ohio Chapter
P.O. Box 175
Mentor, OH 44061
e-mail: watkinsjw@juno.com

Oklahoma
Oklahoma Americans United
P.O. Box 892747
Oklahoma City, OK 73189
e-mail: JAH30@worldnet.att.net

Oregon
Portland Chapter
P.O. Box 3193
Portland, OR 97208-3193
e-mail: sota@teleport.com
http://members.xoom.com/oregonau/

Pennsylvania
Northwest Pennsylvania Chapter
P.O. Box 6579
Erie, PA 16512
e-mail: ASRjr@aol.com

Southeastern Pennsylvania Chapter
P.O. Box 30079
Philadelphia, PA. 19103
e-mail: ausepa@libertynet.org
http://www.libertynet.org/ausepa/

South Carolina
South Carolina Chapter
P.O. Box 21413
Charleston, SC 29413
e-mail: wraptrap@sprynet.com

Tennessee
Chattanooga Chapter
e-mail: sushi@chattanooga.net

Texas
Greater Houston Area Chapter
P.O. Box 60275
Houston, TX 77205
e-mail: amunited@hic.net
http://www.flash.net/~lbartley/au/

North Texas Chapter
1846 Rosemeade Parkway #281
Carrollton, TX 75007
e-mail: ntxamericansunited@activist.com
http://www.flash.net/~lbartley/au/

Virginia
Virginia Chapter
e-mail: ralley@richmond.edu

Wisconsin
South Central Wisconsin Chapter
P.O. Box 55134
Madison, WI 53705
e-mail: auwi@execpc.com
http://www.execpc.com/~auwi/

INDEX